Praise for *Big Data Baseball*

"A useful, entertaining look back at how the Pirates turned a small-market, longtime loser into a playoff team . . . A very illuminating book." —*Baseball America*

"*Big Data Baseball* is a particular kind of nerd heaven, and if you're even vaguely interested in advanced analytics, you should already be halfway through the second chapter by now. . . . Sawchik's real achievement is making the sabermetrics story accessible to everyone, even people who might have been scared off by it at first."

—MLB.com

"This important and highly readable book will introduce the changes in the way the game is being played today to many fans who are not even aware of those changes." —*Spitball Magazine*

"*Big Data Baseball* is a compelling read for those who revel in the game's statistical elements, those curious about their uses, and even those who scoff at the notion that sports and math can exist in harmony. By bridging those gaps alone, *Big Data Baseball* is a triumph."

—*Globe and Mail* (Toronto)

"If you haven't read Travis Sawchik's book on the Pirates, *Big Data Baseball*, I strongly suggest you buy your copy soon. You'll thank me later." —Mike Berardino, *St. Paul Pioneer Press*

"[*Big Data Baseball*] has generated all sorts of buzz in the sabermetrics community and definitely lives up to all the hype that has accompanied it. . . . An intriguing book that . . . has taken the baseball sabermetrics revolution to a whole new level . . . Sawchik seamlessly tells this story and weaves it into its place in baseball history. It's safe to say *Big Data Baseball* is a must-read for anyone with an interest in sabermetrics and big data or even just the casual baseball fan. [It] is the next revolution to the game of baseball, and it seems like the revolution is here to stay."

—Patrick Brewer, *Call to the Bullpen*

"*Big Data Baseball* is one of the best baseball stories I've read. . . . I can't recommend Sawchik's book enough."

—Will Carroll for FanDuel.com

"*Big Data Baseball* reads like a sequel to *Moneyball*. . . . [Sawchik] similarly pulls back the curtain on the analytically inclined Pirates and the ingenuity with which they ended their twenty-year postseason drought. But his book is also about how the flood of data in the last half-decade is not only changing how we think about the game, but also how it is played."

—*Toronto Star*

"The book is a love letter to sabermetrics. . . . It is not just a book for Pittsburgh Pirates fans . . . and it will likely serve as great fodder in strategy sessions for baseball's twenty-nine other teams, and for baseball analysts everywhere. The Pirates were able to change how they go about their business, and Sawchik makes sense of it all from both high-level and nuts-and-bolts views."

—*The Hardball Times*

"At times, the story reads almost like a John R. Tunis baseball book for boys. . . . Tunis's optimism, idealization of character, and overall enthusiasm all are here. Most important is Sawchik's realization, however, that the diamond will never again be so rough—data-gatherers and -analysts are polishing assiduously. Both a comprehensive and a focused look at how computer-recorded data are fundamentally altering America's pastime."

—*Kirkus Reviews*

"How this motley collection of men—from data geeks to throwback coaches to reluctant players—worked the numbers together to mold a winner makes Sawchik's tale as compelling as Michael Lewis's *Moneyball*. Which is saying a lot." —*Booklist* (starred review)

"This enlightening book by Sawchik explains how the team helped redefine the game. . . . Taking cues from Michael Lewis's *Moneyball* and Jonah Keri's *The Extra 2%*, Sawchik wonderfully dissects statistics and the game itself in a style that will score with a broad range of readers." —*Publishers Weekly*

"An author's goal when telling a story like this is to combine gripping storytelling with fresh insight into the wonkish methods an underdog baseball team uses to defy odds and win. The former is a great achievement for anyone, let alone a first-time author. The latter, given how incredibly secretive sports teams have become, is damn-near impossible. In *Big Data Baseball*, Travis Sawchik pulls both off, and he does so masterfully." —Jonah Keri, author of *The Extra 2%*

"In *Big Data Baseball*, Travis Sawchik reveals one of the great untold baseball stories of the early 21st century—how the Pittsburgh Pirates ended a twenty-year streak of futility by using data to revolutionize the way they positioned their defenders. Sawchik's fascinating tale is not merely about numbers, however. It also is about a spirit of collaboration between the new-age analysts and old-school field operatives that elevated the Pirates above other teams with access to the same information. For those who truly want to understand how the game has changed, *Big Data Baseball* is a must-read." —Ken Rosenthal, senior MLB writer for FOXSports

"Some baseball books open your eyes to a whole new way of seeing the game you've watched hundreds or thousands of times—Michael Lewis's *Moneyball*, Jonah Keri's *The Extra 2%*, and now Sawchik's *Big Data Baseball*. Like those spiritual predecessors, Sawchik makes advanced analytical concepts accessible with gripping storytelling about humans and their perseverance against the failures of the past." —Scott Olstad, Public Radio Market Newsletter

"If you are interested in the cutting edge of baseball decision-making, this book is a must." —*Mankato Free Press*

"Sawchik hits a home run with *Big Data Baseball*. It would be far too easy—not to mention lazy—to call Travis Sawchik's debut book *Big Data Baseball, Moneyball* Part 2. Frankly, as great as *Moneyball* was, it's not on the same level of *Big Data Baseball* when it comes to the content. *Big Data Baseball* not only appeals to hardcore baseball fans and Pirates fans, but everyone in general. Sports fans will understand and appreciate the model, while non-sports fans will be able to understand the basic principal ideas, thanks to Sawchik's clear explanations. *Big Data Baseball* is a home-run debut for Sawchik, and is a must-read for all." —*Lebanon Daily News*

"*Big Data Baseball* is instructive on two fronts. It makes a convincing case for why organizations need to staff up on data architects and analysts and invest in software. The book also underscores the importance of culture change. Big data is useless if you're unwilling to act on what it tells you." —*The Hamilton Spectator*

BIG DATA
BASEBALL

BIG DATA BASEBALL

MATH, MIRACLES, AND **THE END** OF A 20-YEAR LOSING STREAK

★ ★ ★

TRAVIS SAWCHIK

FLATIRON
BOOKS
NEW YORK

BIG DATA BASEBALL. Copyright © 2015 by Travis Sawchik. All rights reserved.
Printed in the United States of America. For information, address Flatiron Books,
175 Fifth Avenue, New York, NY 10010.

www.flatironbooks.com

The Library of Congress has cataloged the hardcover edition as follows:

Sawchik, Travis.
    Big data baseball : math, miracles, and the end of a 20-year losing streak /
Travis Sawchik.
        p. cm.
    Includes bibliographical references.
    ISBN 978-1-250-06350-2 (hardcover)
    ISBN 978-1-250-06351-9 (e-book)
    1. Pittsburgh Pirates (Baseball team)   2. Baseball—Statistical methods.
3. Baseball—Mathematical models.   4. Baseball players—United States—Statistics.
I. Title.
    GV875.P5S28 2015
    796.357'640974886—dc23   2015011231

ISBN 978-1-250-09425-4 (trade paperback)

Our books may be purchased in bulk for promotional, educational, or
business use. Please contact your local bookseller or the Macmillan Corporate
and Premium Sales Department at 1-800-221-7945, extension 5442, or by
e-mail at MacmillanSpecialMarkets@macmillan.com.

First Flatiron Books Trade Paperback Edition: May 2016

10   9   8   7   6   5   4   3   2   1

THIS BOOK IS FOR MOM, DAD, AND REBECCA

CONTENTS

BIG DATA
BASEBALL

"A passion for statis-
tics is the earmark
of a literate people."

Paul Fisher

1

THE MEETING

He believed in fearing nothing, respecting everything. He said that often. Still, if Clint Hurdle had felt no apprehension the day he waited for a visitor at his home in early October 2012, it would have been unnatural. Outside his home, the gray sky provided a stark contrast to the vibrant orange, yellow, and red of the trees in the rolling hills in western Pennsylvania. A mild depression fell over many coaches and managers when the season ended. Baseball was something you lived and breathed for nearly eight months, from when pitchers and catchers reported to spring training in February and lasting through the early fall. Then, like that, it was gone. His team, the Pittsburgh Pirates, was no longer playing baseball now that the play-offs had started. Twenty years had passed since the Pirates last landed in the postseason. This was the problem clouding Hurdle's thoughts as he waited.

Before he'd accepted the job as manager for the Pittsburgh Pirates, a number of his closest friends had counseled him against taking the position. He recalled the phone calls: It was a dead end, they told him. The Pirates hadn't made the postseason in twenty years; heck, they hadn't had a winning season in that long, the longest such streak of futility in North American professional-sports history. Not since the 1992 National League Championship Series, when Sid Bream beat a throw home from Barry Bonds for the winning run of Game 7, had the Pirates played in the postseason. That day when Sid slid home was the day baseball died in Pittsburgh.

A lot had changed since those last great Pirates teams. Players, coaches, and executives had come and gone. Attendance declined. The only year-to-year consistencies were the losing and the little money being spent on the club. The revenue gap between large- and small-market teams had grown dramatically since the early 1990s, fueled by the explosion and disparity in regional television dollars. It meant the Pirates had no high-priced free agents to bolster their roster. The Pirates' Opening Day payroll in 2010 ranked last in baseball at $35 million, while the average league payroll was $89 million. Their farm system was also hurting due to a series of missed opportunities in the draft, such as in 2002 when the Pirates selected Bryan Bullington as the number one draft pick over future stars like Prince Fielder, Zack Greinke, Scott Kazmir, Nick Swisher, Matt Cain, and Cole Hamels. Bullington was just one of several great draft busts in recent memory.

Hurdle knew the Pirates had clearly fallen in status to the number three sports team in Pittsburgh behind the Steelers in the NFL and the Penguins in the NHL. Both franchises had recently won championships. Meanwhile, the Pirates had not drawn more than 2 million fans to their stadium since 2001.

Hurdle's friends advised him to wait for another job opportunity with a team that wasn't considered among the worst franchises in North American professional sports. But what his friends wouldn't say, although they didn't have to, was that Hurdle had only one more shot to make it as a major league manager. If he lost this job, he was unlikely to get a third chance at managing. He was no longer a young man, having turned fifty-five in July. So why take a chance in Pittsburgh?

He listened to and processed the many reasons he should turn down the job. But still, he couldn't.

Hurdle had spent the 2010 season as the Texas Rangers' hitting coach. He knew that he wanted to manage, not be an assistant. Like most baseball coaches, Hurdle preferred to wield the ultimate power of a coach: filling out a lineup card. He enjoyed leading. He liked having his hands on different aspects of a club, not being a specialist in one area. Perhaps more than anything else, he thought that rehabbing the baseball club in Pittsburgh could be a special story. He enjoyed a challenge.

After much deliberation, Hurdle decided he wanted the job. He felt it was the right fit, but he had to convince his wife, Karla, that it was the right move for them. They loved living in Denver, where Hurdle previously managed the Colorado Rockies so Hurdle had to convince her that Pittsburgh was not just some cold, undesirable industrial city. He could sell her on the city's renaissance. Pittsburgh had made perhaps the most successful transition of all the Rust Belt cities. After the steel mills closed and so many in the city struggled, a healthy medical industry began to develop along with a burgeoning tech niche. As the coal mines running under the city and its suburban hills quieted, a thriving natural gas industry developed. Home prices had not collapsed and the local economy had not crashed, as in so many cities across the country in the late 2000s.

However, Pittsburgh's baseball club remained in dire need of revitalization. A new stadium, PNC Park, opened in 2001, not far from where the Pittsburgh Alleghenies had begun playing professional baseball in the city in the nineteenth century. But in contrast to the sparkling new facility, the organization itself had fallen destitute on the field. Could its baseball club enjoy a rebirth like the city? Hurdle believed that it could. He convinced Karla that he was confident he could make things work in Pittsburgh.

On November 14, 2010, Hurdle was officially hired by the Pirates. He often spoke of full "buy in" to ideas or practices and to show commitment to the city and the team he became a full-time resident. Hurdle bought a spacious colonial, brick residence, resting on a large plot in the suburban hills of Hampton Township, fifteen miles north of the stadium.

Two years later, he waited in that same home; his confidence in rebuilding the Pirates had been encroached upon by time and doubt. He had just one year left on his contract, and his first two seasons with the team had been losing ones. He had been a major league manager for ten years, first with the Colorado Rockies, and nine of those seasons were losing ones. During games he appeared to go through an entire carton of bubble gum, his mouth constantly chewing like a factory's stamping press, seemingly as a way to reduce stress. This off-season's anxiety however wasn't fixated on just the outcome of one game. Beginning late in the last season, it was difficult for anyone to avoid hearing the public's call for a restart, for a change in the Pirates' leadership. Hurdle could well be on the move again, which would be difficult on his family. The kids, Maddie, ten, and Christian, seven, were settled and comfortable now. Had he made the right decision in coming to Pittsburgh? In truth, it didn't matter now. He vowed to never look back and second-guess himself. He had been through adversity before. He was here now and he had to fix it.

Hurdle's first two seasons as Pirates manager had not gone well. The club had enjoyed surprising winning records through the first half of both the 2011 and 2012 seasons, raising hopes and expectations, then performed horribly in second halves, ending with consecutive-losing-seasons nineteen and twenty. Pittsburghers referred to the second halves of 2011 and 2012 as Epic Collapse I and Epic Collapse II. Hurdle knew he could not afford an Epic Collapse III.

A former major league player, Hurdle was an imposing figure at six feet three and over two hundred pounds. With hands like catcher's mitts and spiked, silver-gray hair, with his presence and size, he commanded most rooms that he entered; but as he waited in his home, underneath that tough exterior he also had to feel powerless when thinking about the realities of his ball club.

Finally, a car made its way down his street, passing the wooded subdivision's spacious lots and approaching his driveway. He knew what was coming, and it was what many of us fear most: the future and change.

★ ★ ★

Approaching the front door was Neal Huntington. Hurdle dwarfed the five-foot-eight, square-shouldered Pirates general manager, whose blond hair and youthful countenance belied his forty-three years. Huntington, guarded and measured in his speech, was a calculating man. Unlike Hurdle, Huntington had come from outside the game, never having a professional at bat.

Huntington had attended an elite school, Amherst (Mass.), though he did not come from the upper class. The son of a New Hampshire dairy farmer, he vividly recalled being in the family barn's stuffy rafters in hundred-degree heat in mid-August, charged with catching hay bales thrown to him by his older brothers. He remembered their laughing as he failed to keep up and was soon overwhelmed and pounded by a peppering of bales. That barn is where he learned the value of hard work.

Huntington had been an excellent student, but his passion was always baseball. He went to college at Amherst because it was the best school that afforded him the opportunity to play the game, albeit at the Division III level. Huntington was never the most talented player, and perhaps because of that he was always thinking about the game's strategy and how to find an edge. From an early age, he was fascinated by the concept of team building. He loved playing the APBA baseball-simulation board game, where he attempted to find flaws he could exploit. APBA baseball came with its own cards that represented every major league player and his skills. Its board featured a diagram of a baseball field with which to advance base runners and show different scenarios—from bases loaded to empty bases—and with its dice you created random numbers. The game was simple. A pitcher's card was matched up with a hitter's card, and a roll of the dice resolved the at bat. The random numbers created by the dice corresponded to an assortment of probability-based outcomes based upon the players' real-life statistical performances. Huntington was always looking for loopholes in the game. He favored speedy base runners when creating his lineups as he learned they could steal bases with ease.

He grew up thinking he would live a simple life; teach somewhere and coach baseball. Instead, Montreal Expos general manager Dan Duquette, an Amherst alum, called Huntington's college coach, Bill Thurston—who had been the head coach since 1966—and asked if he knew anyone who would make a good summer intern. Huntington was recommended. The internship in 1992 led to a full-time position with the Expos. Because of the limited staff and resources in Montreal, many tasks were handed down to Huntington. Some were menial, others were fascinating. In 1994 he served as the Expos' video advance scout. The Expos were one of the first teams to use this method. Most clubs had a scout in the field studying upcoming opponents. The Expos had one of the early, enormous, NASA-sized television satellite dishes installed, which could pluck a limited number of games from the sky. Huntington was tasked with making sure he taped and scouted games from upcoming opponents, as well as the Expos players' performances for when stars such as Moises Alou, Larry Walker, and Marquis Grissom wanted to evaluate their at bats on video after each game. At the time of the baseball strike, on August 11, 1994, the Expos had the best record in the major leagues—despite a paltry payroll of $19 million. The next season, Huntington was promoted to assistant director of player development. He was just one of four full-time employees in the front office along with the general manager, the vice president of baseball operations, and the director of minor league operations.

That experience in Montreal was invaluable. Huntington got to see the smallest-market team succeed in the National League, and he would soon be involved in the infancy of baseball's data revolution in the American League's most challenging environment with the Cleveland Indians.

In the early 1990s, Indians general manager John Hart inherited a team that had reached such a low that it was the subject of the comedy movie *Major League*. Under Hart, the Indians became a powerhouse club that advanced to the World Series in 1995 and 1997. Hart had risen through the ranks as a minor league manager and scout, a traditional path to the general manager's chair. With Cleveland, he faced more challenges and economic limitations than with any other team in the sport, but Hart pioneered a number of innovations, and perhaps the most lasting included what he dubbed a "pilot program." Under Hart, the Indians hired young, hungry graduates of elite colleges to study the emerging data side of baseball to complement what Hart thought was his strength: traditional, subjective scouting. The program helped Hart learn as much as possible about his opponents when he attended the winter meetings each December, which is baseball's annual convention. The winter meetings are where many trades and signings are executed, new products are showcased, and hundreds of hopeful job seekers are visiting, along with players' agents, media members, and many front office executives. At hotel bars gossip and information are swapped until the early-morning hours. Hart wanted to know the contracts, the service time, performance trends, the quality of his rivals' prospects, and he wanted all this information condensed into one three-ring binder of reports that he could easily access when involved in trade or free agent discussions. These tasks were put upon his army of highly educated and lowly paid staff of baseball outsiders, among whom was Huntington, who came aboard in 1998.

Huntington was hired as the club's assistant director of minor league operations and became part of baseball's first wave of data-savvy lieutenants. Like him, none of his colleagues had ever played professional baseball, a highly unconventional path to a major league front office, but despite this, four of his colleagues—Paul DePodesta, Josh Byrnes, Mark Shapiro, and Chris Antonetti—went on to become major league general managers.

"We were definitely on the forefront of that. Now [data analysis] is a huge piece [of the game]," Hart said. "I think we were on the forefront because I recognized my limitations. . . . We developed a pilot program of young, smart guys that wanted to get into baseball. [They] helped provide that cutting-edge stuff that allowed the Indians to be ahead of the game. It was fun. We were embryonic."

However, the competitive advantage of cheap, smart labor fresh out of elite schools was to be short-lived as other teams became interested in the analysts.

"The first guy we lost was Paul DePodesta. He was like number three or number four on our depth chart," Hart said. "I remember [Oakland GM] Billy Beane called me. I knew then that [what we were doing] was working. Billy called me at the 1998 winter meetings and said, 'John, you have a guy over there I'm interested in hiring.' I said, 'Oh, really.' He said, 'Paul DePodesta.' I said, 'Oh, shit. Here we go.'"

Huntington advanced his way to become an assistant general manager in Cleveland and left in 2007 when the Pirates offered him their general manager position. The Pirates liked that Huntington had a variety of experiences, having scouted players, worked in player development, and analyzed data. They liked his tenacity and that he had been around small-market success stories. Huntington and the new Pirates club president Frank Coonelly, brought on shortly before Huntington, were in agreement on a plan to dramatically increase the financial commitment to the draft. But Huntington and the Pirates' leadership wanted to implement something else that was integral to the Indians game. Under Hart, Huntington had been exposed to Cleveland's proprietary database, DiamondView. The first version of the DiamondView software was created in 2000, according to the *Cleveland Plain Dealer,* when Hart's assistant general manager, Mark Shapiro, asked for a computer database to be constructed that could rank each rival club's top players and prospects. It was essentially a computerized and enhanced extension of the reports Hart had asked to be produced for winter meetings. DiamondView predated the *Moneyball* Oakland A's and was the first known comprehensive computer database in the sport, able to quickly sort through large samples of data to identify trends and project performance while uploading new data daily. It quickly evolved to include video, injury reports, and salary figures to accompany scouting reports and performance metrics. Using the software, the Indians made key decisions, such as when they elected not to sign aging star Jim Thome to an extension after the 2002 season, in part because of the database, the *Cleveland Plain Dealer* reported. DiamondView revealed Barry Bonds was the only hitter in the prior twenty-two seasons who produced at an elite level after the age of thirty-five, and Thome was seeking a six-year deal that would take him through age thirty-seven. The Indians balked at signing Thome to a deal that took him beyond his thirty-fifth birthday, so instead he signed a six-year deal with Philadelphia and began a swift decline phase at thirty-four. Moreover, Huntington noted that the Indians found in a payroll analysis that no major league club, dating back to 1985, had won a World Series when committing 15 percent or more of its payroll to one player. This DiamondView finding also influenced the Indians' decision on Thome. DiamondView allowed easy access to and analysis of large amounts of data, helping the small-market Indians avoid making an emotion-based mistake in signing Thome.

Huntington arrived in Pittsburgh to an organization in the dark ages. Four years after the publication of *Moneyball* and nearly a decade after the Indians began consulting DiamondView, the Pirates did not have even a rudimentary analytics department. Under Huntington, the Pirates were finally going to build such a department from scratch. The Pirates were going to build their own DiamondView. To build an analytics department and a proprietary database, the Pirates needed data architects, analysts, and software. This was going to take some time.

Time was a scarce resource in Pittsburgh. Patience was wearing thin and the pressure was on. In each of Huntington's first five seasons, the losing continued. The Pirates had successful neighbors: the Steelers had won Super Bowls in 2005 and 2008, and the NHL's Penguins won the Stanley Cup in 2009. T-shirts were printed with the quip PITTSBURGH: THE CITY OF CHAMPIONS . . . AND THE PIRATES.

★ ★ ★

Huntington and Hurdle both knew that time was running out for them with the Pirates. At the end of the season speculation was rampant that Huntington and his staff would be fired. Many in the public wanted a regime change. Not until November 6 did owner Bob Nutting end that speculation, telling the press that there would be no personnel changes. Nutting was frustrated much like the fans were after the 2012 season. Said Nutting on November 6, 2012, in speaking with the press: "If you're angry, you count to ten. If you're really angry, you count to one hundred. If you're incredibly infuriated and frustrated, you wait four weeks." After the season ended, he began conducting a review of the club examining every aspect of baseball operations. Ultimately, the Pirates' owner decided there would be no scapegoat. Still, Huntington and Hurdle could not afford any more seasons like the last two. They needed to win to save their jobs, but since Huntington was younger, he could more afford to fail. He was part of the new school and would be able to find another prominent role in the business if things didn't work out in Pittsburgh. Hurdle, however, was viewed as a traditional, old-school manager, a stubborn and resistant man trained in twentieth-century baseball orthodoxy. Sure, he might fit as a bench coach somewhere at a dramatically lower salary and in a much less relevant role, but this might well be his last chance to lead a team.

Hurdle and Huntington had scheduled this one-on-one meeting in advance of their organizational meetings to get on the same page, examine their roster assets, and brainstorm some sort of plan—to manufacture a miracle. They met at Hurdle's home, around a dining-room table, to keep it private and to reduce the number of voices involved. Some speculated that they would not only need to produce more wins than losses in 2013, but also make the postseason as well. They needed a dramatic improvement to build public confidence and job stability. They had won 79 games in 2012 and would need to win around 94 games in 2013 to ensure a postseason berth; in baseball, such a 15-game improvement is considerable. Meanwhile most pre-season publications would pick them to finish fourth or fifth in the National League Central Division, and to record their twenty-first consecutive losing season.

After the two men exchanged small-talk formalities, a sobering reality emerged. The Pirates were to be allotted some $15 million for free agent spending on their 2013 roster, which is a relatively paltry amount in baseball, considering that an average starting position player or starting pitcher was commanding $10 million per season in the off-season free agent market. The Pirates had to spread those dollars over at least three vacant spots on the twenty-five-man roster. They would not be able to spend their way to a winning season. They would have to shrewdly allocate the dollars they did have.

Huntington believed teams had to be built through the draft. But typically it takes at least five years for a draft pick to become established at the major league level, and no professional draft is as inefficient and inexact as baseball's. While the Pirates farm system was beginning to show promise, with more depth and emerging impact prospects, the help it offered would not be immediate. From *Baseball America*'s list of the top ten Pirates prospects entering the 2013 season, only pitcher Gerrit Cole was expected to join the club at some point in the season.

Hurdle and Huntington would somehow have to increase the sum of the club's individual parts. But was that even possible when the 2012 roster would comprise 90 percent of their 2013 team? If you consider the roster they reviewed early that off-season, it was akin to a package of baseball cards that contained mostly flawed players.

The pitching rotation was riddled with questions marks, and the club did not have a capable starting catcher. Everyone in the organization agreed that finding a catcher was a priority. The Pirates had declined the $3.5 million option on veteran Rod Barajas, a subpar defensive catcher.

In the infield, at third base, Huntington's first draft pick, Pedro Alvarez, had 30 homers in 2012, but he also had one of the most extreme swing-and-miss rates in the game and played questionable defense in the field. First base was projected to be a platoon between Gaby Sanchez and Garrett Jones, neither of whom was a star-level talent.

Veteran shortstop Clint Barmes was a favorite of Hurdle's. He was a good clubhouse guy, a veteran who wouldn't squabble about playing time, was amiable toward reporters, and had made himself into an above-average defensive shortstop. But Barmes's bat was in decline. They weren't expecting improvement from him, but hoped he would continue to be a quality defensive player.

There were some bright spots. Neil Walker had developed into a solid regular at second base. Twenty-six-year-old center fielder Andrew McCutchen had produced career bests across the board the previous season and finished third in voting for the National League's MVP, but could they rely on him to be even better?

Starling Marte had flashed power and speed as a twenty-three-year-old rookie in 2012. Hurdle planned on penciling him into the leadoff spot as a first-time everyday player. But besides McCutchen, he was the only other player in the lineup with above-average speed. Overall, the club had more question marks than strengths.

At their meeting, Huntington and Hurdle had no dreams or unrealistic hopes. What they had was a 79-win team from the previous year, and on paper, without significant help, it looked as if they would be a sub-.500 team yet again. They were not a particularly young team; young teams carried the hope of improvement through experience. Rather, they were only the twelfth-youngest team in the sport in 2012. The average age of the players on their roster was just shy of twenty-nine years. These were not comforting realities. But they would still somehow have to find a way to add 15 wins without adding much payroll. It was an impossible task.

They asked themselves during the meeting, How do we maximize what we have internally? How do we get the absolute most out of these returning players? What's the biggest impact we can make from a strategic standpoint?

"Sometimes the easy fix isn't to get another player, or to go buy a free agent, or reconstruct this or that," Hurdle said. "You look at what the challenges are. You look at the talent pool that you have. What other adjustments can you make to enhance performance?"

With no money to spend on any big-name sluggers, they could do nothing from a run-scoring perspective, and players' offensive skills were thought to be hardened and difficult to change. You either could hit or you couldn't. The Pirates were stuck with the hitting abilities of their current roster.

At the center of their discussions was one unexplored frontier the Pirates' analytics team believed they might be able to exploit: run prevention. Defense. Preventing runs was one of the untapped areas of opportunity remaining in the game, an area the Pirates had not maximized in the first two years under Hurdle. Their analysts had reexamined the way the Pirates played defense and had developed data-driven strategies for curbing the number of runs scored against them. Executing some of the theories did not require adding any payroll; other data-based ideas suggested they could afford some undervalued players on the free agent market.

What Huntington's data-crunching lieutenants were championing was perhaps the most aggressive, universal approach to defense in baseball history. This new strategy was on a completely different level from the *Moneyball* revolution led by the Oakland A's a decade earlier, or even from the data filtered by DiamondView, which predated the A's approach. The A's had tapped into on-base percentage, an undervalued stat that could be found on the back of baseball cards, visible to any team. Huntington was proposing to take advantage of some possibly significant opportunities in the game revealed by data that had not previously been recorded and analyzed. The strategies demanded Hurdle embrace an avalanche of new data, to trust the millions of new data points that had entered the game and were stored in the Pirates' powerful new computer database. Smarter baseball theory was for so long obfuscated by a lack of data. Now those numbers were flooding in from a variety of places: from an automated pitch-recognition system known as PITCHf/x, which began being installed in major league parks in 2007; from a competing pitch-tracking system from TrackMan, a Danish company that had made its name in golf using radar to track ball flight; and from an army of analysts hired by companies such as Baseball Info Solutions to track play-by-play details that had never before been recorded.

Because so much data had entered the game so quickly, it had overwhelmed teams. Most organizations were employing little of it, but Huntington was paying attention. To enact the defensive plan driven by the front office, incredible change was necessary in several key areas.

Player positioning had to change. Since the dawn of the game, defensive alignment had not been based upon data but rather by placing players equidistant from each other. In the new plan, players would have to shift from areas on the field where they had been stationed their entire careers.

The club would have to improve their pitchers' performance and maximize the defensive alignments behind them. Pitchers would have to learn to trust to change what and where they threw.

Ownership would have to sign off on and invest in the belief that a catcher's most important skill wasn't easily visible and that a pitcher's traditional stats weren't revealing true ability.

Cooperation, collaboration, conversation, and respect had to be the norm from the bottom to the top of the organization. Old-school coaches had to accept data-based decisions and concepts from men who had never set foot in a professional batter's box. The data analysts had to be better integrated into the Pirates culture and clubhouse.

This last point was critical. Over the last decade, almost every major league team had hired at least one number cruncher to analyze data. However, a common grumbling from those analysts was that so little of their research was finding its way to the field. The gatekeeper to implementing the data was the manager. While managers had lost significant influence over roster construction and player acquisitions in recent decades, they still largely controlled on-field strategies. The manager made out the lineup card every day. He decided upon game strategy and had more direct communication with players than anyone else in the organization.

While the front office's plan could be the most elegant and dramatic ever devised, if the coaching staff didn't buy in, it wouldn't work. While many of baseball's executives and front-office staff now had Ivy League roots, and little if any playing experience, coaches were almost exclusively ex-players. Huntington could not go find another manager. He was essentially a lame duck. He had to go into the season with Hurdle fully on board. The Pirates had picked Hurdle in part because of his leadership and communication skills. But also because they thought he might be willing to embrace more new-age concepts. But in many ways Hurdle was a traditionalist trained in the game's twentieth-century thinking, and he had remained largely conventional in on-field strategy in 2012. He referred to his players as "men" and often spoke of the importance of the heartbeat, the human element of the game. He didn't believe in trying to measure everything. He believed in seeing. Yet, Hurdle was being challenged to trust in something that he couldn't see. While much of the plan was devised in the front office, the implementation of the entire plan rested on Hurdle's shoulders.

2

DEMONS

Clint Hurdle's picture graced the cover of *Sports Illustrated*'s March 20, 1978, issue with the headline "This Year's Phenom: Kansas City's Clint Hurdle." The picture was taken as the Kansas City Royals held a morning workout in spring training. His face was youthful, but to this day he boasts the same boulevard-wide, pearly smile. His generous mop of once-brown locks has changed to the silver hair that he spikes up like a porcupine. His complexion, no longer tanned and smooth, is reddened and creased and, depending upon his anger level, morphs to various shades of purple. That his appearance has changed so dramatically speaks to the amount of time that has passed.

That magazine cover keeps showing up. Sometimes it arrives in the mail from an autograph seeker far away; sometimes he is served with one in person. It's a cruel reminder of a ceiling not reached, of potential withered on the vine. Few people are reminded of their past, of their potential, of their previous inability to change, as often as Hurdle.

He looked at the photo on the magazine cover and thought about how much his life had changed since then. He thought about how much he had changed. Every time he sees the cover, he is shocked at how young he looks. He tried to think back at what he was thinking then. What was he doing? Why was he doing it? What where his priorities? He knew that too often back then his priorities were in the wrong place. He tried not to have regrets, at least outwardly. He was a leader after all, and leaders don't express doubts in public.

He jokes that he's not sure if they keep reprinting the *Sports Illustrated* cover as some sort of commemorative edition documenting his baseball failure or if the covers just keep showing up because fans stumble upon them while housecleaning.

"Would I have handled it better [without all the pressure]? There's no doubt," Hurdle said during a press conference at the 2013 winter meetings. "But I believe I am the man I am today from the things I've gone through in the past."

Said Hurdle during a news conference several years earlier when asked about the magazine cover, "I've had many demons I've had to run from. The [magazine cover] isn't a demon."

One of Hurdle's demons was expectation.

In the spring of 1978, Hurdle was one of the top prospects in baseball, perhaps the very top. Spring is a season of promise in baseball. If you squint hard enough, if you dream big enough, anything is possible for any team or for any player. But sometimes you can squint too hard and expectations can become too grand and unrealistic. The perceptions can begin to bend reality. Fans always want to believe what is next holds the promise of being better. Maybe even executives and coaches believe that, too. They're human after all. Everyone in Kansas City that spring thought stardom was not just possible but a sure thing for Hurdle. He was the next George Brett. On the magazine cover, Hurdle appeared to believe it, too. In that moment he looked as if he had not a worry, as if he had never experienced failure. And he really hadn't yet.

When he launched balls with ease in batting practice, teammates stopped and watched, which is noteworthy, considering batting practice is typically mundane. He was gregarious, outgoing, buoyed by the confidence that came with good looks and a lithe, six-foot-three frame that towered above most of his contemporaries.

His route to cover-boy status began in Michigan, where Hurdle was born July 30, 1957, to Clint Hurdle Sr., who had played shortstop at Ferris State. It was there that Clint senior caught the eye of a Chicago Cubs scout, but ended up being drafted into the military after graduation. After several years in the service, he was discharged. Jobs were sparse in his native Big Rapids, a small town located in central Michigan. In 1961, a friend recommended him for a job at the Kennedy Space Center. With few dollars to his name, Clint senior took a chance. He took his pregnant wife, son, and daughter to Florida where the Apollo missions began in October. Clint senior began at the bottom. His first job at the NASA complex was separating streams of paper and their carbon copies being spit out from computer printers. He was introduced to room-sized computers and their noisy, spinning tape drives. He learned computer functions and programming, and worked his way up as a subcontractor with NASA at companies like RCA and Grumman Aerospace. He eventually advanced to become a director of computer operations and maintenance at the complex. His division was responsible for monitoring the computers of the rockets and shuttles up until lift off, when mission control took over in Houston. Clint senior eventually oversaw more than 300 people and once a month, he went around and met with as many subordinates as he could, from top lieutenants to entry-level workers.

"I went around and talked to everyone who worked for me. . . . I wanted to make sure they felt they were part of the program," Clint senior said. "People learn to trust you, you gain credibility."

Said Hurdle of his father: "He was a connector of people. He put people in the right spots."

Hurdle also benefitted from the move south. In the Southeast, because of climate, baseball is played year-round, which is why Florida and the Atlanta area have become some of baseball's greatest hotbeds for amateur talent. Kids there simply can play more often. On Sunday afternoons after church, when Hurdle's friends went surfing at the nearby Atlantic beaches, Hurdle wanted to practice. Clint senior threw batting practice to Hurdle at the Merritt Island High School field. They would hit for hours with his mother and two sisters serving as outfielders to retrieve the balls he launched.

Clint senior gave Hurdle drills to strengthen his swing from swinging a lead bat to constantly squeezing hand grips. When Clint senior was working second shifts, son and mother would play catch after school. Clint played baseball year-round and got a taste of the pro game as a sometimes batboy for the then Cocoa Astros of the Florida State League, meeting future big leaguers such as John Mayberry.

Hurdle grew to tower over his five-foot-eight father and developed a perfect power hitter's frame that gave him a lethal combination of length and leverage to go along with God-given bat speed, the product of quick-twitch muscles and a strong body core. Those innate traits also helped him uncork laserlike throws as a prep quarterback at Merritt Island High, where Hurdle became a top prospect in both football and baseball. The only athletic trait he lacked was speed.

During his senior season, Hurdle put on legendary workouts for major league scouts. Invited to work out at the Braves' spring training home, Hurdle launched balls to places where they were rarely hit by professional hitters: a water-filtration center that was next to the baseball complex, according to an *ESPN* magazine story. Then Royals player-development official John Schuerholz was awestruck. The longtime Braves GM said later he had never seen another such power display by a prep prospect in his forty years of being around the game.

Most teams in baseball had at least one scout following Hurdle. The Kansas City Royals became intimately familiar with him because his high school was near the home of Royals minor league pitching instructor Bill Fischer. Fischer said of Hurdle in the 1978 *Sports Illustrated* cover story: "He was hitting the ball over the fence and into the drainage ditch. I quit working out with him more out of fear than anything else. I was afraid I might get killed."

The Royals brought Hurdle to their minor league complex in Florida, where he put on what Fischer recalled as "the greatest exhibition you ever saw." Fischer recommended to the Royals' scouting staff that they select Hurdle—and early—in the 1975 draft. The team obliged, selecting Hurdle as the ninth overall pick before future stars such as Lee Smith, Carney Lansford, Lou Whitaker, and Andre Dawson. Hurdle signed for $50,000, bypassing a full ride to the University of Miami, where he was signed as a prized quarterback recruit. He was an excellent student, who made only one "B" in high school (and that was in driver's ed). Hurdle had also received a scholarship offer from Harvard.

From there his ascent to stardom only seemed to accelerate. After being named the top prospect in the Midwest league in 1976, Hurdle was invited to big league camp in 1977, where he hit .300. He skipped Double-A and hit .328 with 16 home runs and 66 RBIs in Triple-A Omaha and was named the league's top rookie and MVP in 1977. He made his major league debut on September 18, 1977, starting in right field for a 102-win team. Having just turned twenty, he was the youngest Royal in the club's then nine-year history. In the fifth inning of his first game he smashed a 450-foot home run off Glenn Abbott into the left-center field waterfall at Royals Stadium and spent an hour and a half after the game signing autographs, smiling the entire time. Stardom seemed preordained. He had the look and the power of a franchise-changing force. In his 9-game call-up from the minors, Hurdle hit .308 with 2 home runs and 7 RBIs.

When Hurdle returned to big league camp in the spring of 1978, the spring when he was captured for posterity on the cover of the nation's premier sports magazine, the level of hype and expectation elevated even more. The cover photo was one thing but also consider what was said in the accompanying cover story regarding Hurdle. Royals general manager Joe Burke said of him, "one of the top prospects, I've seen in the 17 years, I've been in the majors leagues." Schuerholz, the scouting director, said, "I bubble inside when I think about his potential." Royals hitting coach Charley Lau called him the best hitting prospect he had ever seen in the organization. "Clint is a lot like me," Royals star George Brett said that spring. "I guess that's one of the reasons we've become close. In 1974 I was the all-American boy trying to make it in the big leagues, and now it's Clint. I can remember the front office asking me not to chew tobacco or go into bars. I was their golden boy. Now the golden boy is Clint, and they'll probably want to protect him, too."

But the Royals failed to protect Hurdle from the pressure and expectation, and they failed to protect him from himself.

The *Sports Illustrated* cover jinx is perhaps not a jinx at all but a mathematical phenomenon: *Sports Illustrated* tends to capture athletes at their extremes, at their highs or lows. From that cover, there was only regression for Hurdle.

Hurdle had a so-so rookie season, batting .264 with 7 home runs in 1978. He spent most of the next season in the minor leagues and appeared to recover in 1980, batting .294. But it was an empty .294 as he hit just 10 home runs in 130 games. The power he had displayed as an amateur and in batting practice did not translate to game action. He was trying to make too many people happy. Lau wanted Hurdle to be a line-drive hitter. Royals manager Whitey Herzog wanted him to hit home runs.

"Clint would call me and really be upset," Clint senior said. "'Dad what should I do?' I said 'Clint, I'll tell you one thing. Herzog is the manager. He's your boss. You need to do what he says.'"

The problem was Kauffman Stadium in Kansas City, which remains one of the most difficult stadiums to hit home runs in today, and Hurdle played there before the fences were brought in.

Questions started to bubble up in the clubhouse from the print media, then grew to a boil as teammates and coaches began to whisper, "What's wrong with Hurdle?" Players and coaches often say they don't pay attention to the media or the public's opinion, but the truth is it finds a way to them. Comments and opinions are either passed along or a player's curiosity is too much to suppress.

In something of an avalanche effect, problems on the field began to contribute to a growing problem off the field. If Hurdle went 0 for 4, he'd try to forget it at the bar, but that would only lead to a sluggish performance the next day. His father had asked him to ease off the nightlife, but Clint wouldn't change.

"Initially it was a release. Maybe it was a hard day. My day wasn't so good, maybe my night will be better," Hurdle said. "The problem was after having good nights, you have days to answer to."

The crushing weight of expectations began to show. Said Hurdle in a 1981 interview with reporters, "If I'd done everything I was supposed to, I would be leading the league in home runs, have the highest batting average, have given a thousand dollars to the cancer fund, and have married Marie Osmond."

His performance began to decline dramatically. He played just 28 games with the Royals in 1981 and was released after the season, just three years after being labeled the game's next star, and just six years after being judged the ninth-best amateur talent in the country. After the players' strike in 1981, during which Hurdle bartended to make ends meet, he was traded to the Reds. He batted .209 in his first season there, was placed on waivers, and claimed by the Mets. He spent most of the 1983 season and all of the 1984 season in the minor leagues. When he did get brief opportunities with the Mets, he failed to bat .200. His bat was slowing, and his lack of speed limited him to few positions on the field. Hurdle appeared in only 3 major league games in 1987 with the Mets. One day that season, according to an ESPN feature story, Mets Triple-A manager Bob Schaefer sat Hurdle down and told him to get himself together or Schaefer might be his last manager. He was. Hurdle's playing career was over. His last major league plate appearance came on June 26, 1987, in Philadelphia, a pinch-hit strikeout against the Phillies' Kevin Gross. He was twenty-nine years old, when he should have been in his prime.

Hurdle had to come up with a plan B, but what could he do? He was smart, but he had no college degree. He had sacrificed that by going straight from high school to professional baseball. But while he had failed at playing the game, it still fascinated him. He enjoyed being around it, enjoyed the strategy, and even enjoyed the drill work. He liked philosophizing and joking with people and the camaraderie of the clubhouse.

"I loved the game and I was a part-time player," Hurdle said. "I asked the farm director if he had any managerial opportunities opening the next year. He actually thought it was a good idea, which was another bad sign. He shared it with other people. I had people calling me up and telling me what a great thought it was. I had two dozen people tell me it was the perfect decision to make at the perfect time."

The following season, in 1988, he became the High-A manager for the Mets affiliate in Port St. Lucie, Florida. This job felt right. He loved the interaction with young players and liked having knowledge to share. "I thought at the time I could be a very good encyclopedia for somebody, personally and professionally: the ups and downs and the sideways. All of it," Hurdle said. "And at the end of the day you watch a game."

He had a commanding presence, a booming voice, a charismatic personality, and his authority was not easily challenged. By 1991, he was promoted to managing the Mets Double-A affiliate in Williamsport, Pennsylvania. He was still drinking, though. Although he had created some order on the field, he was still struggling to find happiness off it. By this point he had burned through two marriages and was still spending too many nights at the local bar.

Hurdle's mother and father were always invested in their son. When

Hurdle played, they followed box scores in the paper. As a manager, they watched the Pirates' games from Florida through the out-of-market television package. Clint senior joked that he would feel "exhausted . . . as if he had played" after each game. They traveled to see Clint as often as they could. When Hurdle was at his lowest point they tried to help. During one visit soon after Hurdle's second marriage ended, Clint senior suggested to his son they take a walk. "I told him life isn't fair," Clint senior said. He told his son sulking about the past did not do any good. He had to move forward. He had to find peace.

★ ★ ★

In the spring of 1991, Hurdle met an attractive, smart brunette named Karla. A local accountant, she was not chasing ballplayers. Hurdle met her while having his taxes prepared. He didn't get a phone number, but he knew he had to see her again. So he made the most important strategic decision of his life: he had a friend host a party as an excuse to invite Karla. His plan worked. After six years of dating, as Hurdle advanced to manage the Triple-A Norfolk Tides in 1992 and then joined the Colorado Rockies as a minor league hitting instructor in 1994, Hurdle asked Karla to marry him, she said no. Hurdle was taken aback. He was a former star, an ex–major league player, something of a celebrity in minor league towns. He knew he was charismatic and joked that he was pretty good at getting married, having already lived through two marriages, but Karla stood her ground. She believed something meaningful was happening between them, but before she could commit, Hurdle had to get his life together. She wouldn't tolerate his drinking binges. Hurdle had to get comfortable with who he was and his past and had to stop trying to run from it. Karla saw a man who was still haunted by that *Sports Illustrated* cover, tormented by his former phenom status and by what he never fulfilled and never became.

"I just thought there were a lot of things he wasn't quite right with," Karla Hurdle said in an interview with ESPN. "He had to put some of his demons to rest that I couldn't help him with."

Former big shots like Clint usually get extra leash slack and extra chances in life. They aren't always challenged and instead are usually accommodated. This time it was different, he had to change. He had to figure out what made him happy. He found he was happiest coaching, managing, and when he was helping people. He discovered that he was happier when he wasn't drinking and reengaged with his faith. He went to Alcoholics Anonymous meetings—Hurdle still attends them from time to time—and learned to recite his favorite Bible verses.

At forty-one years old, Hurdle finally stopped drinking in November of 1998 and hasn't had a drop since. He asked Karla to marry him again in 1999, and this time she accepted. For the first time since he was a top prospect some twenty-one years earlier, his life finally seemed to be rocketing upward. He had joined the Rockies organization in 1994 and was named their major league hitting coach in 1997. In 2002 he was promoted to manager, but the success and happiness was fleeting.

In Colorado during Hurdle's first season as manager, Clint and Karla had their first child together, Madison Reilly. She was born prematurely and diagnosed with the genetic disorder Prader-Willi syndrome. Hurdle said he learned of the diagnosis during a road trip to Houston. He told a reporter he went to his hotel room and "cried more in three days than I had in twenty-five years." He learned about the disorder's litany of frightening characteristics, such as cognitive disabilities, behavioral problems, and a chronic feeling of hunger, and that there is no cure.

Early in the 2007 season when the Rockies were struggling, a Denver TV reporter asked Hurdle if one particular loss "was crushing." Hurdle entered the season on the hot seat and had yet to produce a winning season as Rockies manager. Months later in October, when the Rockies were in the midst of an improbable run to the World Series, Hurdle recalled that question. Said Hurdle: "Crushing was when a doctor told me my little girl was born with a birth defect. Baseball is a game. And I've learned that. And I've embraced that and I've tried to share that with my players."

While he had found perspective, he reached another professional crossroads in Colorado. In the spring of 2009, two years after guiding the Rockies to the National League pennant, the team stumbled to an 18–28 start to the season, and Hurdle was fired on May 29. In eight years with the Rockies, he had produced just one winning season. He had presided over nearly a hundred more losses (625) than victories (534).

While Hurdle had changed dramatically off the field, he was mainly traditional on the field. Following the tenets of tradition helped him become a top prospect, then go on to rise through the coaching ranks. He was raised on and believed in old-school, twentieth-century baseball orthodoxy, which suggested that statistics often lied and that subjective decisions were most important, and that only those who had played the game could understand it meaningfully. Maybe it was denial or willful ignorance, but Hurdle had never investigated the available data that was constantly pouring into the game early in the twenty-first century.

He had gone to the World Series with one of the most traditional franchises in baseball, the Rockies, who didn't employ a single stat-crunching front-office employee. For an example of the Rockies' adherence to conventional wisdom, consider sacrifice bunting. It is a traditional strategy and almost always reduces a team's probability to score a run. Yet, even in hitter-friendly Coors Field, no major league team had as many sacrifice bunts as the Rockies from 2004 to 2006. And with the Rockies he became the most traditional of baseball scapegoats. Though managers have little control over roster construction or player performance, they are often the first to be blamed for failure and the first fired.

After being fired by the Rockies, he finally had something in his life for the first time in a long while: he had time. Hurdle was able to reflect on where he had been and what he wanted to do, and he had no obligations. But he could only be idle for so long. He still wanted to be in the game, he knew that much. To pass the second half of the 2009 season, Hurdle became an analyst for the fledgling Major League Baseball Network. He was a natural for television with his booming voice, lively personality, and library of anecdotes that he easily retrieved as if he were going through a neatly organized drawer. He figured the gig would be a fun way to pass the time until the next opportunity came along.

Hurdle had no idea what waited for him at the MLB Network headquarters, housed in a nondescript, warehouselike building in a business park in Secaucus, New Jersey. But here his sabermetrics enlightenment began. *Sabermetrics* is a term for data-based, objective analysis of baseball.

In the television studio Hurdle was exposed to new age baseball thought and sabermetrics data. He couldn't ignore or avoid it there. Flat-screen computer monitors were everywhere, along with data-savvy interns and analysts. He was in an alien environment, surrounded by elements of the game that he had ignored. Sitting in broadcast booths and preparing for shows, Hurdle was struck by how much data on-air analysts were fed. He had assumed analysts were bright people who did their own research and found their own trends, but he was taken aback by the support network and the information-gathering infrastructure of the MLB Network. For example, he could ask for how often a pitcher threw his slider, what its average speed and inches of vertical break were, and have the answers in mere moments.

His colleagues directed him to the Web site FanGraphs.com, which was a public treasure trove of data, where Hurdle began conducting his own investigations, often looking for statistical data to support a theory or hunch he had for an on-air segment. The young analysts and assistants at the network clued him in to the statistically based theory that was being produced at Web sites such as *Baseball Prospectus* and *The Hardball Times*. Hurdle learned which players the sabermetrics community thought were underrated and overrated.

"It was kind of like being in a *Wizard of Oz* setting with no ramifications," Hurdle said. "It goes back to that saying 'the more you learn the less you know.' Once I got started, it was hard to stop."

Hurdle was not out of a coaching job for long. He was hired by the Texas Rangers to be their hitting coach on November 4, 2009. In Texas he employed some statistical-based scouting reports on pitchers' tendencies to help create game plans for his hitters. By the time he interviewed for the Pirates managerial job after the 2010 season, he talked a good game. The Pirates liked his leadership and passion. They were surprised by the depth of his knowledge and his interest in new age, statistical baseball thought. While he admittedly wasn't on the cutting edge of analytics, he felt he was in play and that he had an understanding of the new data entering the game.

But as Huntington and Hurdle met on that chilly day in October of 2012, Hurdle had put little of the Pirates' statistical findings from the analytics department to use on the field in his first two seasons.

Despite the struggles of the Pirates, he was having trouble breaking from tradition and trusting what he couldn't see. He had always trusted his instincts.

"I think at times I can get hardened or callous to straight statistical analysis because that's not my comfort area. I didn't go to school there," Hurdle said. "I don't have the depth and knowledge and understanding. I've had to rearrange my furniture to have a better understanding of that."

The Pirates needed the conflicted Hurdle to break from tradition. All over baseball the manager and his staff were holding back the big data movement, and it had been no different in Pittsburgh. Huntington and his analytics team needed a complete buy-in to change from Hurdle. And if they needed convincing evidence to make their case, they believed that they finally had it.

3

PROVING GROUNDS

The experiment began far from the spotlight in late February 2010, on the back fields of the team's spring training home in Bradenton, Florida. The fields are remote, behind the dorms, batting cages, and office space at the Pirate City complex, and surrounded by chainlink fences and windscreens erected in vain to try to tamp down the relentless Gulf breeze. The complex is completely private, with the parking lot gated and the perimeter of the property obscured by palms, wax myrtles, gum trees, and undergrowth.

Here, the director of player development, Kyle Stark, behaving curiously, held a map of sorts, a diagram of a baseball field with X's marked at various positions. He walked the infield holding a can of white spray paint and marked an X roughly equidistant between second and third base deep on the infield skin. The tall, brown-haired, and blue-eyed Stark paced some more, then marked another white X just behind second base, then set off into shallow right field between first base and second base and made another mark. What the hell was he doing? wondered the gray-bearded minor league coaching staff as they watched. Was he searching for buried treasure? In a way, yes.

Stark had traded e-mails all winter and early spring with the creator and director of the Pirates analytics department, Dan Fox. Fox, a profoundly unknown Pirates employee, was a former *Baseball Prospectus* writer and Chevron data architect who is never interviewed before or after games, and whom the public and players know little about. He has the last bio in the 2013 media guide at the bottom of page 14, which includes a mug shot and brief paragraph of text that explains in a hundred words that Fox is responsible for the "architecture, development and dissemination of information systems and quantitative analytics" within baseball operations. Most of the coaches on the field that day watching Stark had never even heard of Fox. But Stark was intrigued with Fox's research. Months of dialogue between the two men had led Stark to this field, at this moment, to these markers, which were a guide to hidden value. Stark had in his hands something resembling a treasure map.

A baseball team places nine defenders on a baseball field. Two of those players, the pitcher and the catcher, are in fixed positions. But the other seven are free, in theory, to position themselves at any location on the field. Since the game's beginnings players have taken familiar defensive positions. Infielders and outfielders position themselves not based upon where balls are most often hit but, rather, equidistant from other fielders. Patches of outfield grass are worn down from players' being stationed there so often. It was counterintuitive to leave large swaths of the field unoccupied, considering that the average baseball field covers just under three acres.

This traditional defensive positioning has for more than a hundred years been based on anecdotal evidence. From the nineteenth century through the twentieth, players and managers were often armed with only personal history and observations to make decisions on defensive positioning.

But what if since the game's origins, everyone—players, coaches, executives—*everyone*, had gotten defense wrong? Throughout baseball history some brief, isolated deviations from tradition have been tried. The first recorded defensive shift—generally defined as when three or more infielders are positioned to one side of second base— occurred in the nineteenth century. On May 9, 1877, the *Louisville Courier-Journal* reported a curious defensive strategy by Hartford manager Bob Ferguson against the Louisville Grays. Not only did Ferguson shift infielders, he occasionally moved all three of his out- fielders to one-half of the outfield.

But shifts largely vanished until the 1920s, when several National League managers shifted three infielders to the right of second base to defend against pull-heavy Cy Williams, according to the Society for American Baseball Research. The left-handed Williams was power and pull conscious, meaning that he often hit the ball to right field, his pull-side. He was the first National League player to hit 200 career home runs and was one of only three players, including Babe Ruth and Rogers Hornsby, born before 1900 to hit 200 home runs in his career. But Williams and the effectiveness of the shift against him were forgotten over time.

The other Williams Shift is often credited as baseball's first radical departure from traditional defensive alignment. Though some teams had shifted on the great Ted Williams as early as 1941, the Ted Wil- liams Shift is often credited to have been born in the second game of a doubleheader on July 14, 1946, at Fenway Park. In the first game, Williams had gone 4-for-5, homered 3 times, and driven in 8 runs against Cleveland. So when Williams came to bat in the second game, Indians player-manager Lou Boudreau moved from his usual shortstop position to the traditional second-base position. Cleve- land's second baseman was deployed to shallow right field, and its third baseman moved to the right of second. The alignment was so radical a photo of the shift appeared in *The Sporting News* later that month. Against one of the first documented shifts of the postwar, modern era, Williams went 1-for-2 with a double and 2 walks. Maybe Williams's successful work in a single game against a radically aligned defense helped delay the proliferation of shifts by another sixty-five years.

"Somebody was telling me a story about Ted Williams," Hurdle once told the *Pittsburgh Tribune-Review.* "It was an umpire relaying a story from another umpire. [Williams] stepped to the plate at Fenway, and they had the tremendous shift for him. First time it had happened. He stepped back and looked at it. The umpire goes, 'That's interesting,' [and Williams] said, 'Not really. They can't play me high enough.'"

But as before, shifts mostly vanished from the game after that. Why? Because there was no hard evidence that teams should shift, no data proving that shifts were effective. Any successful moves away from traditional alignment would be based upon anecdotal evidence since no one was tracking batted balls statistically. And even if somebody was, another barrier remained: fear. Going against conventional thought requires courage and conviction because, when such an unorthodox attempt fails, public criticism is intense. For most of the game's history and for the entire twentieth century, teams played defense the same way they always had. Then came John Dewan.

★ ★ ★

On a bright Saturday afternoon in 1984, Dewan was eating lunch in the kitchen of his Chicago home and enjoying the latest *Bill James Baseball Abstract,* a book of in-depth and original statistical research of baseball published each year from 1977 to 1988. James wrote about baseball in a way no one had before and measured things that no one else had. For instance, in the 1985 *Baseball Abstract* he introduced a system to translate minor league batting performance of prospects into future major league production. He wrote about how ballparks shape statistics, how career length varies at different positions, and of course the importance but lack of understanding of defensive play. Like Dewan, Bill James was a baseball outsider. He began writing while working as a night-shift security guard at Stokely–Van Camp's pork-and-beans cannery in Lawrence, Kansas, in the 1970s, and his work is often credited as being most responsible for bringing objective and scientific thought to baseball. In the early 1980s, James was attracting a niche following, those who had similar interests in advancing baseball thought. While James was poring over box scores and counting things that had not been counted before, it was not big data, which *Wikipedia* defines as an information set so large and complex it is impossible to process using traditional tools. What James and Dewan understood was that to advance the understanding of the game more data was needed. In the 1984 *Abstract,* he proposed beginning a grassroots effort called Project Scoresheet, which would employ a network of fans to score every game in more detail, with the information then entered into a computer database. Wrote James in the 1984 *Abstract*: "When Project Scoresheet is in place, all previous measures of performance in baseball will become obsolete and an entire universe of research options will fall in front of us . . . there is no need for the next generation of fans to be ignorant as we are." Dewan stopped eating his lunch when he read that James was looking for volunteers to help out with his Scoresheet stringer network. "I remember going, 'Oh, my gosh, this is what I've always wanted to do,'" Dewan said. This was similar to Dewan's dream to computerize the play-by-play information in all sports. Personal computers were becoming more practical, powerful, and affordable, making the project possible. Dewan had graduated with two degrees from Loyola University in mathematics and computer science, and this was right up his alley.

Dewan left his kitchen table in search of a telephone directory to look up James. Three weeks later, Dewan was entering and collecting data for Project Scoresheet, and a year after that he was the project manager, writing the software and organizing people all over the country to input data. He gave his stringers scoring templates that broke the field into zones and educated his network on how the plays should be coded. By 1994, the project, under various caretakers, had collected ten years' worth of games (1984–94), which covered 23,000 games and 1.7 million plays.

In 1987 Dewan decided his hobby had become too engrossing. His wife, Sue, had even quit her job to put more time into the data-gathering. He had to either lessen his commitment or make it a career. He was so committed to Project Scoresheet and statistical analysis of baseball that he left his successful career as an insurance actuary. He invested in a small company called STATS—an acronym for Sports Team Analysis and Tracking Systems—and became its president. His first headquarters was a spare bedroom in his Chicago home. He then moved his company into a basement office and later rented a proper office space as the company expanded.

Dewan still often works out of that spare bedroom, though his hair has turned white and his thick, black eyebrows have grown fuller. Back in 1987, STATS supplied research to NBC for its postseason-baseball coverage and was doing the same for ESPN regular-season broadcasts in 1989. James and Dewan helped dramatically increase the game's data.

In 2000, Dewan sold STATS to News Corps. and two years later formed another company, Baseball Info Solutions (BIS), which recorded batted-ball and pitch-by-pitch data at a more detailed level.

At BIS, Dewan hired a group of video scouts to review every play of every major league game—all 2,430 per year. Consider BIS's plus-minus statistic, which is an important metric in understanding how the evaluation of individual defensive performance has improved. Plus-minus measures how many balls individual defenders reach compared to a league average at their respective positions. BIS video scouts record the exact location on the field where every batted ball lands or is caught, then convert those locations into coordinates, storing the information in a computer database. James's Project Scoresheet simply noted what zone a ball landed in using a uniform grid overlaying the field. In 2009, BIS began more accurately measuring how hard balls were hit. For fly balls and line drives, BIS times, stopwatch-style, the batted ball's hang time until it lands or is caught. For ground balls in the infield, the time from when a ball is hit to when a fielder first intercepts the ball is timed. Based on that data, BIS records how many balls a fielder reaches compared to the league average at his position. The fielders are debited or credited points. The plus-minus points are then converted into a run value to quantify how many runs an individual player was saving above or below league average, a statistic called defensive runs saved.

Up until that time defenders had been judged largely on the subjective statistic of errors. An error is a judgment by the official scorer. Beyond anecdotal evidence, no one was accounting for more important factors such as how much ground a defender could cover after the ball was hit.

When Dewan was a softball-league infielder, he loved playing defense, which is why he focused so much on it. He prided himself on his defensive play, choosing to play shortstop and third base, the two positions on the more difficult left side of the infield. He was also an enthusiastic player of the baseball-simulation board game Strat-O-Matic, which, like APBA baseball, assigned probabilities to each individual player card that reflected the actual player's skills and used dice to create random numbers and outcomes. While baseball had simplistic methods of measuring defensive value, via errors and fielding percentage, Strat-O-Matic gave each player a defensive rating, and it was important to field a strong defensive team. This all helped Dewan appreciate defensive value, while most in the baseball world were concerned with batting average and home run totals for position players.

"It made me want to appreciate what the best players are really worth, because the eye can be deceiving as with anything. Anything you do, anything you perceive, is not always the reality," Dewan said.

Baseball's perceptions on where to place defenders in the field were wrong.

Dewan and his team unearthed interesting data about the nature of balls in play. For instance, BIS found that major league hitters hit ground balls to their pull-side 73 percent of the time, meaning a left-handed batter hits toward the right-side of the field an overwhelming amount. Batters also hit line drives to their pull-side 55 percent of the time. The only type of balls major league hitters did not pull the majority of the time were fly-balls, which went to their pull-side only 40 percent of the time. Those numbers changed little year to year over a decade of study.

"When we got really in-depth data from Baseball Info Solutions," Dewan said, "that's when I also started looking very closely at shifting."

Dewan's database taught him some valuable lessons, which he began sharing with baseball after the 2011 season. In March of 2012 at the Society for American Baseball Research (SABR) Analytics Conference, Dewan demonstrated the value of shifting to officials from twenty major league teams. Dewan revealed that of the eight most shifted-upon hitters in 2011, their combined batting average when shifted upon declined by 51 points. All eight of the players were power-hitting, left-handed batters, the only type of batters that the majority of baseball was employing generic shifts against. While teams were shifting on some power-hitting lefties such as Jim Thome and Adam Dunn based upon anecdotal evidence, Dewan found defenses should be shifting for a hundred major league hitters—25 percent of the league.

Pull-heavy, right-handed hitters should also have seen shifts, but rarely did. According to BIS's database, the first shift employed against a right-handed hitter in the modern era didn't occur until June 11, 2009, when the Phillies shifted left against Gary Sheffield. In 2010 and 2011, despite mountains of batted-ball data available from scouting services such as BIS and Inside Edge, teams were only shifting 0.8 times per game, and those shifts were almost exclusively against left-handed power hitters.

In a March 30, 2012, article for BillJamesOnline.com, a Web site of statistical analysis run by James, Dewan noted the Tampa Bay Rays were the top defensive team in baseball in 2011, amassing 85 defensive runs saved. The Rays won 91 games in 2011, and Dewan noted that if the Rays had had an average defense, meaning zero defensive runs saved, they would have won 8 or 9 fewer games, using the standard that 10 runs equals 1 win. The Rays were the most aggressive shifting team in baseball in 2011, shifting their defense 216 times. The next closest team was the Milwaukee Brewers, with 170 shifts. Only two other teams—the Cleveland Indians and the Toronto Blue Jays—shifted more than 100 times in 2011.

Dewan wondered, Was it a fluke the team that shifted the most in 2011 had the best defense?

He looked at an interesting case study: the 2010 Brewers versus the 2011 Brewers. The individual defenders on the Brewers were not as talented as those on the Rays. In fact, the Brewers had the worst collection of defensive infielders in baseball. Milwaukee first baseman Prince Fielder ranked as worst defensive first baseman in baseball in 2010 according to BIS, costing the Brewers negative 17 defensive runs saved. Rickie Weeks ranked 34th out of 35 second basemen, costing the Brewers 16 runs. Shortstop Yuniesky Betancourt—who was acquired from the Kansas City Royals—cost the Royals a whopping 27 runs as he ranked last among shortstops in 2010. Third baseman Casey McGehee was their top defensive infielder, ranking 31st at his position, worth negative 14 defensive runs saved. It was difficult to dream up a worse defensive infield.

So what did new Brewers manager Ron Roenicke do in 2011? Dewan noted the Brewers went from being one of the least aggressive defensive teams—shifting just 22 times in 2010—to the second-most-aggressive shifting, shifting 170 times.

BIS categorizes shifts into two types: the Ted Williams Shift, when three infielders are positioned to one side of second base, and "Other Shifts," when players are out of traditional infield alignment but not quite in a Williams Shift position. Dewan noted the Brewers employed the Ted Williams Shift 45 times in 2011 against the obvious pull-heavy, lefty power hitters, the handful of hitters other teams were beginning to shift against by employing the Williams Shift. But the Brewers shifted 125 times against hitters that no other team in the National League was shifting against, using a variety of more sophisticated, nuanced, data-based alignments, making their defense dramatically better.

According to defensive runs saved, Fielder had saved 8 more runs in 2011 than the season before. Weeks had a 9-run improvement, McGehee had a 17-run turnaround, and Betancourt saved 20 more runs than during his previous season with the Royals.

In 2011, the Brewers infielders made a defensive runs saved improvement of 56 runs and added 5 or 6 wins simply through shifting more often. They went from being a 77-win team in 2010 to a 96-win team in 2011. BIS has found since 2010, when they started measuring batting performance against shifts, that batting average on ground balls and short line drives (BAGSL), the types of batted balls designed to be gobbled up by the shift, declined by 30 to 40 points per season with shifts on, compared to batting average against conventional defense.

Still, while shifting jumped slightly to 1.9 shifts per game in baseball in 2012, most of the shifts were utilized by only a handful of teams—with the Rays and the Brewers as the most devout believers and becoming ever more aggressive.

As early as 2004, BIS sold data-based recommendations to major league teams to optimize defensive positioning. While the majority of the industry was curious, few of the recommendations were reaching the field. Why?

"Because when it doesn't work, it really looks bad," Dewan said. "It goes against conventional wisdom of playing infielders where they have always played for so many years. It's hard to break tradition. But by doing the analytics you can see that it has value. You can see the runs you save when the shift is on, the percent of ground balls that are fielded when the shift is on."

When a team placed three infielders on one side of second base and a hitter beat the shift, intentionally or unintentionally, to the lightly defended opposite side of the infield, it looked really bad and it upset pitchers. It made infielders question why the heck they were shifting, and it tested the conviction of coaching staffs.

Still, here was a glaring inefficiency to be tapped into. In October 2012 teams were still only converting 30 percent of batted balls into outs, a rate relatively unchanged since the beginnings of the pro game. By 2012 the Pirates had only slightly increased their use of shifts and remained below average in defense. According to defensive runs saved, the Pirates were -77 in 2010, -29 in 2011, and -25 in 2012.

The Pirates fielded mostly athletically challenged defenders in traditional alignments, and the numbers demonstrated a stunning inefficiency. They had shifted their infield defense only 84 times in 2010 and 87 times in 2011. As late as 2012, Hurdle was still not buying into wholesale shifting, but perhaps an accumulation of data and indisputable evidence would sway him.

When Huntington first entered the limestone façade of the Pirates front office, which rests just beyond the left-field bleachers at PNC Park, there was a glaring absence. Four years after the publication of *Moneyball*, fourteen years after the Mosaic Web browser was released that popularized the Internet, and some thirty years after personal computers began to proliferate and Bill James began publishing his *Baseball Abstracts*, the Pirates were still in the digital dark ages, lacking an in-house analytics department and proprietary database. Not one employee or proprietary system was devoted to analyzing or processing data.

The metrics used by the Oakland A's in *Moneyball* were relatively rudimentary by today's standards. The A's took advantage of the industry's not properly evaluating on-base percentage, a stat that was easily found on a player's MLB.com profile page or a college prospect's Division I athletic site. But now, because of new pitch-tracking technology, computing power, and detailed-data providers such as BIS, baseball was entering an entirely different age, with the amount of data growing exponentially. If a club fell behind in the data-analyzing game, it would be exponentially harder to catch up.

With so much new data, from thousands upon thousands of batted balls to hundreds of thousands of pitch outcomes, locations, and speeds, the information could not be so easily quantified, processed, or made sense of. It required computer science experts and mathematical minds who could create algorithms and were fluent in database programming language. Analytics-savvy front offices wanted data as raw as possible, so they could spin it into their own proprietary measurements, values, and advantages.

One of Huntington's first priorities was to find a data architect to build a database. During his time with the Cleveland Indians the team had created DiamondView, one of the game's first and most comprehensive databases. With a few mouse clicks the Indians' baseball operations staff could retrieve statistical trends and projections, scouting reports, injury history, and contract status on thousands of professional players. To create such a system Huntington first had to find someone who could build it. He found Dan Fox.

★ ★ ★

You would not know Dan Fox was a formidable force in the Pirates front office if you brushed past him during lunch hour on Pittsburgh's North Shore, where PNC Park is located on the banks of the Allegheny River. Wearing wire-rimmed Oakley glasses and dressed in nondescript khakis and golf shirts, he is mild-mannered and speaks clearly, concisely, and quietly. His most distinguishing characteristics are his height, his lanky frame rising well over six feet, and that he shaves his head completely bald.

Fox was born in Davenport, Iowa, in 1968 and raised in Durant, Iowa, a small, idyllic Midwestern town that's a square-mile grid of ten avenues by ten streets and surrounded by cornfields. While Fox's mother tried to give her two sons, Dan and David, a well-rounded education and a childhood rich with experience, from school plays to participating in the band, Fox and his older brother, David, were obsessed with baseball. They organized games at the neighborhood park, watched the Cubs on Sundays at their grandparents' home, and, like Dewan, spent hours upon hours playing Strat-O-Matic. Like Dewan, Fox was influenced by Bill James's writing and research on finding undervalued players and creative strategies.

The first thing that intrigued Dan Fox was James's examination of left-right splits, how a player performed against left-handers versus right-handers. You couldn't find this information anywhere, it didn't exist, and nobody published it. So James did it himself. He went through *The Sporting News* and calculated the left-right splits and some other splits, such as home-road and day-night, and published them in his *Baseball Abstracts*. Fox thought it was revolutionary and was astounded and fascinated that someone had identified a new statistical subgroup upon which important decisions could be made.

Fox's other great interest besides baseball was the personal computer, and he had early access to one. His father, a banker, had purchased an Osborne personal computer in the early 1980s. The Osborne, one of the first portable personal computers, weighed twenty-three pounds and was about the size of a suitcase. On that machine Dan and his brother learned how to write computer code and were soon using it to analyze Strat-O-Matic cards.

Dan attended Iowa State University, where he majored in computer science. After graduating he worked at Chevron and then in the mid-1990s took a job with Quilogy, a Kansas City–based consulting company. He quickly became known not only for his sharp mind and smart presentations but also for his teaching ability. His being articulate and able to process and make sense of numbers gave him a uniquely valuable skill set. His brother, who runs the analytics department for AMC Theatres, attended several of Dan's seminars on database technology.

He was surprised at how simply yet effectively Fox explained complex ideas and applications to those who might otherwise be overwhelmed.

"People sometimes see IT guys as really down deep in the numbers, but he has a way of getting a thousand-foot view," David told the *Pittsburgh Tribune-Review*. "That's what really helps you communicate. He can grasp the big picture as well as the details."

Those that have worked with and know Dan Fox say that he acted as a sort-of translator for customers. He could take all the jargon and the complexity of the tech side and explain it in straightforward terms and relatable analogies. His peers simply did not see many people in the tech industry who had his communication ability.

Fox understood what one of the first computer programmers, Grace Hopper, knew to be true. Said Hopper in an interview recounted in *The Innovators*, "It was no use trying to learn math unless [you] could communicate it with people."

Because of this innate ability and noting how Fox loved to play around with data and communicate its findings, a coworker suggested he try blogging about software development. Intrigued, Fox created a Web page in 2003 and wrote two blog entries on software development before authoring a piece on baseball. After that he never again wrote another blog entry about software development.

The blog turned into a baseball-first hobby and attracted attention. In 2003, the Web site TheHardballTimes.com, a hobbyist site, offered Fox a regular writing position. While it didn't pay, it broadened his exposure. The platform allowed Fox to impress a fringe audience of smart baseball fanatics outside the game. By 2006, Fox, a devout Christian, had moved his family to Colorado, where he began working as a data architect for Compassion International, a child-advocacy ministry. Fox helped streamline disconnected systems, and the organization grew from $300 million to $800 million per year in donations during Fox's tenure. Then BaseballProspectus.com writer Will Carroll approached Fox and offered him a paid position with the site, one of the finest and most influential sabermetrics Web sites.

Fox titled his regular *Baseball Prospectus* column "Schrödinger's Bat," a nod to physicist Erwin Schrödinger's "Schrödinger's cat" thought experiment about the conflict between behavior of matter at the particle level versus the behavior of matter observable to the human eye. Fox explained the goal of his writing in an article titled "Wins and the Quantum."

"[Schrödinger] made people think deeply about what they knew or thought they knew about the nature of reality itself," Fox wrote. "And while I'm not pretending that baseball has anything profound to say about such matters (it is, after all, just entertainment), I do hope that through this column, at least now and then, we can devise clever experiments that put to the test both conventional and sabermetric wisdom and help us think more deeply about our shared distraction."

Fox wrote a hundred articles for the Web site, focusing on measuring what up until that point had not been accurately quantified. "[Bill James] commented in one of the *Baseball Abstract*s once that everything we need to measure in baserunning is already known, it's just that people haven't gone and quantified it," said Fox, who then attempted to quantify baserunning. "Then I wrote a defensive system to work with play-by-play data and wrote a bunch of articles about that."

BaseballProspectus.com still uses Fox's formula to evaluate baserunning. He used pitch-tracking data to visualize the three-dimensional shape of Barry Zito's and Rich Hill's big-bending curveballs and Derek Lowe's and Roy Halladay's sinking fastballs.

On January 10, 2008, from his Colorado home, Fox investigated defensive shifting theory in an article for BaseballProspectus.com titled "Getting Shifty." For his project, Fox employed Retrosheet play-by-play data. University of Delaware biology professor David Smith began Retrosheet in 1989 as an effort to capture all historical play-by-play data, including data recorded prior to Project Scoresheet, which began tracking more detailed play-by-play data in the 1984 season. Fox examined batted-ball distribution for all left-handed major league hitters from 1956 to 1960. He found left-handed hitters were twice as likely to pull the ball to right field (48 percent of batted balls) as they were to hit to center (24 percent) or left (28 percent). He found Yankees star Roger Maris was the most extreme pull-hitting lefty of the era—batting 82 percent of balls to center or right, but was never known to have been shifted upon.

On January 24, 2008, Fox unveiled a defensive evaluation system he called Simple Fielding Runs Version 1.0, in which he created a defensive metric to measure individual player performance by spinning thousands of data points from Retrosheet play-by-plays into a single number to evaluate each major league player's defensive performance. Wrote Fox of his defensive system, which he created in few hours, "For the software developer in me, the interest in projects like these not only lies in the results (just how bad a fielder was Dick Allen?) but the process (actually the code) through which those results are generated."

Now those inside the industry were beginning to take notice. Three months later, Fox's next job opportunity came from inside the game. The call came from the Pirates, who had been intrigued with Fox's work at BaseballProspectus.com. Fox had spoken briefly with several teams, but this was his first serious phone call. Huntington wanted Fox as an analyst. He appreciated the way Fox thought about the game and how he quantified things that had previously never been measured. Huntington liked not only Fox's mind but the way he spoke and communicated. Huntington wanted to marry objective thinking with subjective opinions from coaches and scouts. But the limited resources of the Pirates meant they could only hire one full-time data-related employee in 2008. Fox would have to take on both roles: that of data analyst and system architect. He would have to build the data-gathering and organizational structure he required to do the analysis and investigations that fascinated him. He agreed to take on the challenge, coming aboard early in 2008.

Fox would have to play catch-up to build such a system from scratch. The first year, 90 percent of his time was dedicated to building the club's database, which was called MITT, an acronym for Managing Information, Tools and Talent. He had to learn where all the data he wanted originated from, purchase the rights to use the data, write software, and integrate all of these elements into a system. Only then could he begin asking the interesting questions and enjoy the pursuit of answers.

But Fox was not the only Pirates employee interested in asking questions and challenging tradition. In 2008, minor league infield instructor Perry Hill had begun his own experiment in altering defensive alignment. Based upon his experiences, Hill thought infielders should play hitters more aggressively toward their pull-side. He began positioning minor league shortstops and second basemen deeper in the hole, meaning shortstops played nearer to third base on the left side of the infield against right-handed hitters, and second basemen nearer to first base on the right side of the infield against left-handed hitters. Hill insisted the alignment be uniform across the entire minor league system of the Pirates, and to ensure this standard throughout, he pounded eight pegs made of sawed-off portions of PVC pipe into the ground in the infields of the Pirates' minor league stadiums. The tops of the pipes were at ground level and were visible only if you knew where to look. These markers would guide the four infielders into the new positions against right- and left-handed batters, and these positions were not to be deviated from.

Kyle Stark had granted Hill this freedom to explore. Never shy about considering an out-of-the-box idea, Stark found himself in the midst of controversy late in the 2012 season when he was criticized for his part in having minor league prospects engage in some Navy SEAL–style training exercises that left one of the club's top prospects with a minor injury. Ownership condemned the military-style practices. Then on September 20, in the midst of the Pirates' second straight last-half-of-the-season collapse, passions in the fan base were inflamed when an unorthodox, motivational e-mail from Stark to minor league coaches and development staff was leaked to the *Pittsburgh Tribune-*

Review and later picked up by national media outlets. But Stark's willingness to depart from traditional practices was key in allowing Hill to conduct his experiment. And its results were intriguing. The number of ground balls the Pirates' minor league affiliates had converted to outs had slightly increased in 2008. Stark wanted to know why, so he sought out Dan Fox.

Fox had just spent nearly all of 2008 creating the club's information database. His first analysis assignments in 2008 were related to the amateur draft, which was the keystone of Huntington's strategy for reconstructing the Pirates. Initially Fox didn't have enough hours to dig into game strategy. But by the spring of 2009, his role was expanding, and while Hill and Stark were interested in tweaking defensive alignment, Fox was curious about a division rival, the Milwaukee Brewers. While Tampa Bay was in the vanguard of shifting in the American League, Milwaukee was the first team in the National League to consistently shift. Stark and Hill wanted to know where balls were most often put in play. Now, with the first version of the club's proprietary software in place, and with his amateur-draft studies behind him, Fox turned his attention to shifts.

"Our data was just not very good, not complete at the time," Fox said. "Knowing Perry would be open to [shifting away from traditional defensive alignment] because of the idea of range, and positioning, and the idea of stakes . . . it fit that that would be an avenue to explore."

Defensive theory and batted-ball research became approved as a key project. Fox began acquiring batted-ball data from vendors and began analyzing every ball put in play dating back to 2004, when the data from companies such as BIS first became more comprehensive. He analyzed tens of thousands of batted balls. Like Dewan, Fox was curious in researching players' batted-ball tendencies. But unlike Dewan, Fox was in the Pirates front office and had direct communication lines with the coaching staff and developmental staff also. He had more sophisticated tools and could analyze the data at a deeper level. He reached the same conclusion as when he'd researched cruder

Retrosheet data for BaseballProspectus.com: shifts were dramatically more effective than the conventional alignment. Against certain hitters it *did* make sense to leave roughly half of the infield undefended and to move the infielders closer to the lines.

After weeks of research, Fox brought compelling evidence to Stark, Hill, and Huntington and recommended the Pirates change the way they played defense. Not only did he suggest that the Pirates shift much more often, but he found that Hill's theory was correct: base defensive alignments should also be changed. Infielders should be playing all hitters more toward their pull-side, meaning against right-handed hitters the shortstop and third baseman should play nearer the third-base line.

The Pirates and major league baseball as a whole had played infield defense conventionally for decades, really since the professional game's origins. What Fox was suggesting was that they throw out a hundred years of tradition and begin something new.

"Getting a longtime, respected baseball guy [such as Hill] to say, 'We might not be in the right spots,' and have Dan Fox say, 'Yeah, I have hundreds of thousands of balls in play that show you are not in the right spots' . . . to have those two pieces in place was critical," Huntington said. "To have our coaches talk about it, to see it work, to hear it work, to understand the difference it could make . . . it was critical."

The major league coaching staff was not ready to embrace these findings. Still, Stark wanted to ramp up this plan and thought that the minor leagues should be the first laboratory to test Fox's theories.

Stark and Fox did not have the data at the minor league level to customize alignment for every hitter. Over the winter of 2009–10 they devised, via e-mail and occasional meetings in the Pittsburgh office, two generic shift and defensive-alignment packages: one for right-handed hitters, one for left-handed hitters. They went back and forth drawing diagrams of what base-level alignment changes and shifts would look like at the minor league level, and they marked off the number of feet players should be from the foul lines or bases. Then on a back field at the Pirate City complex in February 2010, Stark laid the plan out to his perplexed minor league coaches and development staff.

"This is what we are going to do going forward," Stark said. They were adopting a radical new approach to defensive alignment, and it was not optional. Hill's "pegs," his sawed-off PVC pipes, were one thing, but this was going to be another level of extreme. Over that spring, Stark met one-on-one with every minor league coach to go over the plan and its alignments, explaining in further detail why they were adopting this seemingly crazy and counterintuitive departure from tradition. Of course there was pushback and plenty of "Why?" But the final word from Stark was always the same: this is what we are doing. Not everyone was on board, and some faces changed among the minor league staff.

"We try to get better all the time and not be bound by conventional wisdom. Sometimes conventional wisdom is right. Sometimes it's there because it's the way we've always done things," Stark said. "We said, 'This is what the information is. Let's sell out to it.'"

In April the planning and directions had been given and the training had been done. Now Stark and Fox sat back and watched.

Stark began seeing results immediately as he toured the Pirates' minor league stadiums that season. Among sparse crowds in the half dozen minor league labs, far from television cameras and the national media's antennae, he saw ground balls up the middle that would traditionally be singles converted into outs; he saw ground balls deep in the six-hole—between the shortstop and third—turned into outs. He also saw pitchers become frustrated when a slow-rolling ground ball would beat a shift; but watching objectively, he saw that more balls were being converted into outs than beating the shift, and the stats started to back up his observations.

Fox did not see the action on minor league fields, but he was measuring it in his modest office on the third floor of Pirates headquarters in Pittsburgh. Fox found the Pirates' minor league affiliates were turning a higher percentage of ground balls into outs than any other organization in baseball. It was clear: the positioning plan was working.

By the end of the 2010 minor league season others had begun to take notice. Late in the year, while Stark was taking in the Pirates short-season, A-level club in Maryland, he was approached in the press box by the opposing team's media-relations director.

"Are you with the Pirates?" the man asked.

"Yeah," said Stark.

"I've watched you guys play however many times this year, and I've never seen a club turn so many balls into outs. We've never seen a team defend this way."

Not only were Pirates executives and coaches seeing the results, but their minor league players, a future generation of Pirates were becoming familiar with and acclimated to extreme defensive positioning. Shortstop Jordy Mercer was drafted in the third round in the 2008 draft, Huntington's first draft as Pirates GM. When he went to High-A ball in 2009, Mercer was exposed to Hill's pegs in the infield. Then in 2010, as he arrived at the Double-A level, the team started shifting. "It was a little strange at first . . . [but then] I just accepted it. I was all for it," Mercer remembers. "If we are going to play the odds, why not? If it works eight out of ten times, then let's do it."

During the following 2011 season, Hurdle's first year as Pirates manager, shifts were rarely employed against major league hitters. Meanwhile in the minors, Stark and Fox ramped up the shifts and lessened base-defense usage. Pirates minor league affiliates used their generic shifts against a vast majority of hitters and were again first or second in converting batted balls into outs.

Mercer saw the results firsthand. When he started playing up the middle against lefties, directly behind the pitcher, he noted that ground ball after ground ball seemed to find him there. Against right-handed hitters, Mercer would play in the hole between the traditional short-stop and third-base positions.

"I still to this day look over at [infield coach Nick] Leyva sometimes and say, 'You sure? You sure I'm supposed to be right here?' You feel out of place," Mercer said. "The next thing you know, they hit you a ground ball and you're in the right spot. I'll get one right at me, and it's just weird how that happens."

Perplexed opposing Triple-A players began to pepper Mercer with questions. "Why are you playing there?" they'd ask once they'd reach second base and were within earshot of Mercer. "What are you guys doing?"

Said Mercer, "I just play where they tell me."

Through the minor league stress-testing of big data strategies, the idea grew at the major league level. While Hurdle and his staff had still not bought into shifting in a significant way in 2012, the results at the minor league level grabbed Hurdle's attention; they had grabbed everyone's attention in the organization.

Finally that October night in 2012 in Hurdle's home, Hurdle and Huntington again discussed the data analyzed by the front office, the case for a radical departure from traditional defense. Pirates affiliates had finished first or second in defensive efficiency in their respective minor leagues, and the margin was growing as they ramped up their shift usage. They were turning more ground balls into outs than any other team. What if the Pirates could take that approach and customize defensive positioning to each major league opposing hitter? How much better could they be?

Hurdle often says feelings aren't facts, and facts aren't feelings. Hurdle could not run from the data facing him. He had started to challenge his own beliefs on alignment even before the meeting, but that questioning didn't mean it would be easy to change his whole philosophy. He was essentially being asked to hand over an aspect of in-game strategy to a man, Fox, who had never played the game. Hurdle would still be able to steer the team, but now he was being asked to trust a navigator who had never played a professional inning. Could he give up that control?

Hurdle had first met Fox at the 2010 winter meetings at the club's suite at the World Swan and Dolphin Resort in Orlando, Florida. The winter meetings were always a chaotic scene, particularly for Hurdle in 2010 as a new manager, with so many hands to shake, so many people to meet. Much of the entire industry was in one hotel, where ESPN and MLB Network set up live studios and tracked trade rumors and free agent signings in the lobby. On the day Hurdle met Fox, he was just another new face. Hurdle had never worked with such an analyst before during his tenure with the Rockies or the Rangers, and little of Fox's analysis was implemented in Hurdle's first two seasons in Pittsburgh. Hurdle admittedly kept Fox at "arm's length" in 2011. But over time that level of trust changed.

As minor league reports and statistics kept streaming into Hurdle's e-mail inbox about the effectiveness of the shifting, and as he began to hear more stories from the minor league managers—with whom Hurdle communicated frequently during the season—he could not simply dismiss the evidence.

It wasn't just shifting Hurdle heard about. Fox passed along ideas about lineup construction, baserunning efficiency, and bunting strategy. Fox was similar in ways to the analysts who had helped Hurdle at the MLB Network during his brief but enlightening time there. So in 2012, Hurdle decided he wanted to have more face time with Fox. Before the beginning of every home series, Hurdle asked to meet with Fox to go over the advance-scouting materials. Hurdle felt it was time for him to challenge himself. Hurdle's office is in the bowels of PNC Park, connected through a hallway to the clubhouse. The drywalled office has no windows, only fluorescent light, the harshness of which is lessened through the soft, khaki wall color. Hurdle has a number of mementos in his office. Photographs adorn the walls, including a panoramic shot of PNC Park and a portrait of Roberto Clemente. The desk is littered with books on leadership, baseball artifacts, family photos, and a Bose sound system that plays while Hurdle pores over pregame data. Perpendicular to his desk is a leather couch against the far wall of the room. Here Hurdle hosts visitors, including Fox. They were both able communicators. Hurdle wanted information. He asked questions and challenged some of Fox's findings, but also wanted to size up the man who was giving him this unconventional data. They spoke not just of baseball data but of their families, interests, faith, and backgrounds. They shared an interest in military history. Fox had loved to tour Civil War battlefields, many of which—Gettysburg, Fredericksburg, Bull Run, and Antietam—were a day trip from Pittsburgh. Hurdle learned Fox had middle-class, Midwestern roots like himself. Hurdle learned Fox was not some impatient IT guy who seemed to speak another language. These afternoon meetings are when Hurdle was able to put a face, and a person, to the data, and where he learned to trust Fox.

"The comfort level and acceptance level got better," Fox said. "I think most of that is from developing relationships. They are going to trust you more, trust your information more, the more they trust you as a person. I think we saw [the trust level] go up in 2012."

This relationship was critical. While Fox had driven the idea and pored over the numbers and created the alignment recommendations, Hurdle was still the on-field gatekeeper. He could bar or welcome the suggestions. Fox understood nothing could be implemented from where he sat. He could only provide recommendations, but he had no power to make it happen.

Hurdle thought about their conversations, and where he had been and how he had changed. He also thought about the Pirates' limited roster and resources and the daunting challenges ahead. He realized that these concepts Fox had created made sense.

At the October meeting with Huntington, after the case had been made for the data-based defensive plan, Hurdle turned to Huntington and said, "We need to be as aggressive as we possibly can with this."

With their jobs on the line, Hurdle and Huntington agreed to implement perhaps the most unconventional, systematic, and inventive plan the game had ever seen.

Hurdle was in and knew his challenge was just beginning. He would have to get his coaches and players on board and keep them committed to the idea and avoid a mutiny. But there was also a challenge for Huntington. The roster had holes and they couldn't expect to add 15 wins just through spinning their returning players into baseball gold. Hurdle needed not just a plan but some players.

4

THE HIDDEN VALUE

Snow had not yet come to Montreal, but the first week of November was frigid. In the biting air, Russell Martin approached his matte-black BMW coupe. He was just leaving his weekly therapy session at a Nordic spa, where he had been jumping from cold tubs to the sauna; the extreme changes in temperature helped his body recover from a long season. He took excellent care of his chiseled, five-foot-ten, 215-pound frame. As Martin scrolled through his smartphone, he saw that he had a missed call from an unfamiliar number. *A 412 area code? Where was that?* He opened his car door and escaped the cold before he listened to the voice mail. He had heard the unforgettable, booming, rough voice on occasion as a catcher with the Los Angeles Dodgers: Clint Hurdle.

Martin had first heard that voice when Hurdle was managing the Colorado Rockies. They'd met briefly when they were both on the 2008 National League All-Star team. Days earlier, Martin had been surprised to learn from his agent, Matt Colleran, that the Pirates were the most aggressive team courting him early in free agency, which began soon after the World Series ended. Martin's season had been over for several weeks now. The Detroit Tigers had eliminated Martin and the New York Yankees in the American League Championship Series on October 18. Rather than stick around New York to hear and read the public outcry, he immediately returned to his native Montreal, where he made his off-season home. It was quiet in his hometown, a place to escape sports, at least baseball. Baseball had been gone since the Montreal Expos left to become the Washington Nationals in 2004. Montreal was a cultural and cuisine mecca where sports outside of hockey were not paramount. The second-largest French-speaking city in the world after Paris, it shared much of Parisian culture. Martin speaks French fluently and prides himself on being something of a foodie and an urbanite. He was raised in Montreal to have an appreciation for the arts. His father is an African-Canadian jazz saxophonist, and his white French-Canadian mother, Suzanne Jenson, is a singer and actress. He skateboards, takes the metro, and enjoys Montreal's cafés and bistros and its European feel. He can relax and escape here.

That escape was now interrupted as he listened to Hurdle's voice mail, asking for an opportunity to make his pitch. Martin's round face, capped with cropped, curly dark hair, broke into a smile, surprised by the call on a number of levels. For starters, the Pirates? They were young and rebuilding, right? They were always rebuilding. They had twenty consecutive losing seasons. Why did Martin make sense for them? He was also surprised his agent said they were willing to go to multiple years and near eight figures per season. The Pirates never paid for free agents, and free agents were not exactly banging down their door to get in. They had become something of a baseball Siberia.

While surprising and perplexing, the phone call was also reassuring. Entering free agency, having produced a career-worst .211 batting average in 2012 and .143 mark in the postseason, he was worried about the level of interest from other teams. His speed was in decline and he was going to be thirty in February. When the Yankees discussed the possibility of resigning Martin immediately after the season, during the window that the clubs had to exclusively negotiate with their own free agents, Yankees general manager Brian Cashman shockingly told Martin's agent that money was tight. Money tight for the Yankees? It wasn't as if Martin were seeking a nine-figure contract. Wasn't it more likely they didn't want him back after his ugly offensive numbers?

The Texas Rangers were the other club that had showed interest. Martin and his agent were to fly to Dallas soon to meet with the Rangers executives, but the Rangers were not offering the years or dollars he sought. Martin thought he might have to sign a one-year, lower-dollar deal to build back his value. The Rangers were a talented 93-win team the previous season, losing in the wild-card game to Baltimore. But the Rangers weren't as aggressive in courting him. Not only had the Pirates aggressively entered discussions as free agency began, offering two years and more money than the Rangers, but now the club's manager was calling him directly. It as an all-out recruitment.

But the Pirates? Why were they so interested? He was coming off his worst season as a pro and, according to traditional statistics, had generally been in a six-year decline in offensive performance. As Martin drove along an open expanse of highway that ran along the St. Lawrence River on Montreal's south shore, the city's skyline became visible to the north. He freed one hand and reached for his phone.

Back in Pittsburgh, Hurdle knew Martin might not be interested in the Pirates and might not return his call to listen to his pitch. But the Pirates had been so aggressive and Hurdle had reached out so quickly not only because of their interest but their desperation. Hurdle had agreed to implement a radical defensive plan. The beauty of the plan was that the shifts and what the pitching staff would be asked to do had not required adding a single dollar to the payroll. The Pirates thought they could create wins without spending additional dollars; they *had* to. But that plan couldn't fix all the team's issues; it wouldn't push them into the playoffs. They also had to somehow find hidden value externally and pay for it.

After their organizational meetings several weeks earlier, the Pirates had universally agreed that their situation at catcher was untenable. They did not have a starting-caliber major league catcher within the organization, and without one they would be in dire shape. They also agreed they had to bolster their starting rotation. The problem? The Pirates had roughly $15 million to spend on major league free agents in the 2012–13 off-season. Those dollars might seem significant, but an average starting pitcher or position player was then going for $10 million per year on the free agent market. The Pirates would not be able to afford obvious, proven, top-of-the-market commodities. So to reverse their fortunes, for the coaching and front-office staff to save their jobs, they would have to maximize every dollar. They had to find value on the free agent market in places where others did not.

Still, they knew Pittsburgh was not a free agent destination and that other teams would be attractive to Martin. Hurdle's phone had been silent for an hour when Martin called.

After some initial catching up, the sales pitch began. Hurdle sold the city, the park, the team, noting how the Pirates had carried winning records into the second half of each of the last two seasons before Epic Collapses I and II. But what Martin really wanted to hear about beyond the contract details was what they saw in him. Why did they value him? Hurdle said the clubhouse needed a veteran presence. He thought Martin would be great working with young pitchers, who would be less likely to shake him off and go with his game plan. Hurdle said the Pirates liked Martin's toughness and throwing arm since they had been woeful at controlling their opponents' running games.

There was also the contract. It didn't hurt that the Pirates were also offering more money than Martin's other suitors: $17 million for two years. The Pirates had never spent that much for a free agent.

After Martin and Hurdle amicably concluded the phone call, Martin was intrigued. "He helped me shape my decision," Martin said. "I thought, 'Maybe there's something I can do to help them get over that hump.'"

But the Pirates were withholding information. During their conversations, they never revealed a key discovery that had led them to Martin.

★ ★ ★

At the 1906 Plymouth country fair in England, eight hundred people took part in a contest to guess the weight of a particular ox. Statistician Frank Galton noted the average guess of 1,207 pounds was within 1 percent of the actual weight—1,198 pounds. The anecdote is contained in James Surowiecki's book, *The Wisdom of Crowds*, which theorizes that decisions made by a diverse collection of individuals are likely to produce more accurate predictions than even those of experts. With the advent of the Web, never before could so much knowledge, so much data, and so much brainpower be thrown at a problem. The wisdom of crowds' closely related kin are online open sourcing and crowdsourcing. With the Web, companies and institutions are able to outsource problem-solving, giving tasks once performed by employees to the public.

In 2006, Netflix put open sourcing to great use. The movie-streaming company's primary goal was to connect people to the movies they liked and predict other movies users might like. The company asked the crowd to see if it could produce an algorithm better than its own, Cinematch, and offered a $1 million prize. In 2006, Netflix presented the interested parties with a data set of more than a 100 million ratings that 480,000 anonymous users gave to 18,000 movies. Netflix withheld over 3 million recent ratings from those same subscribers. Contestants were required to make predictions for the 3 million more recent ratings and better Netflix's own algorithm's predictive power by 10 percent to win the prize. By June 2007 more than 20,000 teams had registered for the competition from over 150 countries, according to Netflix. The algorithm had to incorporate millions of ratings, thousands of users, and the ever-evolving preferences of those users.

In 2009, after three years of heavy collaboration, hundreds of e-mail exchanges, and long nights, BellKor's Pragmatic Chaos became the first team to beat Netflix's algorithm for predicting ratings by over 10 percent, at 10.6 percent.

Crowdsourcing and open sourcing began impacting an assortment of industries, including baseball. And the phenomenon benefited from baseball's first great automated big-data collection tool, PITCHf/x.

★ ★ ★

Entering 2007, the Chicago-based company Sportvision was best known for enhancing telecasts, bringing the glowing hockey puck to NHL telecasts and the yellow first-down marker superimposed on the field to football. The camera-based, motion-tracking system PITCHf/x was developed to improve for ESPN its K-Zone product, which measured if pitches were in the strike zone.

PITCHf/x was functioning and collecting real-time pitch data in select parks in 2007, and every major league stadium in 2008. That season, three 60 Hz cameras were mounted inside every park. The cameras and object-recognition software capture images of a pitch's flight from the time it leaves a pitcher's hand until it crosses home plate. From the images the speed, trajectory, and three-dimensional location of the ball are calculated in real time. PITCHf/x has a margin of error of less than one mile per hour in speed and one inch of location. Moreover, PITCHf/x labeled every pitch type in real time. For the first time, the exact speed of a pitcher's throws and the exact percentage of times he threw certain pitches could be tracked. Finally, standard measurements existed for pitch speed, type, movement, and location, and this data was made widely available, such as the on Web sites FanGraphs.com and BrooksBaseball.net.

Wrote University of Illinois professor Alan M. Nathan in a 2012 paper on physics and baseball, "[PITCHf/x] records with unprecedented precision such quantities as the pitch speed and the location at home plate. But even more importantly, we have measures of quantities that we never had before."

Database journalist Sean Lahman made a presentation titled "Baseball in the Age of Big Data" at a 2013 Society for American Baseball Research conference in Philadelphia. Lahman explained James's *Baseball Abstracts* had spiked the sport's total data points to more than two hundred thousand per season in the early 1980s. By 1990, Project Scoresheet's play-by-play data tripled the game's total data points to just under 1 million per season. Still, Lahman noted that big data doesn't mean a lot of data. It means collecting every shred of data available and employing complex mathematical formulas to draw conclusions from it. Baseball did not have a true big data tool until PITCHf/x. "James clearly understood that to make advances in our understanding of the game, we needed to make a quantum leap in terms of the amount of information we had available," Lahman said at the presentation. "As far as I'm concerned, that was his real genius."

While Bill James and John Dewan understood the importance of creating more data points, they were manually gathering much of it. PITCHf/x was automatically generating nearly 20 million usable data points per year, nearly as much as all the data recorded in baseball in the twentieth century, a giant leap for the game.

The growth has only accelerated as Lahman estimates new player-tracking technology that was being tested in a handful of ballparks in 2014 could push data points to 2.4 billion per year.

With the creation of PITCHf/x, major league front offices had overnight more data than they knew what to do with and not enough manpower to think of creative ways to employ it. But outside the front offices the game had hundreds if not thousands of creative, statistically inclined hobbyists who, like teams, were curious to search for hidden value in the sport. And hobbyists stumbled upon a use of data that teams had not thought of.

Pitch framing is a catcher's skill to influence borderline ball-strike calls. A batter and a home-plate umpire each have less than half a second to identify a 90 mph fastball as in or out of the strike zone. How a catcher receives the ball is a visual trick, a sleight-of-hand skill that can influence umpires to call borderline pitches as strikes. The ability to frame pitches had always been thought to carry value by managers, coaches, and players, but in the analytical community the skill had not been quantified, so its value was underappreciated. No one doubted that if the ability to turn a borderline ball into a strike existed, it would be immensely valuable. A hitter's batting average changed dramatically based upon whether the count was in his favor or the pitcher's. The difference between a two-ball and one-strike count versus a one-ball and two-strike count is nearly 200 points in batting average.

On April 5, 2008, an article appeared on the Web site BeyondtheBoxScore.com by Dan Turkenkopf. By day, Turkenkopf was a data architect for the software company Apprenda. By night, he was a baseball blogger. His was the first known effort to quantify the value of pitch framing based upon PITCHf/x data. He worked off PITCHf/x research from fellow hobbyists Jonathan Hale and John Walsh. They had published articles in 2007 that used PITCHf/x data to track how accurately major league umpires called balls and strikes. They were curious to identify individual umpires' strike-zone biases. Turkenkopf was most interested in the gray areas, the borders of the strike zone, the areas where Hale and Walsh found, on average, umpires called pitches as strikes 50 percent of the time. This is where the value of pitch framing resided.

Wrote Turkenkopf, "Using Walsh's strike zones, empirically defined as the areas where at least 50 percent of pitches are called strikes, I determined for each catcher how many balls should have been strikes and vice versa. This allowed me to calculate an average rate and then figure out how many strikes above or below average each catcher was."

Reviewing his findings, originally Turkenkopf thought he had miscalculated. The results were staggering. The catchers who caught at least 120 innings in 2007 showed a tremendous difference in the value they added or subtracted in their ability to frame pitches. Gregg Zaun led all catchers by saving 0.85 runs per 150 pitches. Gerald Laird cost his team -1.25 runs per 150 pitches. While Zaun led in the rate stats, the catcher who successfully framed the most pitches in 2007 was Russell Martin, who finished fourth in rate value, saving .63 runs per 150 pitches.

"I'll be the first to admit this is a much larger effect than I expected to see. In fact it's so large that I have to think there's something wrong in the analysis," Turkenkopf wrote. "Over the course of 120 games (a reasonable estimate for the number of games caught in a season by a starting catcher), the difference between Gregg Zaun and Gerald Laird is over 250 runs or 25 wins."

Turkenkopf's findings were astounding, and while imperfect, he was on to something. He had discovered something remarkable. He'd proved certain catchers were better than others at manipulating borderline strike calls and could swing the probable outcome of an at bat dramatically in favor of the pitcher. During the 1990s and early 2000s, catcher defense had been undervalued by analysts. Wrote Turkenkopf, "Maybe we've been wrong the whole time and catcher defense is really that important." Other analysts soon followed with attempts to refine the valuation of pitch framing. BaseballProspectus.com analyst Mike Fast found that the best catchers in 2011 were saving their teams 15 to 30 runs per season through pitch framing, and the worst catchers had cost their teams roughly 15 runs per season. Ranking second on Fast's leaderboard was Russell Martin, who had saved 70 runs through pitch framing over the five years from 2007 to 2011; ranking last was Pirates catcher, Ryan Doumit. Doumit had caught more than 2,800 innings over those five seasons and had cost the club thousands of favorable counts—and 65 runs—due to his faulty glove. Doumit's receiving skills were so obviously poor he earned the nickname Ryan "No-Mitt" in Pittsburgh. The five-year study showed a 135 run difference between Martin and Doumit. The Pirates' 2012 catcher, Rod Barajas, was also a below-average pitch framer according to the study.

Consider the following chart:

EXCERPT FROM MIKE FAST'S CHART FROM HIS SEPTEMBER 24, 2011, ARTICLE, "SPINNING YARN"								
TOP FIVE CATCHERS	Called Pitches	Total Runs Saved	R/120G	2011	2010	2009	2008	2007
Jose Molina	18,788	73	35	10	15	15	26	7
Russell Martin	**42,186**	**70**	**15**	**15**	**10**	**20**	**14**	**11**
Yorvit Torrealba	26,306	40	14	5	14	3	11	7
Jonathan Lucroy	14,205	38	24	17	21	0	0	0
Yadier Molina	39,184	37	8	7	7	1	16	6
BOTTOM FIVE								
Kenji Johjima	19,588	−33	−15	0	0	−9	−9	−15
Jason Kendall	35,772	−37	−9	0	−10	−19	−5	−3
Jorge Posada	17,942	−49	−25	0	−23	−11	−5	−10
Gerald Laird	30,298	−52	−15	−2	−12	−16	−11	−11
Ryan Doumit	**22,861**	**−65**	**−26**	**−9**	**−3**	**−16**	**−36**	**−1**

Max Marchi, then a writer for *Baseball Prospectus,* published more PITCHf/x research on pitch framing, including studies on how the skill improved or declined with age, and found that the skill aged well.

Realizing the value these hobbyists brought to the game, all three, Fast, Marchi, and Turkenkopf, were hired by major league teams to become data analysts or baseball systems developers. One could argue that an analyst such as Fast, who could be procured for far less than the minimum wage of a major league player, was in fact more valuable than many of the players on the rosters. An analyst could identify undervalued players and produce millions in dollars of value for his club.

Wrote NBC baseball analyst Craig Calcaterra in a January 2013 blog post: "For as much crap as the sabermetic and bloggy types take from the mainstream media about how they don't truly know the game because they're not out there at the park or interviewing players in clubhouses and stuff, ain't it funny how the sabermetrics and bloggy types are continually hired by major league teams to work in baseball operations? And did you notice that teams never hire the guys who claim to know so much more about baseball and who continually slam advanced metrics and statistical analysis?"

Just as the game had been closed for so many decades, open to only those who had played, the sport was still exclusive early in the twenty-first century. Only those that played, or had an Ivy League degree, were typically found in front offices. But with the advent of big data, of PITCHf/x, and the accompanying hobbyist research, anyone who showcased talent and creativity could gain entrance to a front office. Data had moved the game closer to a true meritocracy. The race was on for teams to hire the best and brightest hobbyists and to create proprietary metrics. For example, in 2008 Dan Fox—an Iowa State undergrad—was the only data analyst or architect employed by the Pirates baseball operation side: by 2013, the Pirates had five full-time employees devoted to data analysis, collection, and architecture.

With the creation of PITCHf/x, Sportvision had incidentally created a job field in professional baseball that hadn't existed before: data-science departments.

That these hobbyists had access to the PITCHf/x data was unintentional on the part of Sportvision, whose CEO, Hank Adams said, "People get the data by scraping the site. . . . We don't send it out. It's not downloadable per se, but amateurs went in there and figured out how to scrape the [MLB Advanced Media] site. Now many of them have made it publicly available. You're not supposed to commercialize this, but most of these guys are amateurs and hobbyists. We could theoretically shut it down, but at the same time we recognize that these guys have done a lot of great work to highlight the value of the data."

With PITCHf/x's millions of data points entering the game, by 2013 an arms race was on for analysts who could make sense of them. Clubs were after analysts who could craft their own meanings from data using complex algorithms. The data entering the game in the 2010s would be on an entirely different level of sophistication than anything before.

"If [teams] can only use a standard set of data [like PITCHf/x], finding the answers and asking the right questions is going to be key. Teams are hiring very smart people to ask those questions and find those answers," said Ryan Zander, general manager of baseball operations for Sportvision. "We can create the data but not how it's interpreted and how it's used and analyzed. Data has gone from being something where maybe you had one person looking at it, to what we are seeing now, where data is being used as an everyday process for a front office. I think a lot of decisions being made are using data we're creating, whether it's player development or coaching, training players, or understanding the value of players."

In 2012, the Pirates added their second full-time data quantitative analyst. He would become exponentially more valuable than what he was paid.

As a sophomore at MIT studying chemical engineering, Mike Fitzgerald read *Moneyball*. Like so many other mathematically inclined young people, he was awakened to the idea that professional-sports front offices had jobs for people like him, people who had once been outside the game. Fitzgerald wasn't sure exactly what path he wanted to pursue, or how to enter the field, but he had a passion for sports and a strong mathematical mind. When he was a child, Fitzgerald's mother would tote him along to their Boston-area grocery store. She would tell him what every item cost and offer an approximation of the tax.

"At the end I would give what the total bill would cost to a penny," Fitzgerald said. "It used to blow her mind. . . . I knew I could make a career out of [mathematics] after my sophomore year in college."

Like Dan Fox, what set Fitzgerald apart from some of his classmates at MIT was an ability to communicate complex mathematical ideas in simple, relatable ways, an example of which was an assignment that impressed one of his professors. Fitzgerald and his classmates were tasked with writing a ten-page paper that someone with a minimal mathematical background could comprehend. Fitzgerald did not choose an obscure subject; rather, he tackled one of America's most popular sporting and gambling events: the NCAA Division I men's basketball tournament. Fitzgerald's project was how to optimize selecting teams in a tournament. Being a basketball fanatic, he examined a strategy for selecting teams in a traditional bracket pool, where points are awarded for correctly predicting winners in each round. He then examined another optimization plan for a bracket where participants are awarded additional points for picking upsets. For instance, if a No. 12 seed beats a No. 5 seed, and the participant had selected the No. 12 seed (the underdog), the participant was awarded the seed differential of seven points. Fitzgerald chose a topic that made the mathematical concept he was studying—conditional probability—accessible to a wide audience.

Conditional probability, simply defined, measures the probability of an event given that another even has occurred. Conditional probability led Fitzgerald to the Pirates' most important free agent signing in club history in the 2012–13 off season.

"The notion that if we are looking at a situation and we bring new information into the situation, how does that change the possible distributions of outcomes you could have?" Fitzgerald said. "So I think my mind works pretty quickly through those types of things, which is cool, because baseball is a game where you are constantly getting more and more input data, which changes our initial thoughts. There is so much data entering the game."

Fitzgerald is an enthusiastic Boston Celtics fan. As a sophomore at MIT in 2008, Fitzgerald and several of his cousins traveled from Boston to watch the Celtics play the Pistons in Games 3 and 4 of a play-off series in Detroit. They split a $100 hotel room in suburban Birmingham, Michigan. Across the street the Pistons were housed in luxury accommodations. In a park near the hotels, Fitzgerald and his cousins were tossing a football on an off day when to their delight Celtics forward Glen "Big Baby" Davis approached them. Soon a pickup game between Davis, Fitzgerald, his friends, and several local Michigan kids emerged. The spectacle drew the attention of ESPN television analysts Jeff Van Gundy and Marc Jackson, who were staying at the Celtics' hotel and came down to the park. Van Gundy had been a coach with the Houston Rockets, and although he was fired after the 2007 season, he remained friendly with Rockets GM Daryl Morey, who had brought analytics to the NBA.

"Van Gundy asks me if I had ever thought about getting into analytics in basketball," Fitzgerald recalled. "I had no idea [analytics] were breaking into basketball. I said, 'That's interesting.'"

That conversation helped Fitzgerald land an unpaid basketball internship with the Celtics that fall. He then took a paid internship with the Danish company TrackMan, a burgeoning rival for Sportvision. TrackMan had made its name in golf, using radar to track the trajectory of golf balls. In 2009, TrackMan was in the early stages of an effort to use radar to track pitches and batted balls in baseball. They had begun testing their technology in three major league parks.

"Basically the goal was to clean the data and come up with some very elementary information for the clubs," Fitzgerald said. "The biggest thing that jumped out to me was the effective velocity. TrackMan readings are basically the same as PITCHf/x except they measure the [entire] flight of the ball instead of picking up the ball at [twenty] different points starting at fifty feet . . . and they get pitchers' extension."

Pitchers' extension was one of the primary reasons teams were interested in the TrackMan product, along with tracking bat speed and exit speed of balls in play. PITCHf/x gives teams a pitcher's vertical release point, but it does not produce a horizontal release point, meaning, it doesn't read how closely a pitcher is releasing a ball to home plate. This is important because if a pitcher releases the ball closer to home plate, his effective velocity can become greater. For example, a 93 mph fastball traveling 53 feet instead of 55 feet is effectively a faster pitch.

The TrackMan system was installed for Arizona Fall League play in 2013, quantifying that Angels lefty Michael Roth had the top extension on his delivery of all pitchers in the league, releasing his pitches seven feet five inches from the pitching rubber, according to MLB.com, shrinking the distance from the mound to home plate. Perhaps this extension explains how Roth helped the South Carolina Gamecocks to two College World Series titles and rocketed through the Angels system although his fastball averaged only 85 mph.

"The offsets aren't as large as you'd think they'd be, but they can add two miles per hour. That's pretty substantial," Fitzgerald said. "If you're looking at batting averages against ninety-four [mph] compared to ninety-seven, you are seeing some significant differences."

Fitzgerald worked with TrackMan for only six months, but his time there would prove critical. In the 2011–12 offseason, the Pirates were installing TrackMan at PNC Park when Dan Fox asked TrackMan officials if they knew of any bright young minds they had worked with who could help the Pirates. Fox was seeking a full-time assistant analyst to help him deal with the incredible amount of data flowing into the game. Fitzgerald's name was dropped. The Pirates interviewed the tall, slim, green-eyed, dark-haired, fast-thinking, and quick-speaking Fitzgerald at the MIT Sloan Analytics Conference in early March of 2012. Fox liked that Fitzgerald had never worked in baseball, was a true outsider, and was willing to be more radical.

The twenty-three-year-old was hired, and Fitzgerald would quickly add value to the club. Just as he had become curious about the seemingly insignificant aspect of a pitcher's extension with TrackMan, Fitzgerald had become fascinated by the impact of pitch framing.

"That was one of the first projects [Fox] and I kind of tackled," Fitzgerald said. "How do we implement it? How do we improve upon it? What do we look for? We had a model we thought we liked to accurately evaluate pitch framing. . . . We looked at it for two weeks, just trying to poke holes in it."

At first, like Turkenkopf, they couldn't believe pitch framing could create that great of an impact. They had conversations in Fox's office asking each other, "Can it really be that big? Can the effect be that significant?" They kept vetting their model. They tried to account for all factors that could play a role in a catcher's opportunity and ability to frame pitches. For instance, what types of pitchers, and umpires, were catchers paired with? They kept being surprised at how significant and important this skill was.

Whom did their model keep identifying as by far and away the best pitch-framing catcher on the 2012–13 free agent market? Russell Martin.

"We said, 'Okay, we have to get this guy,'" Fitzgerald said.

Huntington encourages subordinates to "pound the table" for players or ideas they believe in. By the second half of the 2012 season, a sanguine Fitzgerald was pounding the table for Martin. There was no need for formal presentations. Each night during home games, Huntington opened his suite in the club level behind home plate to his front-office staff. Everyone from the assistant general manager to the veteran graybeard scout, or fresh-faced, quantitative-minded intern, was welcome. Front-office staffers filled up to-go boxes in the media dining hall and headed up to watch the game and throw around ideas. They were free to talk openly and often, as just watching the game would spark a thought.

This in-person exchange of ideas and collaboration was important. The intersection of people and their thoughts is where the next big thing is often born. So in Huntington's suite Fitzgerald began to make the case for Martin late in 2012 as the Pirates unraveled toward another losing season.

Fitzgerald can be animated when he's excited, speaking quickly and enthusiastically, and he was adamant about the value of pitch framing. He said pitch framing was the biggest bang for the buck and completely undervalued. Heck, no one seemed to be making player-acquisition decisions based upon it. He was emphatic that Martin was the best value they could target in free agency. Fitzgerald and Fox argued that Martin should be their top free agent target, and he would represent a massive upgrade over the two starting Pirates catchers over the previous five seasons. They argued Martin would make every pitcher on the staff better.

The one big problem in convincing ownership that they should invest in Martin? In 2012 Martin had batted .211. While batting average is hardly an ideal tool to judge a player's total worth, it was still by and large the number one statistic used by the general public in evaluating a position player's value. Batting average was the one statistic displayed on every major league scoreboard when a player came to bat, and Martin's was well below average. Huntington already liked Martin's reputation as a quality defender and as a positive, veteran clubhouse presence, but the data from Fox and Fitzgerald would help sell the owners on a player with a questionable bat. Fox and Fitzgerald wrote a report on their findings on the value of pitch framing, and they also supplied anecdotal evidence of its value. Huntington took that report to the ownership of one of the lowest-spending teams in the game and asked for the most money the Pirates had ever given to a free agent.

"It helped that we had this information to supplement it," Fitzgerald said. "I think it made it easier for [Huntington] to go to ownership and say, 'Yes, I want to acquire a guy who hit .220 last year, but here is the reason why, and here is the value he brings.'"

On November 28, 2012, after a workout, Martin returned to his friend's two-story town house in a hipster-populated neighborhood near downtown Montreal. The town house's stone façade rested along a tree-lined street. On the first floor was a tattoo parlor, and above it were two levels of apartments with a rooftop terrace. Until work on his Montreal condo was completed, Martin was residing at his friend's home. He liked it there. He liked the view of the skyline from the rooftop, where AstroTurf had been installed along with netting so one could hit golf balls. Here Martin made his decision.

Martin had been wined and dined in Texas by the Rangers, and the Yankees had made a halfhearted attempt to keep him. However, the Pirates had been the most enthusiastic and aggressive. Once he made his decision, Martin called his agent and related a story of how he had been at a Foot Locker earlier in the week to buy a new pair of workout shoes. The pair that caught his eye were black and gold: Pirates colors. He did not think of himself as superstitious, but he felt it was some sort of pull to Pittsburgh. In some ways, it was easy. The Pirates offered the most guaranteed money, and what if they were able to turn it around in Pittsburgh? That would be an amazing story to be a part of. At the least he wanted to rebuild his value.

The Pirates had just outbid the rest of the industry for Martin. Once the two-year, $17 million deal was agreed upon, an outcry came from the fans and media. Many in the local media thought it was a desperate move. *Pittsburgh Tribune-Review* columnist Dejan Kovacevic wrote in November 2012 of the Martin signing, "Let's not pretend this transaction was anything other than what it was: An overpriced desperation move that's going to hurt the Pirates in more ways than one." By June, Kovacevic admitted his error noting Martin had been "masterful" and worth "every penny."

But initially, the public did not understand, did not see Martin's pitch-framing ability. And the rest of the industry wasn't quite ready to buy into pitch framing the way the Pirates had. What the public wasn't able to see was that Martin had just improved the Pirates by nearly 40 runs per season over their previous catchers, and it had nothing to do with his bat—which everyone kept judging him by. It had nothing to do with performance stats that could be found on the back of a bubble-gum trading card. It had everything to do with his framing skills. According to BaseballProspectus.com, in 2011 Martin saved 32 runs for the Yankees through framing. In 2012, he saved 23 runs. In 2012, Barajas had cost the Pirates 9 runs through framing. In 2011,

Doumit's glove had cost the club 15 runs. This value was hidden, and that's the only way the Pirates could afford it.

But Martin's would not be the only free agent signing by the Pirates that caused head-scratching that off-season.

★ ★ ★

Back in 2001, baseball hobbyist and blogger Voros McCracken published what at the time was a radical idea. Wrote McCracken in an article published at BaseballProspectus.com, "'You're insane.' That's generally the response I get when I present the information you're about to read. I've been accused of being the epitome of 'pseudo-stat fan gibberish.' I've even been accused of being Aaron Sele (a woeful Boston Red Sox pitcher) writing under a pseudonym. I'm not entirely sure why my little way of doing things stirs the emotions of people to such a large extent, but apparently it does. My belief? Well, simply that hits allowed are not a particularly meaningful statistic in the evaluation of pitchers."

McCracken found that pitchers had significant control over their strikeout rates, walk rates, home runs allowed, and hit batsmen. However, his radical idea was that hits allowed by a pitcher were largely dependent upon the defenses behind him. That meant that earned run average, ERA, the gold standard to judge pitcher performance, was faulty.

McCracken continued, "I looked at the behavior of Hits Per Balls in Play. That's where the trouble really started. I swear to you that I did everything within my power to come to a different conclusion than the one I did. I ran every test, checked every stat, divided this by that and multiplied one thing by another. Whatever I did, it kept leading back to the same conclusion: There is little if any difference among major league pitchers in their ability to prevent hits on balls hit in the field of play. It is a controversial statement, one that counters a significant portion of 110 years of pitcher evaluation."

Hits not being dependent on a pitcher's performance? That seemed counterintuitive. What was undoubtedly true was pitchers had control over the location of pitches—that is, whether their offerings were balls or strikes. Pitchers therefore had considerable control over whether they struck out or walked a batter. But if a ball was put into play, McCracken theorized a pitcher's influence over whether a batted ball was converted into an out or a hit was largely subject to the ability and placement of the defenders behind them, while also tied to the dimensions of the ballpark they pitched in. McCracken was onto something as major league hitters had for decades produced a batting average around .300 on balls put in play. For instance, in 1920, major league hitters produced a .297 average on balls in play. Ninety-three years later, in 2013, major league hitters hit .297 on balls in play. Eight defenders in fair territory—not including the catcher—could only cover so much ground. With those defenders aligned nearly the same way for a hundred years, the amount of balls they were converting into outs had become something of a mathematical constant. McCracken found even the best pitchers of the modern era, pitchers such as Greg Maddux and Pedro Martinez, had little control over the outcome of a batted ball. The idea that some pitchers could allow fewer batted balls to become hits than others did not seem to hold up.

This thinking influenced teams from the *Moneyball* A's to the Pirates, and outside hobbyists, to become more interested in measurements such as strikeouts and walks per inning, measurements they thought pitchers independently controlled and were more telling of true skills.

By the 2012–13 off-season, the Pirates had largely removed traditional statistics to measure pitchers' performance. Neal Huntington rarely cited ERA, wins, or hits allowed when evaluating a pitcher. The Pirates tried to separate a pitcher's performance from his environment as much as possible. *Indicator* became an often-used word by Huntington. The Pirates were thought to be paying particular attention to a new age metric created by baseball analyst Tom Tango and inspired by McCracken, something that was not found on the back of baseball cards, a metric focused on what pitchers did control and a better indicator of what a pitcher's true ability was: fielding independent pitching or FIP. Dave Studeman, a writer and analyst for TheHardballTimes.com, took FIP a step further to estimate how many home runs a pitcher should have allowed. Home-run-to-fly-ball rates generally fluctuate over time, so one bad-luck home run year can also dramatically impact a pitcher's ERA. Studeman called his refined FIP "xFIP," a further attempt to isolate a pitcher's true ability.

For example, in the season before the Pirates traded for A. J. Burnett, he had produced a 5.15 ERA with the Yankees, but his xFIP—on a scale designed to be similar to an ERA—was 3.86, which said he was unlucky because of factors out of his control. In his first year with the Pirates, Burnett's ERA fell to 3.51 and his xFIP remained relatively constant at 3.40. It seemed like magic but it was simply math.

When the Pirates speak among themselves about a perfect pitcher, they talk about a big, physical pitcher who racks up strikeouts and ground balls and does not walk batters. They do not mention wins or losses or ERA, traditional standards for pitchers. The Pirates also knew they were not going to sign pitchers that carried all three elite skills—high strikeout rate, high ground-ball rate, and low walk rate—on the free agent market. Those types of pitchers were costly and contended for Cy Young Awards. So they asked themselves, What do you sacrifice? What's easier to get? What's harder to get? What's harder to fix? What's easier to fix?

For example, you can't fix the height of a five-foot-nine player. You can't make him six-three. You can't make a right-handed pitcher left-handed, and you can't make a pitcher throwing 85 mph increase his velocity to 95 mph. You typically can't make a pitcher learn to develop an elite breaking ball. Of all the skills McCracken found to be independent in a pitcher, the ability to strike out batters was the most difficult to improve and typically most costly in free agency. The Pirates thought they could perhaps improve other independent skills of pitchers.

In the 2012–13 off-season, finding and signing a pitcher with upside was on the Pirates' to-do list right after getting the team buy-in on the big data strategies and finding a free agent catcher. Specifically they required top-of-the rotation arms, the kind of pitchers that could consistently impact games. The kind of arms also labeled as aces, pitchers who struck out a lot of batters and did not walk many. But, of course, they ran into their usual problem of not being able to afford proven top-of-the-rotation arms, since starting pitchers enjoy the highest average salary in the game. For example, winter free agent ace Zack Greinke signed a $147-million deal with the Dodgers, roughly a third of the value of the Pirates franchise before the season, as estimated by *Forbes*. The game's top pitchers were routinely earning $22–$25 million per year on the free agent market, or a third of the Pirates 2013 payroll.

The Pirates had just spent half of their available free agent funds on Martin, after which they retained the major league equivalent of pocket change. With their limited free agent resources, they had to make a choice between flawed but high-upside, bounce-back candidates, or durable but league-average, back-of-the-rotation arms. The Pirates opted for upside, and to find upside, as with Martin, they had to look beyond conventional numbers and take on risk. Huntington liked to say they had to pay for projected performance—really, projected improvement by a player—and not for successful history.

Some teams were still paying for successful history. They were paying in part for traditional, back-of-the-baseball-card statistics in the free agent marketplace, which meant that they were paying for wins, saves, innings, hits allowed, and earned run average. These results were in large part influenced by the defense behind a pitcher and the home park he pitched in. The Pirates and other analytically savvy teams went in search of something else. Value rested in the independent skills pitchers possessed. Forget earned run average and wins, the traditional statistics with which to judge pitching performance. As the Pirates analysts and scouts scoured the free agent marketplace for a starting pitcher with upside, they went back to one pitcher they could afford with intriguing indicators whom, they thought, their coaching staff could improve, and whom they specifically thought Russell Martin could improve. They kept coming back to Francisco Liriano.

Liriano was once one of the most prized young arms in baseball. He had a six-foot-two frame, broad shoulders, and a slim waist, the ideal V-shaped torso scouts looked for in an athlete. The San Francisco Giants saw him work out first as an outfielder in the Dominican Republic, but were most intrigued with his rocket arm and that he threw left-handed. He converted to pitching and hit the upper 90s with his lightning-quick arm. He was more of a dream, a project, a raw and unrefined pitcher with potential, when he was traded to the Minnesota Twins in 2004 in a package for catcher A. J. Pierzynski. With the Twins he developed a wicked slider, polished his command, and demonstrated a precocious feel for a changeup. He rocketed up through the Twins system, overwhelming hitters in such places as Fort Myers, Florida, and New Britain, Connecticut, and was ranked as the sixth-best prospect by *Baseball Prospectus* and *Baseball America* entering 2006. He began the year with the Twins, featuring a fastball that averaged 95 mph along with a swing-and-miss slider, and a fall-off-the-table changeup. *USA Today* published a feature on Liriano headlined "Scarier than Santana," as in Liriano's older teammate Johan Santana, who would go on to win his second American League Cy Young Award in 2006. The excitement was washed away in August of 2006 when Liriano felt pain in his left elbow. He tried, unsuccessfully, to pitch through the injury. Doctors found he had torn the ulnar collateral ligament in his elbow, meaning he needed Tommy John surgery. The procedure is often viewed as an automatic cure for an elbow injury, with its sole negative side effect being the time a pitcher will miss while rehabbing, as if the surgery were merely an inconvenience. Liriano's case was a reminder that the surgery is not a perfect science, and not every pitcher returns to his previous ability, at least not initially.

In his first full season back in 2008, Liriano lost 4 mph from his fastball and his slider was not biting as it had prior to the injury—the pitch had a more rounded shape. After one start that season, he lamented solemnly to reporters, "I don't throw hard anymore." Batters had extra fractions of a second to decide whether to swing. His command suffered as he had never had ideal mechanics or control, but had previously benefited from limiting opponents' reaction time with elite fastball velocity. In 2009 Liriano struggled again, and was well below league average in both 2011 and 2012. In five seasons since returning from his injury, he had only one productive season, in 2010. As he entered the 2012 season, his velocity was still 2–3 mph below his rookie speed, and his walk rate hovered at 5 per 9 innings. Liriano had become not a prized major league pitcher but a cautionary tale, a reminder of the bust rate of top pitching prospects and the uncertainty of performance following surgery.

The Twins had seen Liriano's promise and were slow to give up on him. They still dreamed that what he once was, he could be again. You could count on one hand the number of left-handers in the game who had shown the ability Liriano had as a rookie. They tried reworking his mechanics, lessening his reliance on his slider, and they tried sending him to the minor leagues to see if he could regain confidence. Nothing worked. Liriano kept walking too many batters and allowing too many fly balls to leave the stadium. All too often he was giving the ball to Twins manager Ron Gardenhire prior to completing 5 innings of work, walking off head hung in shame from the mound toward the Twins dugout. The Twins finally grew frustrated with Liriano and gave up on his potential in July of 2012, trading him to the White Sox for marginal prospects. The Twins couldn't fix Liriano and neither could the White Sox. By September, Liriano found himself demoted to the bullpen at U.S. Cellular Field and looking for answers.

If you looked on his baseball card going into the 2012–13 off-season, it was ugly. He had posted ERAs over 5.00 in three of his last four seasons, well above the average major league ERA. Liriano's ERA in 2012 was an unsightly 5.34. But if you looked elsewhere, if you looked in the right areas, you could see a player with unrealized potential, who was a click away from re-creating magic. Looking closely at Liriano's history you could see that that he had worked with some of the poorest receiving catchers in the game, and he was a pitcher who could benefit from being paired with Martin.

The most difficult thing to acquire in free agency was a strikeout pitcher. Strikeouts were the most expensive skill set. After all, strikeouts kept the ball out of play and eliminated any chance of a batter reaching first base. Strikeouts were largely the product of excellent swing-and-miss off-speed pitches, or premium velocity that made batters more susceptible to off-speed pitches, skills that were largely innate.

Through the noise and clutter of Liriano's inconsistency, Fox and his analytics staff noticed some encouraging trends. Liriano's velocity had ticked back up to 93 mph in 2012, still 2 mph off his heyday, but well above the league-average fastball he had shown in 2008, 2009, and 2011. Also, his slider had shown more life in the second half of the season, when he had averaged 10.5 strikeouts per nine innings, his best rate since his rookie year. The number of swings and misses he generated (13.2 percent of his pitches) ranked number one in baseball among starting pitchers, ahead of the four ace-level pitchers, Yu Darvish, Matt Harvey, Anibal Sanchez, and Cole Hamels, who rounded out the top five.

The indicators went deeper than strikeouts and whiff rates thanks to PITCHf/x and TrackMan data, both of which were employed by the Pirates. The club could study trends and changes in movement, release point, location, and spin rate of pitches, and they could study Liriano's pitch movement relative to that of other pitchers, or league average rates. They could also study movement in his good years versus his bad years. The PITCHf/x data verified the subjective view of Pirates scouts: Liriano had slowly become stronger since his 2007 surgery, and had three above-average pitches in his fastball, slider, and changeup. But the obvious and significant flaw with Liriano since he'd returned from Tommy John surgery was his struggle with his command. That made him a discounted strikeout pitcher since he was walking more batters than almost every other major league starting pitcher.

But perhaps Liriano could throw more strikes not only if paired with Pirates pitching coaches Ray Searage and Jim Benedict, whom the club had marrow-deep trust in, but also with an adept pitch-framing catcher.

In 2012 at catcher, the Twins fielded Joe Mauer, an average pitch framer, and two below-average framers in Drew Butera and Ryan Doumit. Liriano had a 10.57 ERA in two games working with Doumit. Butera, who was most often paired with Liriano, cost Twins pitchers 10 runs per 7,000 pitches in 2012, according to *Baseball Prospectus*. Mauer saved a negligible 0.4 runs through framing in 2012. By comparison, Martin's glove over those five years had saved 70 runs by turning balls into strikes. After Liriano was traded to the White Sox in midseason, he was caught by A. J. Pierzynski, another below-average catcher at turning balls into strikes.

While the Pirates didn't think they could transform Liriano into a control artist, they did believe that Martin and their coaching staff could better help him throw strikes, avoid walks, and more often get in favorable two-strike counts to make opposing hitters more susceptible to his slider.

"[Fox and Fitzgerald] liked his indicators: the strikeouts, the ground balls," Huntington said. "It was a good team effort: a good combination between our scouting and our [statistical] information. [Scouts] really liked the arsenal. They believed in the slider and changeup and talked about fastball command being key."

In the 2012–13 off-season, only one team offered more than a one-year deal to Liriano: the Pirates. After agreeing initially to a two-year, $14 million deal with the Pirates, Liriano broke his right arm—his nonthrowing arm—during an accident in his home in the Dominican Republic. Liriano claims he broke his arm against a doorframe while trying to scare his children during a prank. The Pirates and Liriano then renegotiated the contract with Liriano signing a one-year deal with a club option guaranteeing him only $1 million in 2013. On paper, it made little sense. Liriano produced a 5.34 ERA in 2012 and a 5.09 ERA in 2011. He had been one of the least effective pitchers in baseball. As with Martin, the signing drew criticism from fans and the Pittsburgh media as another bottom-of-the-barrel selection, another scratch-off lottery ticket. This bargain shopping concluded the club's most significant off-season signings in an attempt to upgrade the roster externally. Any other improvement had to come from within.

5

POINT OF NO RETURN

In late February on the first day of full-squad workouts at spring training, the entire Pirates major league team assembled in the Pirate City cafeteria. The Pirates major leaguers spent the first few weeks of spring training working out and going through drill work at the Pirate City complex on the outskirts of Bradenton, Florida, before migrating to their March home of McKechnie Field in downtown Bradenton, where major league spring training games are held. Pirate City is the hub of the club's minor league, player development, and amateur draft operations. Every player in the system begins rehab there after surgery, and the lowest levels of minor leaguers are housed in its dorms when they begin play in rookie ball.

Clint Hurdle had called this meeting in the cafeteria, a vast room lit by fluorescent lights and several floor-to-ceiling windows, with cream walls and little personality. The space was designed for utility not atmosphere.

This meeting would set the tone for the rest of the year. Every year at the beginning of spring training Hurdle delivered a different message. Such speeches are often cliché-ridden and filled with corporate-style motivational messages and are quickly forgotten. This time, Hurdle knew it had to be different. It had to resonate. Leadership is about persuasion, and he had to persuade his players to play the game differently from the way that had got them to the major leagues.

Communication was key, and Hurdle knew he possessed this strength. He understood what it was to be everything from a highly rated prospect to a bench player struggling to earn regular playing time. As the manager of the Rockies, Hurdle had often posted an inspirational message in the Rockies clubhouse before each game, pinning the words near where the batting-practice groups were listed on the clubhouse bulletin board.

"It lets us know how he's feeling about things. And a lot of times they provide a lot of insight as to where the game ranks in life," Rockies first baseman Todd Helton told *Sports Illustr*ated in 2002.

With the Pirates, the messages went from paper to electronic as Hurdle sent out daily e-mails to the players, staff, and friends on his list. The messages are rarely Hurdle's words, but rather from motivational speakers, historical figures, or one of the many leadership books that scatter his office. He ends each e-mail with the same words, his own *Make a difference today. Love Clint.* The e-mails were another way to connect with players, to broaden perspective, while also, hopefully, offering motivational fuel.

Hurdle looked around the room and saw the stubby, gray beards of his coaches and the eyes of his players, some attentive, others wandering or looking down at a table. Some players were chuckling in conversation. Hurdle's sonorous voice ricocheted around the room as he asked for attention.

Still regarded as a player's manager, one who rarely criticized his players in public, Hurdle had changed his leadership style. Clint Barmes played under Hurdle in Denver and Pittsburgh. With the Rockies, Barmes noted Hurdle spent considerable time in the clubhouse interacting with players, being one of the guys. In Pittsburgh, he gave that space back to the players and kept more to the coaches' quarters. With more separation, there was less chance of complicating decisions or relationships.

Hurdle began his speech by telling his players this spring they were going to be open-minded and break from tradition. Hurdle often said traditions can be wonderful and meaningful, but also a vision killer. Tradition was preventing the Pirates from realizing their true run-prevention potential.

Hurdle had two men join him at the front of the room. Most players rarely interacted with these nondescript employees and most did not know them by name. Hurdle introduced Dan Fox and his assistant analyst Mike Fitzgerald.

Fox and Fitzgerald stood awkwardly before a room full of professional athletes, in contrast to Hurdle, who typically doesn't stay still when he works a room. He paces back and forth by a podium, walks up and down aisles, makes eye contact. He wants to feel omnipresent. Hurdle told everyone these men knew how to do much more than turn on a computer, and they were going to do everything they could behind the scenes to help the whole team. They were meant to be resources. The Pirates were going to dramatically change how they played defense, and Fox and Fitzgerald could explain why. Have a question? Are you curious about something? Ask them. The team could expect to see both of them in the clubhouse. They were going to be in the video rooms. They were going to be a part of every pregame meeting with the coaching staff in Hurdle's office for home games, and on the road they would at least be on conference call for the meetings. Instead of speaking with only Fox before every home series, Hurdle planned to include Fox and Fitzgerald in every advance scouting meeting, which occurs before the first game of a new series when Hurdle and his assistant coaches review and game plan for a new opponent. Later in the season, Fitzgerald even began traveling with the club, which would become the norm in 2014. They were going to become as common a sight in the clubhouse as one of the team's trainers or assistant coaches. Just as Hurdle had gained more trust in the analysts in 2012, just as he saw them less as invaders and more as assets, he wanted the same for his team this coming season. The Pirates were pioneering: few if any major league clubs had attempted to integrate analysts into the clubhouse so comprehensively.

Hurdle spoke briefly about Fox's and Fitzgerald's backgrounds and their work on defensive shifting. But there was one catch about Fox and Fitzgerald: they had never played professional baseball.

Some of the Pirates players turned to each other, rolled their eyes, and shook their heads in amusement. Who were these guys? They're going to influence how we play in the field? Right. Sure they are. They've never dug their cleats into a professional baseball field. What did these guys know about playing defense on a major league field? This lack of respect for nonplayers had prevented so many smart ideas from quantitative analysts from reaching the field. Some analysts, likewise, did not respect traditional baseball thought. One of Hurdle's primary challenges was to create a culture of respect. With Fitzgerald and Fox flanking him, Hurdle told his assembled players and staff that they were not better than these analysts. They were to be thought of as equals.

To some in the room this presentation seemed desperate or crazy, maybe the first fostering the latter. That was true to a degree. Hurdle and the Pirates were desperate and were willing to try just about anything. But if the team thought they would be able to brush off Hurdle's mission from day one of spring training and quickly forget about this meeting and radical defensive alignment, they would be mistaken. That would quickly become apparent. The next day saw a round of meetings of smaller groups, including pitchers and infielders—the two groups most affected by the two mysterious men introduced at the previous day's meeting. They reconvened in the cafeteria with infield coach Nick Leyva.

It wasn't just the players. Hurdle also needed his assistant coaches to become more familiar and more trusting of the data. Hurdle encouraged his coaches to "initiate some dialogue" with Fox and Fitzgerald. The analysts were "good people," Hurdle assured them. He told the staff the analysts would be spending more time with them so it would be best if they became more comfortable with each other, believing that most of his assistants would be receptive to change.

Leyva's job was to explain in more detail the defensive-positioning plan and sell the whole group on it. From now on, on the first day of every series in the regular season, Leyva was to meet with Pirates infielders in a clubhouse video room and go over the defensive-positioning plans in great detail. He would show video, if necessary, to reinforce why they were positioning against certain hitters in certain ways. Leyva had never before had so much alignment responsibility, and he wasn't sure if even he was completely comfortable with the plan.

Leyva had been given access to defensive-positioning data as early as 2011, when Hurdle hired him, but he was never pressured to use any of the findings on the field. He had resisted much of the data Fox had made available to him the previous two seasons. But now Leyva had direct orders to consistently stick to and implement the data-based alignments.

Leyva, stocky, tawny-skinned, gray-haired, was a self-described "old-school" baseball man. In a 2012 interview with FanGraphs.com, he acknowledged that the Pirates had the analytical tools at their disposal, but often ignored them: "As coaches—and I think Clint would tell you the same thing—a lot of it still comes down to gut feeling. I set the defense on the infield and I can see how our pitcher is throwing and how a hitter is swinging. I know if he's hot, and a lot of times you can tell by someone's swing what he's trying to do."

That subjective way of aligning defenders was to come to an end. The transition was not easy for Leyva, a former minor league shortstop. He was drafted in the twenty-fourth round of the 1975 draft by the Cardinals. Although he never reached the major leagues, he worked his way up over the years to become the Cardinals' first-base coach in 1985 under Whitey Herzog. Leyva first met Hurdle in St. Louis when Hurdle's career was already in a surprisingly early decline. On the Cardinals coaching staff Leyva told the *Pittsburgh Tribune-Review* he witnessed Herzog track where opponents hit balls off Cardinals pitchers. Herzog would use orange pencil for balls hit off Cardinals starter Bob Forsch, and black pencil for John Tudor. Leyva copied that practice and was exposed to early rethinking on defensive positioning. Still, he wasn't comfortable stripping his infielders of autonomy and having them ignore their instincts on where to go, but he understood his place in the chain of command, and these were orders from the top.

Leyva wasn't alone; he undoubtedly felt what a vast majority of coaches and players were feeling as well, but the data suggested that their instincts and subjective judgments had little predictive power on where a ball thrown at 95-plus mph, hit off a bat swung at 90-plus mph, would go. The number of balls in play converted into outs was almost like a scientific law, a constant for the first 130 or so years of professional baseball. You could count on major league hitters batting around .300 when they put the ball in play against a conventional defensive alignment. Even when Leyva had directed traffic in a game based upon anecdotal evidence, he was still only moving fielders several paces from traditional positions. Now Leyva was being told to set aside not only his gut feelings, but to direct his infielders to do the same.

Hurdle and Huntington wanted Leyva to direct his players to follow a specific plan, but it was by no means guaranteed to happen on the field. For example, Washington Nationals manager Matt Williams had pledged in the 2013–14 off-season to increase shifting. He even hired a new type of coach, a defensive coordinator, Mark Weidemaier, to align the defense based upon data and shift the infield defense more often. But the Nationals finished 2014 with the second fewest shifts in baseball. Players resisted departing from tradition. Would Leyva be able to get his infielders to jump on board? These early meetings were key as the barrier threatening the whole plan was lack of communication. Coaches, and ultimately players, were the gatekeepers deciding what new ideas would reach the field.

So on the second day of full-squad workouts Leyva had his infielders gather, flanking him at a table in the quiet cafeteria. The presentations to players had been planned long before these early spring training meetings. The new presentations had helped sway Leyva to a degree, and the Pirates needed them to influence the infielders also.

"Presentation to players is always of critical importance: when you make the presentation, and how you make the presentation. It's new, it's different. It's change. Change can bring about controversy," Hurdle said. "But we can lay out information that is black-and-white. There is no gray area. We showed [them] why it's going to be beneficial. Here are the adjustments we need to make to make it happen."

Leyva brought with him an example of the data-based scouting reports he would be positioning his infielders with that April. He showed his players not a statistical spreadsheet on Cincinnati Reds left-handed hitter Jay Bruce, a familiar foe, but a colorful visualization of the data. Leyva was not going to recite numerical percentages of balls to certain parts of the field while his infielders lost attention and daydreamed. Bruce was nine times more likely to pull a ground ball to the right side of the infield than the left, and Leyva showed a chart with hundreds of colored lines emanating from home plate and fanning out over the right side of the infield. The left side of the infield was nearly unblemished. After examining the data-visualization map, where the lines indicated the path of ground balls hit off various types of pitches, it was tough to argue against overloading the right side of the infield.

Once Fox and Fitzgerald had learned that the front office and coaching staff were committed to employing more of their defensive-alignment recommendations, they worked to make the data more accessible. They had to democratize the data and turn it into something that not only stat wonks understood, but athletes, too. Fox and Fitzgerald knew they might lose players if they just passed along numerical data. They had learned in their limited conversations with players in the clubhouse in 2012, and in going over video with players, that they absorbed visual materials amazingly fast and retained the information. It made sense, especially if you subscribed to the theory of multiple intelligences. Baseball players would logically have higher visual IQs since they are adept at tracking pitches thrown at 95 mph and at plotting courses in milliseconds to intercept fly balls and line drives.

In the off-season Fox purchased an analytical platform from TruMedia that allowed for easy creation of data-visualization charts Leyva showed to his infielders. Fox and Fitzgerald happily dug into the work. This was their chance to make a difference in the game if they could clear just one final step: convincing players this was the right track to take.

"We did a lot of work on the visuals," Fox said. "If they can visualize it, it's a lot easier to accept and say, 'Okay, that's not radical. That fits with where the ball is actually going to go.'"

The visual data-based scouting reports weren't just key for defensive positioning; they helped in nearly every aspect of game planning. For instance, say Pirates pitching coach Ray Searage is going over an opponent's lineup. Instead of saying San Francisco Giants star Buster Posey is 0 for 15 against a certain pitch in a certain location, a heat map, which is a color-coded chart, would show Posey's strengths and weaknesses clearly and efficiently. Using the TruMedia tool, pitchers could then, with a mouse click, filter to video of those pitches in those locations for further evidence. The entire Pirates clubhouse was also given a printed package of applicable, visual-based scouting reports prior to every series.

As Leyva went over Bruce's scouting report with infielders Neil Walker, Clint Barmes, Pedro Alvarez, and Gaby Sanchez, it showed his hitting pattern wasn't a one-year phenomenon. While Bruce was nine times more likely to hit a ground ball to the right side of the infield than the left in 2012, he was ten times more likely to do so for his career, which covered more than 2,500 batted balls put into play.

But still, the infielders had questions. Yes, the presentation was clear as day when presented visually, but they wondered, if they left roughly half the infield undefended, wouldn't the batter simply go the other way? Wouldn't he adjust? He was a major league hitter after all. Heck, he could just drop a bunt down. However, the coaching staff explained that if the batter bunted, he would be eliminating his chance for an extra-base hit. This would take him out of his preferred approach. Moreover, the coaches noted how pitches on the outside of the plate were more likely to be hit on the ground to a batter's pull-side, into the teeth of the defensive alignment, given the swing plane, the path of the bat, and the angle to the ball. Coaches explained outside pitches hit into play to the opposite field were more likely to be lifted into the air due the angle of the swing.

Studies of hundreds of thousands of balls in play showed little evidence of hitters' changing their batted-ball profiles. Based upon anecdotal evidence, even the few lefties that were shifted against continued to try to pull the ball and to hit home runs because that's what they were paid to do. They were not paid to hit opposite-field singles. Let them try to change their approach, the Pirates were told. Let them go away from their strengths. Still, some doubt remained as the training began.

★ ★ ★

In the days after the meetings, on the back fields of the Pirates City complex, before the major league club departed for its downtown-Bradenton home for the remainder of spring training, the Pirates infielders began taking ground balls at unusual positions on the field. The plan not only required players to buy into the concepts, but to rewire the neural circuitry that is muscle memory. The infielders now stood at the unusual white X's Kyle Stark had spray-painted on the ground several years earlier for the minor league players. But now the major leaguers stood there.

Throughout their amateur and professional careers, the infielders had taken thousands upon thousands of ground balls at traditional locations. They were accustomed to making throws from certain locations on the field. Now they were learning new positions, new bounces, and new throwing angles and distances.

Pirates second baseman Neil Walker began taking ground balls essentially in shallow right field between first and second base, while Clint Barmes began spending more time behind second base, where he had to navigate more tricky opportunities, since batted balls could more often be obstructed by base runners, umpires, and pitchers and could also be redirected by the pitcher's mound. Third baseman Pedro Alvarez spent time taking ground balls at the traditional shortstop position. To prepare for right-handed hitters, Barmes was hit ball after ball deep into the six-hole, making the long throw across the diamond, the longest throw in the infield. Often in their training they would leave one-half of the infield with just one defender or sometimes none at all. Hurdle and Leyva believed if they had the middle infielders fall in line with the plan, the rest of the defense would follow.

Early on, Walker was on the fence. He was looking around to see whether others would buy or reject and contest the philosophy. Walker remembered looking toward Barmes early that spring and asking, "Are you really going to do this?"

Fortunately for the Pirates, they had an open-minded player at the infield's most important position.

★ ★ ★

The first thing evaluators want to see from a shortstop is his arm. Can he make a throw from the hole, the area between the traditional starting setup of the shortstop and the third baseman on the left side of the infield? Then scouts and coaches want to see lateral speed, to see a player gracefully and quickly range to both his left and right, and they want to see soft hands that act with vacuumlike efficiency. Barmes had few of these ideal traits. He does not have an elite first step, meaning he does not have the quick-twitch muscles that allow for fast acceleration in his initial movement. Barmes did not have an elite arm like that of Atlanta shortstop Andrelton Simmons, but he did have the requisite hands. That was his one natural gift.

Barmes also understood the game's geometry and timing. He understood the nature of placement and angles more so than any of his teammates. Observers praised Barmes's baseball instincts, but instincts are hardwiring that we're born with. Baseball instinct isn't quite like that. Players are born with certain physical gifts, but what is called instinct is really experience, the by-product of doing an exercise over and over. It comes from intensive, meaningful practice. It's about creating that instant-recall memory. To remain at shortstop Barmes had to understand the nature of the position, where to be, and the timing of the game better than any other player at the position. So when Leyva first huddled his infielders that spring and handed them spray charts—including their own spray charts, produced by Fox and Fitzgerald, that showed where they most often hit the ball against what types of pitchers—Barmes intuitively understood and embraced the data.

"The spray charts are huge," Barmes said. "You look at it and see all these [batted balls] and see one or two that spray up the middle and a ton of balls and lines that were hit in that certain area and you think, 'Yeah, I'm going to stand there; it only makes sense.' Having it on paper and going through that [visually] has been a big part, especially for guys to buy into that aren't used to it."

Barmes had first learned to appreciate the geometry of the game while coming up through the Colorado Rockies system. Barmes felt he had shifted away from tradition years ago as a minor leaguer with the Rockies when he heard time after time, "Know who is on the mound. . . . Know who is at the plate." If a sinker-ball pitcher was up against a pull hitter, Barmes would move more toward third base. To quicken his timing from catch to throw, he took thousands upon thousands of balls to his backhand side in extra defensive work and during batting practice. By taking balls on the backhand side, he did not have to shift his feet to throw to first base. For Barmes, it was an important half second to shave.

"I've been taking balls in unconventional positions for a long time. That's a big reason for my sticking at shortstop. I really like going to my right. I'm really confident in my backhand. I'll work on balls in the hole, balls up the middle. I'll work in those different spots, different throws and different angles and different spots in the field," Barmes said. "After practicing and doing it every single day, I've got it. It's muscle memory in a lot of ways. There is no thought now."

Despite not being able to rival many, if any, of his peers in first-step quickness, sixty-yard-dash speed, or arm strength, Barmes was one of the most efficient shortstops in the sport, according to advanced defensive metrics. He finished second to Brendan Ryan in defensive runs saved from 2010 to 2013, a defensive statistic created by BIS that measures the number of balls a defender converts to outs compared to peers at his position. BIS tracked where balls were hit in the infield, how hard they were hit, and measured how many balls defenders reached compared to the average shortstop. Barmes was elite. The statistic was a key reason why the Pirates targeted Barmes in free agency after the 2011 season. Another reason was that he had the respect and trust of Hurdle from their time together with the Rockies.

The importance of positioning was increased by the altitude of Coors Field and the makeup of the Rockies staff. For years the Rockies have targeted different types of pitchers, hoping to find some way to combat the thin, mile-high air of their home park, in which fly balls traveled farther, making it a dangerous place for fly-ball pitchers. During Barmes's time there, the Rockies had begun to collect ground-ball pitchers with the thought that there had never been a ground-ball home run. But the thin air also made for drier conditions, which meant harder, quicker infields, lessening the reaction time and range of infielders on ground balls. Not only did Coors Field typically surrender more home runs than every major league park, but more ground balls also got through its infield. Barmes got tired of seeing sharply hit ground balls by right-handed hitters get through the infield to his right. So at shortstop he began positioning himself farther to his right when a sinker-ball pitcher was on the mound and when a right-handed hitter was at the plate. He had stored up a library of anecdotal evidence and it helped him be worth 25 defensive runs saved in 2006, and it helped him be open to the idea of comprehensive shifting in 2013.

But there was a significant difference between what Barmes did in Colorado and what he would be asked to do in Pittsburgh in 2013. Like many other teams the Rockies weren't employing data-based defensive theory on the field. Data was not making its way into the clubhouse. Many of Barmes's decisions to play out of traditional position were based upon his own findings and were done sporadically against select hitters. What was happening with the Pirates was different.

Barmes didn't like that his subjective decision-making was to be reduced, if not eliminated. The shifts would be data-driven and extreme in number. For the shifts to work, everyone had to subscribe to the plan on every pitch; there could not be impromptu deviations from the concepts. This tested even an open-minded player such as Barmes.

"I think guys were pretty open [in the spring]. But at the time maybe we didn't realize how extreme it was going to be until we got involved and started doing it," Barmes said. "It's not uncommon for one player [to shift]; it's uncommon for an entire team."

While it was difficult at times for Pirates infielders to accept, it was perhaps more difficult for Pirates pitchers. Hurdle knew that the greatest chance for mutiny against this plan was not from his infielders but from his pitchers. He thought they would be irked when they saw the occasional ball trickle through an undefended part of the infield where an infielder would traditionally have played. Such a batted ball wouldn't hurt a defensive player's traditional defensive statistics, but a pitcher would it see it as affecting his earned run average, hits allowed, and future earnings. Getting the pitchers to buy in to the second part of this defensive plan was going to be a challenge.

When the Pirates unveiled their defensive plan in the spring of 2013 to their players, resistance bubbled up mainly from the pitchers, who took comfort in having defenders positioned equidistant from each other on the field. It seemed counterintuitive to leave large swaths of the infield undefended. It's one reason the data-savvy Cardinals had shifted little in 2013. Their pitchers were not comfortable with the idea of shifting. In the spring of 2013, neither was the Pirates staff.

The Pirates pitcher who had some of the greatest disagreements with shifting was one of their most influential players, A. J. Burnett. This was the player who could lead a mutiny. The thirty-six-year-old Burnett carried veteran and alpha-dog status in the clubhouse. Burnett is tall and lithe, sporting spiked blond hair and tattoos. He possessed a cutting scowl and a sometimes-prickly demeanor, which he frequently used to try to intimidate reporters and opponents. He had presence.

Burnett had been in the game a long time and had made more than $100 million in his career. He was not easily influenced. He was stubborn. When he came up with the Florida Marlins, their coaching staff had harped on Burnett to develop a changeup, a third pitch, to better neutralize left-handed batters. Burnett refused. He trusted two pitches: his mid-90s fastball and a knuckle-curve his grandfather had taught him in his native, rural Arkansas. He had never changed the grip, and he had never felt the need to develop another off-speed pitch. Tired of the Marlins nagging him to throw a changeup, he threw 44 changeups in a start just to show them. Then he went back to his stubborn ways.

He was an outspoken opponent of the radical defensive alignment. During a game in Texas later in the 2013 season, his disdain for the shift bubbled over into public view. After a ground ball trickled through the left the side of the infield for a run-scoring single for the Texas Rangers, a ball that would perhaps have been converted into an inning-ending, double-play ball with a traditional alignment, Burnett screamed and motioned toward Barmes. The argument continued in the dugout between innings. Explained Burnett later to a clubhouse full of reporters, "I don't have a problem with Clint Barmes. I had a problem with the fucking shift!"

However, that spring the Pirates pitchers mainly kept their opinions to themselves and did not talk much openly about their distrust of the defensive alignment. But during games, they often wore expressions of bewilderment and disbelief when they surveyed the field, seeing their infielders overstuffing one side of the field and leaving the other half of it barely defended.

Every time a shift was burned by a base hit the other way, it pissed off pitchers, and at that moment they tended to forget about the hits the shift turned into outs. No one seemed annoyed more than Burnett, and no other pitcher was looked up to more by the young pitchers in camp. They were watching him, waiting to take his lead. Would Burnett buy in?

The Pirates coaches kept having to cool off their pitchers, stressing that they needed to focus on the pitches that were turned into outs. "I think initially they all looked around once in a while [at the infield defense] and said, 'Hey, wait a minute. Where are we?'" Hurdle said. "And we just told them, 'You have to get through that.' There has to be trust. There to be buy-in. Every once in a while we're going to get crosscut. But in the big picture as it plays out, hopefully we can show tangibles of the effectiveness and how much better it makes us as a club."

Pirates relief pitcher Mark Melancon was a polar opposite in personality and temperament to Burnett, but he, too, had his reservations about the shift. A video room adjoins the Pirates clubhouse both at McKechnie Field and at PNC Park. Players were encouraged to ask Fox and Fitzgerald questions and to challenge Fox and Fitzgerald's findings. More than any other player, Melancon could be found near a computer and video screen with them. Melancon felt too many weakly-hit, bleeding, seeing-eye singles were being hit against him. He was different from most Pirates pitchers. He relied on a cutter, which moved away from right-handed hitters. Melancon wondered if the shifts should be based not on a hitter's overall spray chart, but upon a hitter's spray chart versus a particular pitcher. The problem was, that was too small a sample to study. Few hitters accumulated more than a few dozen plate appearances against any one pitcher, particularly a relief pitcher. However, he brought up a good question. So in part because of Melancon's concerns and curiosity, Fox and Fitzgerald dug deeper into the data. Defensive alignment recommendations are a blend of batter and pitcher's batted-ball tendencies. But for pitchers with an outlying repertoire like Melancon, Fox and Fitzgerald made the alignments anchored more to the pitcher's batted-ball tendencies than the individual batter's. They also refined their recommendations for starting lineup construction. They looked at their hitter's profile against fifteen or so pitchers comparable to that day's opposing starting pitcher based upon handedness, velocity, and pitch types. There were examples of the data and recommendations being refined and improved through bottom-up communication. It wasn't just analysts thinking up areas to study and delivering the results. The players could ask a question that led to changes or interesting data findings. These interactions proved that the old school and the new school could not only coexist but could enhance each other. Fox welcomed the challenging questions and the interactions that ensued. It helped him to think about new areas to explore or disregard.

"Just sitting in the video room in spring training and having players come in and out, that's an opportunity when you're able to say, 'Hey, how do you approach this particular aspect?' Players are usually more than happy to share the information they have," Fox said. "Through some of those conversations in the spring, we provided some different information as part of the scouting reports and [game strategy] recommendations on other teams."

Hurdle knew there would be plenty of questions beginning with *Why* that spring; that's in part why he wanted Fox and Fitzgerald around. He couldn't afford a revolt against the plan by his players. Not now. This was a last chance.

Hurdle occasionally thought of the story of Hernán Cortés, the Spanish conquistador, who upon reaching the shores of the New World burned his ships to keep his men motivated. He gave them no alternative but to go forward. That was one way to avoid a mutiny: eliminate an option. Hurdle wanted his players to understand why they were doing this, and that's why the presentations to the players that spring were so methodically planned. But he also realized the need for other motivations so there would be no going back to the team's old, unsuccessful ways. The pitchers could buy in and throw where they were directed—more on this concept in upcoming chapters—or they could watch their ERAs and hit totals inflate as they went against the plan and opposing hitters took advantage of the often-undefended opposite field. The Pirates infielders understood that if they resisted the shift, then they would not only be going against a mountain of convincing data but be giving up even more hits since the pitching staff was adopting a specific philosophy. Hurdle was burning his ships the best he could.

6

SHIFTING THE PLAYING FIELD

Spring training is a time to renew hope. Maybe this player will bounce back, maybe this prospect will shine, maybe this will be the year. But for twenty consecutive years, building hope and optimism as a Pirates fan was a fool's endeavor. At the end of March 2013 the Pirates' spring training ended, and they left the sunshine and Gulf breeze of Bradenton for the unpredictable weather of Pittsburgh. On April 1, Opening Day, there were snow flurries. The winterlike weather was in a stark contrast to the warmth of spring training and helped hammer home that the hope and goodwill of March was over. The weather gods seemed to be saying, "Welcome back to reality." Now was the time for doing. This was the beginning of the last chance for many in the organization.

None of the Pirates, from management to the players, had much sense of how this season was going to play out. Would their radical plan work? No other franchise in the league had ever turned around its fortunes based almost entirely upon a run-prevention plan like the one they were going to implement. The team knew that they were going to be a guinea pig. The playing field had been financially tilted against small-market clubs such as the Pirates for years. They couldn't afford evaluation mistakes, and they couldn't attract stars like the Yankees, Red Sox, or Dodgers. Instead, the Pirates were literally going to attempt to shift the playing field in their favor.

Clint Hurdle's favorite time during game day is thirty minutes before the first pitch. He likes to come out to the dugout and sit there alone. He likes that the field is in immaculate condition, freshly lined and watered. He likes to watch the crowd file in, bubbling with energy. He likes that anything is possible. There's always a different energy on Opening Day. It was one of the few days you could count on a sellout crowd in Pittsburgh. It was one of the few days the city did not associate a negative feeling with its baseball club. There's anticipation before the first pitch, a joyfulness, a release for Pittsburghers, who were finally enjoying an outdoor activity after enduring western Pennsylvania's typically harsh winter. In these pregame minutes, music thumps from the sound system, and the aroma of grilled meats wafts about. The beer vendors make their rounds and calls as the crowd settles in. Hurdle soaked it all in on this frosty day and tried not to think about it potentially being his last Opening Day as a manager.

Hours before the first pitch, Nick Leyva met with the infielders in the cramped video room. There Leyva showed the players where they should position themselves against the Cubs hitters. They focused on the projected starting lineup and he supported the positioning with data. Each player was given the same printouts that Leyva had prior to the series. He showed them the Cubs regulars' spray chart versus the Pirates' Opening Day starter, A. J. Burnett, and right-handers similar to him. A particularly dramatic spray chart was that of Cubs first baseman Anthony Rizzo, a left-handed pull hitter. On the left side of the infield was nothing, a few stray lines. On the right side was something resembling the NBC peacock logo, a variety of warm and cool colors expanding out from home plate, color-coded to denote where ground balls were most concentrated. Any ball Rizzo hit on the ground was incredibly likely to go to the right side of the infield.

After the meeting, the players went back to their lockers to grab their gloves and bats for batting practice. Now Hurdle and Leyva would have to wait several hours before the first pitch to find out whether the players would actually follow the alignments Leyva had mapped out.

The home dugout at PNC Park, along the third-base line, is about four feet below the playing surface, with several steps leading up to the field. To watch the experiment play out during the game, Hurdle took his usual spot in the Pirates dugout. A three-foot-tall nylon net rises at field level around the dugout to protect the players and coaches from line drives. The netting also makes it difficult to see the field from the dugout bench, so Hurdle occupied the top step at the corner of the dugout nearest home plate. He usually stood with his folded arms resting on the slim layer of green padding that rests atop the rail supporting the netting. He could get a better view of the field there. He would take that position and chomp on bubble gum for seemingly the entire length of a standard three-hour game. He chews so often a Twitter account with the handle #ClintHurdlesGum has been created. Gum chewing is his iconic in-game characteristic, but on that Opening Day in 2013, perhaps he chomped with more nervous vigor as he stood and wondered, *Will they move?* Would his infielders accept the alignment plan?

In the top of the first inning, Hurdle watched his infielders as the public address announcer introduced the first batter of the season, the left-handed David DeJesus. Would they shift? Would they move? Would there be a mutiny? When shortstop Clint Barmes began moving to his left, Hurdle could exhale.

Barmes took the first step toward second base and Walker followed his lead, swinging closer to the right-field line and moving deeper into right field. Barmes slid into place just to the left of second base. While they were not in a Ted Williams Shift—when three infielders are placed to one side of second base—they had significantly altered their alignment plan. But they couldn't shift high enough. Two batters later, Rizzo launched a towering fly ball off Burnett that went over the center-field wall for a home run, also scoring Starlin Castro, who had reached on a single. The Cubs' early 2–0 lead was all the support Cubs starter Jeff Samardzija needed to cruise to a 3–1 victory.

Fans muttered, "Here we go again," as they filed out of PNC Park on the cold, overcast day. Despite the loss, what was most important was the Pirates' infielders had shifted, they had followed Leyva's direction, and they were giving the plan a chance. Now all his team needed was some evidence, some positive rewards, for their unusual alignment movements. They would soon have it.

After a day off, the Pirates returned to play on Wednesday, April 3, another cool night. The hitters must have felt as if they were swinging at rocks with their numb and frozen hands. Pirates starter Wandy Rodriguez had not allowed a run in over 6 innings, and McCutchen and Starling Marte had produced RBI hits to give the Pirates a 3–0 lead going into the top of the ninth inning. The stadium was half-empty, and those that were still witnesses in the grandstand seemed to be frozen to their seats when Rizzo came to the plate to lead off the inning against Pirates first-year closer Jason Grilli. Barmes again moved to the right of second base, while Walker plotted himself twenty feet to the right of where he would traditionally be stationed, then moved several steps back deeper into the right-field grass. Walker was positioned perfectly.

Rizzo blistered a one-hop ground ball just to the left of Walker. Walker snagged the ball and threw to first for the out. It was just one play of thousands in that season, but it delivered the first positive reinforcement for the shifted infield. Had Walker been in his traditional position, Rizzo would have reached first base on an infield hit.

"There are certain times you feel like you're in no-man's-land as a middle infielder," Walker said of shifts. "You're in certain spots that when you catch the ball, you kind of feel like you don't know where you're at, and that's kind of a strange feeling."

Sure, teams had been shifting on select lefty power hitters for a number of years, but that season the Pirates began shifting on nearly every lefty hitter to different degrees, and many right-handed hitters. Against every hitter, at least some slight variation from the traditional defensive positioning was made. And in the season's first month, a mountain of evidence showed that the shifting was turning hits into outs.

"There were more instances [of shifts working] than you care to count," Hurdle said. "There were two dozen of those that were electric eye-openers early in the season where the ball is hit and the initial thought is 'There's no way it's an out,' but then you have a guy right there. I just continue to remind them I played in an era where a hard-hit ground ball up the middle was a base hit nine out of ten times. Now a hard-hit ground ball up the middle might be a hit two out of ten times. The game is changing. Sometimes you need to change with the game or it will pass you by."

On April 10 at Arizona, Barmes was positioned deep in the six-hole, closer to third base than the usual shortstop position, and Walker was shifted to nearly behind second base. The Pirates weren't in a Ted Williams Shift by definition—where three infielders are to one side of second base—but it was still a shift away from traditional base defensive lineup. The Pirates were tailoring defensive positioning to each batter. The infielders always moved prior to the beginning of an at bat. The defense never looked the same for any two opposing batters. Arizona slugger Paul Goldschmidt smashed a ground ball into the hole, which would traditionally have been a base hit, but Barmes was there to field the ball and throw across diamond.

"There was talk between infielders: 'Why are we giving a right-hander the four-hole [between the traditional alignments of the first and second basemen] and the whole right side? Why do we have Walker stand straight up the middle in situations where they can drive runs in? That was a tough one for all of us to swallow at times," Barmes said. "They are big league hitters, too. They can jam themselves and hit a ball weakly through the four-hole and it scores a run from second. Why are we giving them that?"

Still, the evidence for why to do it grew.

Early in the season against the Detroit Tigers, left-handed hitter Don Kelly bounced a sharp ground ball up the middle of the infield, which for the first hundred-plus years of the game's history would have rolled into center field for a single. Instead, Barmes was there to gobble up the ground ball, step on second for one force out, and throw to first to complete the double play. Through experiences like that the team strengthened its resolve to enforce the new game plan. But it wasn't just those experiences that strengthened the belief.

One white-haired coach on staff was a bit different from the others and because of that acted as something of a liaison between the analytics team and the rest of the staff. Dave Jauss, fifty-five, with piercing blue eyes and gray stubble, looked like the other coaches. But he had never reached the major leagues. The son of a *Chicago Tribute* sportswriter, Jauss had graduated Amherst with a degree in psychology and later earned his master's in sports management. He had captained the baseball team at Amherst and became a longtime coach and minor league evaluator under Dan Duquette with the Montreal Expos, where he met Huntington. Jauss suggested to Fitzgerald that atop the data-based scouting reports given to players prior to each series should be an anecdotal example of the data's working in a recent game. This important communication, a positive reinforcement, helped build acceptance.

Not only were the players beginning to believe more and more through circumstantial evidence; the coaches, schooled in twentieth-century baseball thought, were starting to believe as well. Said the sixty-year-old Leyva, whose coaching career began with rookie-level Johnson City of the Appalachian League in 1978, to the *Pittsburgh Tribune-Review,* "When I first came over to the Pirates, you could consider me as an old-school guy. But numbers don't lie. Halfway through 2012, I was probably using maybe fifty, sixty percent of what I was getting from stat guys last year. [In 2013] I was close to one hundred percent."

The Pirates would increase their use of shifts by nearly 500 percent in 2013. For baseball, being such a conservative game with a culture that is often slow to accept change, this was a stunning pivot in strategy. In the first year under Hurdle, in 2011, the Pirates shifted 87 times. In 2012, the Pirates shifted only slightly more often, 105 times. In 2013, the Pirates shifted *494 times*. This remarkable increase was a previously unheard-of one-year change in philosophy.

Just a few years earlier, only the Brewers and the Rays were shifting more than 100 times per season. The Pirates advanced from being in the bottom third in baseball in shift usage to sixth in 2013, and that helped them to a winning first month. The Pirates were 15-12 at the end of April. They had not fallen out of the gate. The infielders had seen more examples than not of shifts turning hits into outs, and their acceptance was growing. Pirates players had paid close attention to the anecdotal results in the first month of the season. More wins and more anecdotal evidence of the shifts' success piled up in May, another winning month for the Pirates.

The Pirates' aggregate improvement was from a collection of individual defenders who were more efficiently converting batted balls to outs. According to BIS, Pirates second baseman Neil Walker improved from -4 defensive runs saved in 2012 to +9 in 2013, a 13-run improvement equal to 1.3 wins. The dramatic improvement was tied to simply getting to more balls in play. Walker made 32 more plays in zones outside traditional areas played by second basemen in 2013 than in 2012. Being positioned more intelligently, Pirates third baseman Pedro Alvarez improved from costing the Pirates 5 runs in 2012 to saving them 3 runs in 2013 and was involved in 71 more defensive plays despite the same amount of playing time. Pirates first baseman Garrett Jones was worth -5 defensive runs saved in 2012, then improved to a league average value in 2013, or 0 defensive runs saved. Despite playing in 400 fewer innings due to injury and the emergence of rookie Jordy Mercer, shortstop Clint Barmes's out-of-zone plays remained the same, as did his total defensive runs saved—telling of more efficient defensive play.

The Pirates also altered outfielders' positioning, though less dramatically. Pirates center fielder Andrew McCutchen improved from costing the Pirates 5 runs in 2012 to saving 7 runs in 2013. It all added up to more wins with the same players.

"I think [shifts] are something that's going to be universally kind of implemented in the game of baseball," Walker said prophetically after the 2013 season. "But if you ask me, it's going to take some time, because most people don't want to give in to it."

It took much less time for baseball to evolve than even Walker could imagine.

Two thousand fourteen marked the year of the shift in baseball. The use of shifts skyrocketed across baseball in part because clubs witnessed the one-year jump in shift usage—and resulting defensive improvement—by the Pirates. Baseball saw 7,461 total shifts in 2013, according to BIS, but by July 1, 2014, halfway through that year's season, there had been 8,800 total shifts. According to BIS, teams shifted 13,294 times in 2014, a threefold increase from 2012's 4,577. More and more teams were signing on to the concept, seeing how they could cut their runs allowed without adding a dollar to payroll.

The St. Louis Cardinals had employed little shifting in 2013, with Cardinals manager Mike Matheny citing his starting pitchers' discomfort with them. However, the Cardinals announced plans to gradually increase shifting at the major league.

"We have shifted and I think that's going to continue to happen as people get more information," Matheny said. "Statistics might not tell the whole story, but they don't lie."

In 2013, shift-heavy Tampa allowed 230 fewer hits than traditional-minded, anti-shifting Colorado. Shift-heavy Milwaukee allowed 154 fewer hits than shift-resistant Philadelphia. That's roughly just 1 hit per game, a seemingly trivial number; however, hits add up to runs, and runs add up to wins, and the industry has taken more and more notice of this. After the 2013 season, the Reds replaced the anti-sabermetrics Dusty Baker with Bryan Price, a manager more open to shifts and analytics.

The Astros, under the new leadership of general manager Jeffrey Luhnow, are now one of the most cutting-edge analytical teams and set a record for shift usage in 2014.

By 2013, 1 percent more of batted balls were being turned into outs compared to 2007 levels across baseball. Over a season that's 2,540 fewer base runners in baseball. Such numbers are fueling a rapid increase in the use of shifts.

Consider the team-by-team increase in shifts from 2013 to 2014 according to Baseball Info Solutions:

TEAM	2013	2014
Astros	496	1,341
Rays	556	824
Yankees	475	780
Orioles	595	705
Blue Jays	249	686
Pirates	494	659
Brewers	538	576
Royals	386	543
White Sox	73	534
Indians	312	516
Red Sox	478	498
Rangers	355	490
Athletics	311	488
Twins	84	478
Mariners	261	411
Cardinals	107	367
Giants	149	361
Angels	249	357
Cubs	506	316

TEAM	2013	2014
Phillies	45	291
Diamondbacks	191	252
Padres	88	241
Mets	177	221
Braves	160	213
Reds	290	212
Marlins	180	208
Dodgers	51	208
Tigers	139	205
Nationals	45	201
Rockies	95	114

Said Baseball Info Solutions' John Dewan, "In baseball when one team does something and they are successful, other teams try it out. . . . Shifting was way up last year [in 2013]. Our analytics are showing it has value."

Some teams, however, are still resistant to fielding more smartly aligned defenses. The Rockies had not shifted once in the first month of the 2014 season. The Phillies and Padres were also resistant to moving away from tradition and were some of the worst clubs in the sport in 2014.

While the majority of baseball was catching up to the Rays, Brewers, Pirates, and other shift-heavy teams, advanced analytical teams were already employing the next generation of shifting. In their first series against the Cardinals in 2014, the Pirates weren't just shifting their defense per player, they were shifting alignment *per pitch*. For example, against Cardinals third baseman Matt Carpenter, who is one of the best contact hitters in the league, Pirates infielders were in near-constant motion. On various counts—the number of balls and strikes on a batter during a plate appearance—they altered their alignments to Carpenter's tendencies, overloading one side of the infield for one pitch, then balancing into a more straight-up alignment for another.

"There's still a lot left out there," says John Dewan. "Even the most aggressive shifting teams are not shifting often enough, that's the first thing. There are other elements that are very, very important. For example, the count. When the count is in favor of the hitter, almost every hitter becomes a pull hitter. Vice versa, when the count is in favor of the pitcher, almost every hitter becomes a nonpull hitter. That's very, very important. Also, the type of pitch. The second baseman and the shortstop need to read the sign from the catcher. If it's a fastball, it's less likely to be pulled. It's almost common sense, but not every player does this: read the sign and anticipate where the ball is going to go. I think the more progressive teams are starting to do some of that."

The Pirates also began more aggressively aligning their outfielders in 2014, with left fielder Starling Marte sometimes within thirty feet of the left-field foul line, an unusually extreme position.

However, outfield shifts were trickier to employ. When you see data clusters of batted balls in certain areas of the infield, the data points meant that they were mostly either ground balls or short line drives: they were often hit at similar speeds and were on the ground or low to the ground. But in the outfield, optimizing fielding position was more difficult since the cluster points included batted balls with different trajectories, hang times, and speeds—with the need also to try to calculate the range of an outfielder along with the dimensions of the field to determine optimal positioning.

"The outfield was difficult for us because where you see clusters isn't always where you optimize fielding," Fitzgerald said. "For balls in the outfield you might see a huge cluster in left-center field. I may see twelve balls to left-center, but the four balls down the line end up being more important [because they could be extra-base hits]."

Pirates analysts used visuals to plot the different types of balls in play and where they suggested positioning each outfielder, and Fitzgerald said, "Visually it jumped out to each of the guys."

Cincinnati Reds slugger Joey Votto is one of the most cerebral and feared hitters in the game. The Pirates, however, found Votto had specific tendencies on fly balls. When Votto came to bat, the Pirates had

Marte hug the left-field line as if Votto were a pull-heavy right-handed hitter.

"Outfield shifts have made a difference. I've lost some hits. I've lost quite a few more than I've gained," Votto said. "The Pirates have always shifted heavily. There's been numerous occasions . . . when I've hit to left field, and down the left-field line . . . those [batted balls], which are usually hits, have been outs against the Pirates. They are taking away hits."

Another consequence of big data is that it has tilted the playing field toward the defense since most big data entering the game has been tied to maximizing run prevention. The proliferation and increase in shifting and enhanced scouting information has played a role in the decline of offense. Shifting, along with the increase of strikeouts, has endangered traditional batting average standards and warped the run-scoring environment. In 2013, the major league batting average fell to .253, the lowest in baseball since 1972. For decades, a .300 batting line was the gold standard of a good hitter, but that standard is now in jeopardy.

Of course the batting average decline was tied in part to strikeouts. To isolate the effectiveness of shifts, consider batting average on balls in play. From 2006 to 2008, the major league batting average on balls in play hovered between .303 and .300, around the historical average. The number fell to .295 in 2011 and to .293 in 2013. Ten points in average might not seem significant, but that is hundreds of what would be hits against traditional defenses being turned into outs.

The ultimate proof of runs being cut down due to big data is the scoreboard. The average number of runs scored by a team per game has declined every year since 2006, from 4.85 then to 4.2 in 2013, the lowest rate since 1992. In 2014, scoring fell again, to 4.07 runs per game, the lowest since 1981. The major league batting average has fallen every year since 2006, from .269 then to .251 in 2014. And this is with only about a quarter of the league significantly shifting, including the Pirates, who in 2013 were ahead of the curve. They, along with such teams as the Brewers and the Rays, enjoyed a considerable competitive advantage—for the moment.

The Pirates learned early in 2013 that the shifts were working, and their success influenced the rest of the sport in 2014. But for Hurdle to keep his job, and for Huntington and Fox to remain in the front office, the Pirates would need to do more than smartly align their defenders.

7

ATTRITION

In 2012 the Pirates were badly in need of quality pitching, so they sent several of their promising prospects—including Robbie Grossman and Colton Cain, who were each signed to $1 million bonuses as draft picks under Huntington—to the Houston Astros for veteran, left-handed pitcher Wandy Rodriguez. Rodriguez was under contract for two and a half more seasons. The Pirates were banking on Rodriguez to be a stabilizing force in their 2013 rotation. Other than A. J. Burnett, Rodriguez was the only Pirates pitcher to have logged 200 innings in a major league season. In the four previous seasons, Rodriguez had pitched at least 191 innings in each season.

On a balmy afternoon at Turner Field in Atlanta, Georgia, on June 5, 2013, the Pirates' season fell into a precarious position. On his fourteenth pitch of the game, Rodriguez threw a fastball that seemed to slip out of his hand, traveling high and inside to the left-handed hitting Freddie Freeman. The errant pitch, an uncharacteristic throw for a man who rarely misplaced his pitches, hit Freeman in the shoulder. Rodriguez motioned to the visitors' dugout with his gloved hand, his right hand. The motion transcended any language barrier—Rodriguez was summoning the training staff. Russell Martin was the first to reach Rodriguez. As Martin reached the mound, Rodriguez motioned to his left elbow and muttered something. Pirates trainer Todd Tomczyk was second to arrive, rushing to the center of the diamond, where he was flanked by a mass of gray road jerseys as the entire Pirates infield congregated. Rodriguez again raised his left elbow. Tomczyk looked at it and consulted briefly with Rodriguez before they slowly walked off the field to the Pirates dugout. The crowd in the middle of the infield wore long, serious faces as Rodriguez was examined. Players and training staff knew it was rarely a minor issue when a pitcher complained of elbow pain. It was the last time Rodriguez pitched in 2013.

This was just one in a string of injuries that had been plaguing Pirates players recently. Three days earlier, starting pitcher Jeanmar Gomez, who had begun the year as the Pirates' long man out of the bull pen, had to leave a game with a right forearm strain. Gomez had replaced another starting pitcher, James McDonald, who went on the disabled list May 1 with a shoulder strain. McDonald had pitched like an All-Star in the first half of 2012, but then struggled in the second half of the season along with the rest of the team. McDonald's shoulder began to bark in late April 2013 as his velocity and performance declined. Like Rodriguez, he missed the rest of the season.

To make matters worse, earlier in the season Jonathan Sanchez, another member of the team's Opening Day rotation, had been so ineffective that he had been let go on April 30. In a thirty-five-day span, the team had lost 60 percent of their Opening Day rotation *and* their first reserve starter in Gomez.

The Pirates were in trouble.

They could little afford and had little control over injuries. They could design the most elegant defensive plan ever and extract more hidden value from the free agent market than any other team, and their front office and coaching staff could pull all the right levers, but none of that would matter if they lost too many key players to injury or underperformance. And beyond star Andrew McCutchen, they could least afford injuries to their starting rotation.

This left the Pirates with little room for error. Entering the season, the club possessed the game's fourth-lowest payroll at $66 million, and nearly one-fifth of that, tied to injured pitchers, was now dead weight. The Pirates could not take on bad contracts or sign free agent stars to white-out misfortune. When the Pirates lost a player, they often had to look internally, not externally, for help. And they needed help badly.

The night Rodriguez got injured, the team lost to Atlanta, 5–0, their third straight loss, and they had fallen 3½ games behind St. Louis in the National League Central Division, and one game behind Cincinnati. They had surprised many observers with a strong first two months of the season, winning 35 of their first 60 games, but the injuries threatened to end the feel-good story. Perhaps they were at a high-water mark.

Another problem of attrition was haunting the Pirates organization: the erosion of interest in Pittsburgh in its baseball club. For two decades, layer after layer of trust had broken down between the Pirates and their fans. Despite the early-season success, PNC Park stood half-empty during the first two months of the season. A sea of empty deep blue seating remained in the upper deck. Many in the city viewed those first two winning months as a fluke. Pittsburghers were teased by the previous two seasons when the Pirates towed winning records into the second half, only to see them evaporate into consecutive losing seasons number nineteen and twenty. Though the Pirates thought they were onto something new and promising with their defensive plan and free agent acquisitions, they couldn't discuss their plans in public and thus lose their secret advantages. Even if they did broadcast their plans, since most of it wasn't plainly observable, it would be a tough sell: an extra batted ball caught here and an extra ball turned to a strike there didn't have the splash of signing a big-dollar slugger or an ace pitcher. The value didn't show up on the back of a baseball card and couldn't be sold on a billboard.

The Pirates had hoped wins would boost attendance, but the fans had not come.

A number of Pirates ownership groups throughout the last two decades hadn't trusted that increased spending would make fans show up. This lack of trust was perhaps reinforced as attendance fell from 2 million in 1990 to nine hundred thousand in the strike-shortened 1995 season. Attendance had crept above 2 million only once in the last two decades—in the inaugural season of PNC Park in 2001. Only a last-minute funding agreement in 1998 had ensured a new stadium would be built on Pittsburgh's North Shore and that baseball would remain in Pittsburgh. Support for the club had fallen so quickly since the breakup of the Barry Bonds–led teams of the late 1980s and early 1990s. Ownership groups were reminded again and again that Pittsburgh was a football town, and when it wasn't a football town, it was a hockey town.

Even though Bob Nutting had only owned the team for a handful of years and had little role in the organization's losing streak, he was perceived as more interested in his other investments, such as the Seven Springs Mountain Resort, which became a frequently cited property on local sports-talk radio. Fans joked that since Nutting wasn't spending money on players, he must have been spending cash on ski lifts. Pirates management spoke often of small-market limitations, but the city didn't hear the Steelers or Penguins making similar excuses, though the NFL and NHL employed salary caps to promote parity. Fans sensed that Nutting would not spend on a big trade or any significant free agents. Even a former longtime minority owner of the club, Jay Lustig, doubted that Nutting would ever spend enough to bring winning baseball to Pittsburgh. Lustig sold his stake in the Pirates in 2012. Interviewed by the *Pittsburgh Tribune-Review* in April 2013, he said, "If you are a small-market franchise, if you want to win, you have to be willing to lose [money]. . . . [Nutting's] problem is, he is a rational owner in an irrational business. People say he is a cheap owner, but nothing is further from the truth. He allocates the money properly. He wants to make enough money to keep us from going into the red.

"Now did Bob Nutting and I have personality clashes? Absolutely. I've talked to him several times and tried to convince him that now is the time to sell to a multibillionaire who is willing to come in here and spend more money and see if he can make the Pirates win. [But] Bob Nutting told me something that his grandfather told his father and his father told him. And that's when the Nuttings own something, they own it forever. I just felt I'm too old to find out how long forever is."

The public's confidence was further tested when Pirates management's competence was questioned after revelations of their Navy SEALs training practices and after the image of a poster outside the minor league players' spring training clubhouse in Bradenton with the phrase *Embrace the Suck* was leaked to the press. It was a military phrase designed to encourage subordinates to embrace their trying work. The team was urging their minor leaguers to embrace hard work as beneficial. Instead, the phrase was represented by some in the local media as a snappy, humorous slogan to sum up twenty years of losing.

The empty seats in PNC Park felt like a boycott, expressing the erosion of trust and the desire for change. Clint Hurdle saw this broken trust when he came to Pittsburgh late in 2010. He often spoke of his mission to rebond the city with its baseball team. He had first known the Pirates as a great organization, the "We Are Family" Pirates of the 1970s that had won a pair of World Series with stars such as Dave Parker and Willie Stargell. Pittsburgh had not always been a football town. It had not always been a place where the hockey team had been the number two sport of choice. Pittsburgh had once been a baseball town. Before the Steelers were winning Super Bowls and the Penguins were winning Stanley Cups, the Pirates had won championships.

To be an ambassador for the Pirates, to be the face of the franchise, Hurdle thought he should not be a part-time Pittsburgh resident. So he bought a home and lived year-round in the city, even through its snowy and slushy winters. He made daily stops at a Starbucks, where his name was written on his cup without a barista's asking. You could find him at North Hills grocery stores and barbershops near his suburban home. He noticed when he was out in public that most kids wore Ben Roethlisberger Steelers jerseys and Sidney Crosby hockey sweaters. He saw far fewer kids adorned in Pirates gear. It was as if they were embarrassed by their baseball club, and he knew that had to change if he was going to stick around. This was a business. It was about selling tickets, jerseys, and compelling people to turn on their televisions. The Pirates had to win.

What the public did not see were the data-driven, smart decisions that were making a real difference in the season's first half. Hurdle believed if the Pirates could continue this play into the second half, it would be impossible to ignore, even in a town obsessed with its more successful franchises, the Steelers and the Penguins. He felt the Pirates could capture the city's imagination if they kept winning. He also knew he could not afford another second-half slide. He already had two strikes and couldn't afford a third. The injuries to the pitching staff were threatening to guarantee Hurdle's third strike and a twenty-first consecutive losing season. The Pirates and Hurdle had to find a way to overcome the loss of 60 percent of their starting rotation through just the first third of the season. Such a rash of injuries would have threatened the prospects of even the game's most talented and deep-pocketed teams.

Baseball is often called a game of attrition. Hurdle knew it was a specific type of attrition: pitching injuries. Pitchers broke. It was nearly a scientific law in the game. The teams that won either had better luck in keeping their pitchers healthy, more pitchers in reserve, or the money to acquire additional pitchers via free agency or by taking on large contracts in trades. Los Angeles Dodgers head trainer Stan Conte was one of the first medical officials in the sport to study injury data. Conte found a starting pitcher has a 50 percent chance of being injured in any given season. A team without pitching depth is therefore highly unlikely to succeed. Moreover, starting pitchers are the game's highest-paid players, with major league teams devoting a disproportionate share of payroll to pitchers. From 2008 to 2013, teams spent $1.3 billion on pitchers disabled by injuries, according to journalist and sports-injury expert Will Carroll. No type of injury has been more costly than ulnar ligament tears in the throwing elbow, which require a reconstruction of the ligament, a procedure known as Tommy John surgery, which that can take a year to eighteen months to rehab.

One-third of pitchers on Opening Day 2013 rosters had undergone Tommy John surgery. Pitchers, particularly young ones, were needing the surgery more than ever. Through September 2014, seventy-six pitchers had had Tommy John surgery, breaking the previous record of sixty-nine to undergo the operation in 2012. There were no signs of improvement in injury prevention.

Part of the increase in injuries is believed to be tied to the arrival of the first generation of pitchers who were raised and overused in a sports-specialization culture. Today's pitchers threw in year-round programs as kids and overexerted themselves for scouts and college recruiters as teenagers at showcase events. That was the hypothesis of a 2013 position paper by the American Sports Medicine Institute, which studied the epidemic of Tommy John surgeries.

Velocity is perhaps another culprit. The average speed of a major league fastball has increased every year since 2007, according to PITCHf/x, which began tracking pitch data that year. Perhaps the human body simply cannot keep up with the increasing stress placed upon it. In 2008, the velocity of the average major league, four-seam fastball was 90.9 mph. By 2013 it was 92 mph. In 2014, it increased again to 92.1 mph. In 2003, Houston Astros reliever Billy Wagner was the only pitcher to throw at least 25 pitches at 100 mph or faster. In 2013, eight pitchers hit 100 mph at least 25 times, and Reds closer Aroldis Chapman threw 318 pitches at 100 mph or faster, according to CBSSports.com

While pitchers are taller and stronger than they were a generation ago, and while they can strengthen their muscles, they cannot strengthen their tendons and ligaments. The ulnar collateral ligament, about two centimeters long and one centimeter wide, is made up of bundles of fibers and frays like a rope. The ligament doesn't snap on one throw; rather, it's believed to wear down over time, and clearly the ligament has never been under more stress.

While the increase in injuries is well documented and there is a better understanding of why injuries occur, there is little understanding of how to prevent them. Baseball is still largely using rudimentary tools—raw pitch counts—as the universal preventive practice. The Pirates knew they needed pitching depth, but the club couldn't afford proven, above-average pitchers on the free agent market. They had few easy fixes, but they thought they had identified one.

8

SPINNING GOLD

Hurdle's background was in hitting. A former power-hitting prodigy, he had advanced to manager from minor league coach and major league hitting instructor. Despite his personal experience, he was obsessed with pitch efficiency. Perhaps he had witnessed too many pitchers become exhausted in the thin, run-scoring air of Coors Field or wilt in the oppressive, sweat-soaking August heat of Arlington, Texas, where he was briefly a hitting coach with the Rangers. He was not enamored with strikeouts, despite managing in an era of record strikeout totals. Rather, he preferred generating outs in "three pitches or less." He wanted his pitchers to be more contact-oriented than swing-and-miss focused. He wanted to decrease pitch counts and increase innings from his starters and keep them and the bullpen fresh. He had recommended this approach since his arrival in Pittsburgh, and now he saw his opportunity to sell this philosophy to his pitchers.

Hurdle had taken a collective risk with a pitching staff before. The thin air of mile-high Coors Field had helped create a tremendous offensive environment in Colorado and helped give Hurdle a good reputation as a hitting coach. It springboarded him to being named Rockies manager early in the 2002 season. The thin-air environment was also a considerable barrier to creating effective and efficient pitching. Since the award of an expansion team to Denver in 1993, nothing had worked to make pitching effective at its mile-high altitude. Nearly every season, Coors Field ranked as the most friendly home-run and run-scoring ballpark in baseball. Placing the balls in a humidor prior to games to soak up humidity before use helped a little, but Coors Field remained a hitter's paradise.

At first, the Rockies had forsaken pitching and loaded up on offense, but that was a difficult way to win, particularly in the postseason. The team then tried signing high-dollar free agent pitchers Mike Hampton and Denny Neagle, but that wasn't effective either since their signature breaking pitches were not as effective at the higher altitude, where the lesser air resistance on the ball made it break less. So on August 15, 2005, Hurdle and the Rockies decided to try something that hadn't been done in twenty years: they dropped the fifth starter from their pitching staff. It was difficult to attract and develop pitchers in Colorado, and besides, their fifth starters were horrendous. Denny Stark and Jeff Fassero were a combined 0-3 with a 17.47 ERA. Dropping them should improve the club's overall pitching performance. To keep a four-pitcher rotation fresh, the Rockies' four starters would also throw fewer pitches per start. This was important as a batter's performance in a single game tends to improve with each subsequent plate appearance against a starting pitcher. The more looks a batter gets at a pitcher's release point and pitches, the better he typically performs. Part of sabermetrics ideology is that starting pitchers should pitch fewer innings. By employing four starters the Rockies would slightly reduce their innings per start, thus their batters faced, with the bull-pen arms soaking up more innings.

"We were at a point in time where the fifth starter's record, for a year and a half, was horrible," Hurdle said. "The ERA was horrible. The [performances] weren't anywhere close for what you'd ever hope.

We kind of looked at each other and said, 'Let's eliminate it. Let's see where it can take us.' Tradition is a wonderful thing. There are reasons for honoring tradition and staying with tradition. But tradition can also be a vision killer."

No team had employed a four-man pitching staff for an entire season since the 1984 Blue Jays. The 1995 Royals were the last team to experiment with a four-man staff for a significant portion of a season.

"We've batted the idea around for more than two years but have been too scared to try it," Hurdle told reporters at the time. "It's time for us to be a bit more creative to get our pitching right."

Unfortunately, the four-man rotation didn't last and neither did Hurdle. The pitchers were uncomfortable with the setup and the Rockies continued to lose. The Rockies ditched the four-man rotation by the end of the season. Hurdle failed to find a way to improve pitching effectiveness at Coors Field, and lost his job in 2009. But it wouldn't be his last attempt to employ a radical theory with his pitching staff. He still believed it was the right approach, and had a successful team first adopted the philosophy, it might have gained traction. Baseball is a copycat game. Teams copy the practices of successful teams. In the spring of 2013, Hurdle was desperate again and ready to try another radical experiment. Not only would the Pirates place their infielders in untraditional positions, they would ask pitchers to change what and where they predominately threw. What if the Pirates pitchers could not only have more efficient outings, logging more innings using fewer pitchers, but could also create more ground balls? And what if those ground balls were hit into a more smartly aligned defense? Remember, ground balls were pulled by hitters nearly 80 percent of the time.

Hurdle discussed this idea with his pitching coach, Ray Searage, and organizational pitching guru Jim Benedict: "What if we could get more ground balls hit into the shift?" Hurdle and Searage and Benedict all agreed upon the merits of the three-pitches-or-less doctrine. They could sell it to their pitchers by telling them they'd pitch deeper into games, log more innings, and thereby have more opportunities to earn wins.

"It made sense when framed [that way]," Hurdle said. "And if that is your focus point, if you really bite into that and buy into that, the two-seam fastball becomes your best weapon."

Some believed that whether one was a fly-ball or a ground-ball pitcher was an innate trait. The difference was based upon what a pitcher threw and how he threw, what angle the ball was delivered from, pitch movement, etc. These traits were thought to be hard to change. Moreover, for most of the game's history no one had been recording ground-ball rates of hitters or pitchers.

Groundball data was not available until more detailed play-by-play records began being kept in the 1980s. BaseballReference.com has ground ball-fly ball ratios on pitchers dating back to only 1988. The batted-ball data showed beyond a doubt that pitchers and batters each tended to either produce more fly balls or ground balls. The batted-ball data, combined with one of the game's great technological innovations, its first true big data tool, PITCHf/x, explained why pitchers had groundball or fly ball tendencies. PITCHf/x demonstrated that not only could some pitchers change, but how they changed. PITCHf/x not only measured the speed, trajectory, and location of every pitch, but also accurately labeled every pitch type. For the first time analysts could see a clear statistical correlation between certain pitches and certain results, including pitches and ground balls. Anyone with an Internet connection could study the year-to-year changes in how often pitchers threw certain pitches and their corresponding ground-ball rates. While the fastball has been the most commonly thrown pitch in baseball from the sport's beginnings to the present day, the two-seam, sinking fastball and variations of it produce more ground balls than the more commonly thrown four-seam fastball.

The four-seam fastball can be thrown with the most velocity and has therefore traditionally been the game's most common pitch. Intuitively, pitchers want to throw a fastball as fast as possible. But four-seam fastballs also travel on a straighter plane toward home plate, making such pitches more likely to be squared up and lifted into the air by hitters. They are called four-seam fastballs because of the grip; the pitcher holds his index and middle fingers perpendicular to the seams. When the ball is released from the pitcher's hand, all four of the ball's seams are rotating, face front, end over end, toward the batter. Two-seam fastballs travel with slightly less velocity; but because of the way they are gripped, with a pitcher's index and middle fingers overlapping two seams, their spin and air resistance create more downward and horizontal movement. The two-seam is more difficult to hit cleanly, and therefore the pitch produces more ground balls.

By simply changing pitch grips, some pitchers could change the nature of the balls in play against them. This was known naturally to some, but PITCHf/x demonstrated without a doubt through data how dramatic the change could be. So if a pitcher could produce more ground balls, combined with a smarter defensive alignment behind him, he should theoretically be able to lower his hits and runs allowed.

Producing more ground balls was the third prong of the most radical defensive plan in the game's history—to be implemented along with the shifts and pitch-framing. There was little talk that spring of improving run production. Instead the entire off-season and spring training was focused on preventing runs. That's where Fox, Huntington, and Hurdle believed opportunity resided, with all three of these opportunities rooted in data-based evidence.

Curiosity and desperation were recurring motivational factors in Hurdle's career. They had led him to implement the four-man rotation in Colorado and to the MLB Network and exploring sabermetrics Web sites such as FanGraphs.com and finally to the two-seam fastball. That blend of curiosity and desperation had allowed Hurdle to change as a person and as a manager. He believed his pitching staff had the power to change, too. He had the PITCHf/x data to prove pitchers could improve their ground-ball rates, and the Pirates had witnessed one of their own make a remarkable transformation.

★ ★ ★

Charlie Morton had not pitched in a major league game in more than a year when he left his suburban home north of Pittsburgh to drive to PNC Park on a muggy, overcast afternoon on June 13, 2013. He was several hours away from making his first appearance since returning from Tommy John surgery. Headed south on I-279, winding through the northern hills of the city, he was already perspiring.

Morton wasn't sure if his arm would ever again be the same thanks to the six-inch scar on the inside of his right elbow, the telltale sign of Tommy John surgery. The previous May, his career was placed in jeopardy just when he thought it was turning around. After a disastrous 2010 season, he'd rebounded with a much better campaign in 2011, posting a 10-10 record and 3.83 ERA with the Pirates. But after a start against Cincinnati in late May 2012, he felt that he had hyperextended his right elbow. Tests revealed he had torn the ulnar collateral ligament. He was headed for Tommy John surgery and a lengthy rehab and recovery.

Morton traveled to Birmingham, Alabama, to have ligament-reconstruction surgery done by Dr. James Andrews. The new ligament was a tendon extracted from below his knee and threaded through small holes drilled near the ends of the humerus and ulna bones where they connect at the elbow. He returned to Pittsburgh for a week, then headed for the club's Pirate City complex in Florida to begin his rehab. One challenge of rehab is being away from the spotlight and the familiar faces and fellowship of coaches and teammates. And rehab is monotonous. The early weeks feature isometric therapy, where an athlete does simple exercises while remaining in static positions. In the back training room of the Pirate City complex, Morton stood against a wall and pushed against it at different angles, with different levels of resistance.

"I made good friends with the wall in the back training room," Morton said.

Not only was his repaired elbow sore and stiff, but the area below his left knee where the replacement ligament was harvested was also uncomfortable, weak, and in need of strengthening. Rehab was tedious and painful, and tangible results were slow to come.

Perhaps the toughest part for Morton was the lack of a competitive outlet. To fill the void he invited other rehabbing players to come over to the four-bedroom, single-family home he had purchased in Bradenton for marathon video-game sessions, most often playing the military-themed, shoot-'em-up game *Call of Duty*. On Tuesdays they went to Gecko's, a Bradenton bar and grill, where they played trivia. They called their team the Red Barons, after the red T-shirts the rehabbing players wore to distinguish themselves from the healthy players.

"Rehab was just driving us insane because we were competitive by nature," Morton said.

Morton is different from many of his teammates, an oddity in a professional-baseball clubhouse. While he looks like a prototypical right-hander, long and lean at six-feet-four and athletic from having played a number of sports in high school—his father played basketball at Penn State—Morton is cerebral and introspective. He pauses to scratch his closely cropped black hair as he searches for the right words to articulate his thoughts, never relying on canned, clichéd responses when speaking with reporters. He feels compelled to be honest and interesting. He'd have loved to attend college, and would have, had the Braves not made him a third-round pick in the 2002 draft out of Barlow High in Redding, Connecticut. He looked at pitching as science. He loves numbers and examines data and is concerned not just with results but the hows and the whys of his craft. He is a thinker.

And during rehab he had more time to think about his uncertain future.

That summer of 2012, Morton worried about things he'd never worried about before. He was careful with how he shut doors at home, how he closed the trunk of his car, worried about damaging the reconstructed ligament. He treated his elbow as if it housed a Fabergé egg. He knew that Tommy John surgery usually places pitchers back on the field, but it is not an automatic cure. Not every pitcher comes back. Morton even worried that he might not be tendered a contract for the 2013 season by the Pirates. He was entering arbitration and was becoming more expensive. However, he would eventually agree to a one-year, $2 million contract with the Pirates for 2013. It was a pay cut from his $2.4 million salary in 2012, the first time he had earned above the league minimum.

As he drove to the ballpark now, his thoughts wandered back to early that spring when he first threw off the mound in an extended spring training game, after the big league club had broken camp and headed north. He had no idea how hard he had thrown that inning against an assortment of Toronto Blue Jays minor leaguers. He knew that if his velocity was below 90 mph, he was in trouble. He completed his first inning of work in the dark about exactly how his arm had performed on the quiet back-fields of the Pirate City complex. It was the first time he had really cut it loose since the surgery. He approached Pirates pitching guru and special assistant to the general manager Jim Benedict in the makeshift, chain-link dugout. Benedict had worked with Morton throughout his rehab, rebuilding his mechanics and confidence. Morton considered Benedict not just a coach but a friend. The tall, broad-shouldered, and mustached man had stood behind the plate and put a radar gun to Morton's pitches in that first inning back. An anxious and eager Morton asked what the top radar-gun reading was. Benedict broke into a smile and said, "You sat at ninety-four to ninety-six mph. You touched ninety-eight." Morton hugged him.

"I hugged him, one, because I was happy and it was a relief," Morton said. "And two, he was there with me the whole time [during rehab], working with me, putting in as much time as anyone."

Morton's sinker was consistently in the mid-90s that day, putting one fear to rest: his elbow had successfully been reconstructed and the grueling process had not been in vain. But on this June afternoon as he wound through the hills on the outskirts of the city and the skyline opened up before him, a different fear emerged: Could he get big league hitters out? This was no longer just about his rehab. The Pirates were playing well and he knew they needed him since Rodriguez and McDonald were both injured. In a rehab start a day earlier, McDonald allowed 5 runs in 6 innings at Triple-A Indianapolis. McDonald's velocity was still down, his shoulder was still hurting. The Pirates' first reserve, Gomez, was also out. The club was running out of arms. Morton was okay during his four rehab starts with Triple-A Indianapolis, but the Pirates needed him to be better than that.

There was little room for error in the National League Central Division. The Reds had made the play-offs a year earlier and were off to their best start since 1995. The Cardinals, perhaps the game's model franchise and winners of the 2011 World Series, were off to another excellent start. The Pirates, Cardinals, and Reds all had .600 winning percentages or better entering June—the first time that had happened in any National League division since 1977. And those three teams continued to play .600 baseball twelve days into June. But would the Pirates be able to continue a winning season with the staggering amount of injuries that were accumulating?

Morton walked from the bull pen with his catcher, Russell Martin, a pregame routine after a pitcher had completed his warm-ups. Morton tried to relax and shake off nerves. The lineups had been introduced. Fans were taking their seats. Pregame music blared through the PNC Park speakers. A buzz was in the air that he had not felt in more than a year as he walked across the outfield grass to the home dugout. His career had been five years of uneven performance. In some ways this was a last chance with the Pirates. An added pressure was that his wife was seven months pregnant. He was out of options, and if he struggled, he could be released. He had already made enough money to be comfortable. But he wanted to pitch, he wanted to compete, and he wanted to be great. He had gotten by on potential for so long—would he produce results? Morton wondered. He knew the Pirates could no longer afford to be patient with him.

The Pirates had a huge stake in Morton, too. They needed pitching depth. While Morton's elbow was rebuilt after surgery, the club's pitching coaches had also reconstructed him as a pitcher. They had changed what he threw, where he threw, and how he threw. Would the new model work?

Morton had first tried to throw a two-seam fastball in 2006 with the Myrtle Beach Pelicans, the Atlanta Braves' High-A minor league affiliate. On a hot afternoon, under a searing sun on the South Carolina coast, Morton experimented with the pitch in a practice session between his starts. Pitch after pitch, two-seamer after two-seamer, came out of his hand as straight as an arrow. Observing quietly in the bull pen was the pitching coach Bruce Dal Canton, a grandfather figure. The sixty-four-year-old had been around the game forever. He had pitched for the Pirates from 1967 to 1970, after he was discovered by a Pirates scout in an amateur league while working as a high school science teacher at Burgettstown High in southwestern Pennsylvania. He later pitched for the Royals, White Sox, and Braves. After his playing career ended he began coaching, working his way up to become the Braves' pitching coach from 1987 to 1990. He was instrumental in the development of the Braves' pitching greats Tom Glavine and John Smoltz. Dal Canton had seen about every kind of pitcher and every kind of problem. He was kind, patient, and observant. Over the years Dal Canton's hair had turned a brilliant white, and his long, narrow face had thinned. Dal Canton was dying of esophageal cancer.

He asked Morton to stop throwing and walked across the crushed red brick and artificial turf of the bull pen under a searing sun to demonstrate how to get inside the ball. That means, if you are right-handed and you hold a baseball straight in front of you, the force is applied to the inside, left-hand side of the ball. He showed Morton how to grip the ball more off center. Morton copied the grip and returned to the mound; suddenly the ball began diving.

He gained more and more confidence with the pitch and started throwing the sinker in 2007 in Double-A, then with even more regularity in 2008 with Triple-A Gwinnett. He reached the majors in the second half of the 2008 season and produced an above-average ground-ball rate, 51 percent, in 15 starts. He thought his two-seamer could develop into one of his better pitches as batter after batter pounded the top half of the ball, driving it into the dirt in front of home plate. After his starts, it looked as if a toy army had landed an artillery barrage in front of home plate. But he was soon to be stripped of his new weapon.

In June of 2009, the Pirates acquired Morton in a three-player trade with Atlanta. The Pirates sent outfielder Nate McLouth to the Braves for two young pitchers, Morton and Jeff Locke. McLouth was having a fine season, he finished with 20 home runs, 19 steals, and a .256 batting average. He was one of the club's most popular players, but McLouth was not likely to be part of the club's future as he did not have a long-term contract. The pitching-bereft Pirates needed arms and they liked Morton, whose four-seam fastball could touch the mid-90s. Morton had gone 7-2 with a 2.51 ERA with Atlanta's Triple-A affiliate in 2009 and went 7-2 with a 2.29 ERA with Indianapolis, earning a call-up to finish the season with the Pirates.

However, when the Pirates acquired Morton, one of the first things they did was strip him of his two-seam fastball. The Pirates coaches were troubled by all Morton's thinking, tinkering, and assortment of pitches. They wanted to simplify things for him. The Pirates were intrigued with something else, too: radar-gun readings. Morton's four-seam fastball routinely touched the mid-90s. His average fastball was

93 mph in 2010. Morton's four-seam fastball possessed velocity, but it was also straight.

"There was an organizational decision made that I wasn't going to throw a two-seamer at all," Morton said. "Four-seam, curveball, change-up; I did not have input. I think it was interpreted that my two-seamer was my four-seamer, just slower. So I went with it. That was the decision that was made."

The decision was a disaster. Morton started 17 games in 2010, the first season he broke camp with a big league club. He went 2–12 with a 7.57 ERA. He had the worst winning percentage and ERA in baseball. He allowed more fly balls than he ever had before. Those straight fastballs were hit hard and far, with 18 percent of the fly balls he allowed going for home runs. He didn't throw a single two-seam fastball that season.

"I respected that decision. Unfortunately, it didn't work out. It took a weapon away from me. I think that year really exposed some things about me that I needed to improve upon," Morton said. "I needed to get tougher. I needed to grow up. I needed to mature. It wasn't just about getting by. I didn't want to be a guy that didn't really have an identity."

When Morton was demoted to the minor leagues that summer, he was told he could experiment. He began to think again about the sinker he had learned in Myrtle Beach in 2006. In the spring of 2011, Morton met a new coaching staff and welcomed a new voice: the scratchy, Long Island–accented tones of Ray Searage, the new Pirates pitching coach.

When Hurdle was named Pirates manager late in 2010, one of his first and most pressing goals was to assemble a staff. Like any other CEO type, a manager must delegate. He must surround himself with competent assistants. In baseball, perhaps no other assistant is more important than the pitching coach, who must be part psychologist, part mechanic. He watches bull-pen sessions and work in games and identifies and quickly fixes mechanical flaws. He must make strategic and psychological adjustments in real time during mound visits.

When Hurdle took the Pirates managerial position, he did not know Searage well. Searage had been named the interim Pirates pitching coach at the end of the 2010 season. His and Hurdle's playing careers and coaching careers had rarely intersected. Hurdle interviewed Searage, and other external candidates. When Hurdle spoke with Searage, and people who knew him, he was drawn to Searage's natural communication ability and his familiarity with a number of the young arms coming through the system who would impact the Pirates under Hurdle's watch.

There was something else striking about Searage: his story. As a boy, Searage accompanied his father to construction sites on Saturdays near his native Freeport on the shores of southeastern Long Island. His father directed the construction of department stores and commercial buildings. Searage remembered how his father addressed everyone the same way, treated everyone the same way, from the sweaty, sawdust-covered workers who were lowest on the food chain to his suit-wearing superiors. It left an indelible imprint on Searage, who described his father as a compassionate man.

Searage also remembered how throughout his own baseball career, every pitching coach had tried to change him. It seemed like everyone knew what Ray Searage was supposed to be. He was a left-handed reliever for the White Sox, Dodgers, Brewers, Mets, and Indians; and every time he arrived to a new organization, its coaching staff tried to change him. The most extreme change came at the end of his career, with the Indians in 1991. That spring the Cleveland staff wanted Searage to adopt a high leg kick like Len Barker. Searage did as instructed but struggled to throw strikes. He was traded to the Mets that winter and after the 1991 season he was out of baseball, having thrown just 287 professional innings. He vowed, if he ever coached, he would be different. He had been in pitchers' shoes and didn't want them to go through the same things he did. If he coached pitchers, he wanted them to keep their identities.

That's just what Morton was seeking: an identity. Searage wanted Morton to go back to feeling comfortable. Searage felt his best skill, the one that allowed him to communicate so well with players, was empathy. He knew what it was to feel like a broken player, and he inherited one in Morton in early 2011.

Searage and special assistant Jim Benedict studied video on Morton. The first thing they noticed was that he was not throwing from his natural arm slot. This was not uncommon. Pitchers were told ideal mechanics began with an over-the-top motion, meaning the ball should be released high above their head, the idea being to create as much downward angle or downhill slope as possible. However, Searage believed that pitchers have natural arm paths and that they weren't designed to throw as robots. The other thing they noticed from watching video and from speaking with those familiar with Morton was that he had been stripped of the two-seam fastball by the previous coaching staff. Morton lit up radar guns, but his four-seam fastballs were straight.

In February 2011, Searage and Benedict called Morton in for a meeting to reveal their plan. Searage and Benedict told Morton that they were going to lower his arm slot and give him back his two-seam fastball. He trusted them because he felt, intuitively, that he should. Searage was a bit like Dal Canton, patient and soft-spoken, doing more watching than talking during bull-pen sessions. Searage didn't overwhelm you, and he was positive. Morton felt that they cared about his success. Coming off the worst season of his career, what other choice did he have but to follow their advice? He was down to his final chances with the Pirates, and it was either succeed or else.

Their presentation to Morton included video of All-Star pitcher Roy Halladay, whose arm slot they wanted Morton to emulate. Like Morton, Halladay was demoted to the minor leagues early in his career after severe struggles. He had to discover a new arm path to become the perennial Cy Young contender he became in the late 2000s. They told Morton when Halladay dropped his arm slot, he was able to throw around his body, better keeping his head still. If your head isn't still, the target isn't still, and command over the ball suffers, they reasoned. Morton was contorting his body and kicking his head left in his delivery to try and create that desired throwing plane. Morton agreed to try Benedict's and Searage's plan. The experiment began along the left-field foul line on field No. 2 of the back-fields complex at Pirate City, the same complex where Kyle Stark had experimented with spray paint and defensive alignments. The nondescript, windswept field enclosed by chain-link fencing was generally used for minor league spring training and Gulf Coast League games. With no one watching, no pressure, Morton began throwing with his new mechanics, and he was astounded by how natural it felt.

"It killed me to feel it because it was like, 'Oh, my goodness, I wish I had known earlier,'" Morton said. "That's pretty much all they did. Keep your arm working around your body, keep your head still. It was incredible really. It was instantaneous. I knew something had changed."

In the second key part to the plan Searage wanted Morton to trade in his four-seam fastball for a two-seam, sinking fastball. Morton returned to placing the ball in the two-finger grip he had learned from Dal Canton. Morton got on the mound, coiled his body in his windup, and unleashed a ball that traveled on a plane that seemed to include an invisible cliff near home plate, where the ball dropped late and steeply at 93 mph.

"It was just incredible. I got on the mound and it was unbelievable," Morton said. "The sinker is a pitch I need to throw. They understand that's part of who I was on the mound. I was just a totally different dude."

Pirates first baseman Lyle Overbay, a former teammate of Halladay's in Toronto, took live batting practice against Morton that spring. He told Morton his motion was identical to Halladay's, and then he told *Sports Illustrated* separately, "This is Roy Halladay with better stuff. Roy's location makes him the elite of the elite. Charlie's not there yet with his location. But once he is . . . "

Morton was now a different pitcher. He essentially tabled his four-seam fastball for his sinker.

What made Morton's sinking two-seamer so special?

"The spin angle. Its angular rotation," Morton said. "It's just the angle of the ball, the way it rotates, the rpm of the ball. The way the air resists the ball, the way the seams are spinning, it just allows the ball to run and sink. It's interesting. If you slow down a sinker on video, you'll see the actual rotation. It's almost like on an axis. The two seams are rotating and it rides like a rail."

In his first start of 2011, Morton faced the Cardinals. In the first inning of his first start, his confidence still fragile after the challenges of the 2010 season, he faced the National League's most feared hitter, Albert Pujols. This was the first great test of the sinker, the first great leap of faith. Morton got the sign to throw the sinker. He went into his new windup, coiled, and unleashed a pitch that left his hand with his fingers applying pressure to the inside of the baseball. The pitch's initial trajectory was to the inner third of the plate, then it suddenly dove down to the right and compelled Pujols to jackknife out of the way and drop to his knees. The pitch didn't result in a weak ground ball or a swing and miss or even in a strike, but it had rare movement. Its movement had surprised Pujols, who barely had time to avoid being hit by it. For the first time against an elite major league batter, Morton saw the pitch had life.

Morton's teammates watching from the dugout were also intrigued. The starting pitchers, who usually congregate near the rail at the end of the dugout to watch games together when they are not assigned to pitch, broke into smiles and buzzed after the pitch seemed to fall off an invisible escarpment. They told Morton to watch the pitch on video after the game. He saw then the movement and saw the game's best hitter react late to the pitch's movement. He realized that if he could throw that pitch in the strike zone, it would result in swings and misses and ground balls thanks to its unconventional flight path. It wasn't just video that buoyed Morton's confidence. In 2008, when PITCHf/x went online in every major league stadium, there were, for the first time, standards of measurement for velocity, movement, and release point available to front offices, coaches, players, and fans. PITCHf/x could do more than label pitches and report accurate velocities, it could help a curious player such as Morton gain trust and confidence. It could give a data-savvy player a competitive edge.

Beginning in 2009, Morton had begun employing PITCHf/x tools to study changes in his release point, pitch rotation, and velocity. His father studied Morton's PITCHf/x readings, too. They discussed them and looked for changes and progress. As with Hurdle, this was an illumination period. Morton had objective data to study, and this data helped Morton to buy in to the Pirates' plan.

PITCHf/x gave Morton an objective baseline with which to evaluate himself, something that's often difficult for a pitcher since so many variables are outside a pitcher's control. He doesn't control the defense behind him, the ballpark he is pitching in, or the lineup he's facing. A pitcher could pitch exactly the same way in two separate outings and get completely different results. The resulting peaks and valleys of performance can be maddening, particularly to an analytical pitcher such as Morton. But with PITCHf/x data, he had an objective standard. He could see his location, release point, pitch movement, and velocity, factors he could control and judge his performance upon. He knew he could make the ball sink and run as well as any other pitcher in baseball. For instance, according PITCHf/x data at BrooksBaseball.net, Morton's two-seamer averaged 93.1 mph in 2013 with 9.63 inches of horizontal movement, a rare combination of movement and velocity. Morton could see the results in real time in 2013. While pitchers had for years been able to look at the scoreboard to see their velocity, in 2013 at PNC Park, Dan Fox had the PITCHf/x horizontal and vertical movement for each pitch shown on the thin, ribbonlike auxiliary scoreboards that were on the façades of the upper decks along the first- and third-base grandstands. The hard science, the measurable pitch movement, the big data that PITCHf/x provided, resulted in a soft-science benefit: confidence.

PITCHf/x also told Morton an important data-based story. In 2011, his curveball wasn't good, his changeup was a nonfactor, his cutter wasn't cutting, and his four-seam fastball was flat. Morton saw he was a one-pitch pitcher, but it was an above-average pitch, and this one pitch changed the Pirates.

In 2010, he had thrown only four-seam fastballs. In 2011, his four-seam fastball rate fell to 6.6 percent, and he threw his sinker 65.8 percent of the time, spiking his ground ball rate to 58.5 percent. He produced 3.1 ground balls for every fly ball, a remarkable ratio, even more so considering his ratio the previous year was 1.5. Morton finished the season 10-10 with a 3.83 ERA and went from one of the National League's worst pitchers to one of its best ground-ball pitchers simply by changing pitch type and arm slot. Some took to calling him Ground Chuck.

Morton was reinvented simply by his returning to a pitch he was comfortable with and adopting a new arm slot. It was an interesting case study for Hurdle and the Pirates, who were trying to improve their pitch efficiency beginning in the spring of 2012, and who in 2013 wanted to increase the number of ground balls hit into their infield shifts. Morton was a sort of test case; he built confidence in the two-seam plan. What if more pitchers could be like Morton? What if the Pirates could improve their own pitchers—and better prevent runs—through one pitch? What if every Pirates pitcher could generate more ground balls to be hit into a more smartly aligned defense? If they could make Morton a dominant ground-ball pitcher, who else could they change? A. J. Burnett became the second test case.

On February 17, 2012, the New York Yankees so wanted to be rid of the final two years of A. J. Burnett's five-year, $82 million deal they agreed to trade Burnett to the Pirates—and pay half his salary—for two marginal prospects. Burnett had not fit well in Yankee

Stadium or the American League East Division. He had posted ERAs above 5.00 in back-to-back seasons in 2010 and 2011. He was stubborn with his approach. And he had lost a tick on the fastball that had made him one of the game's top young flamethrowers with the Marlins earlier in his career. Thanks in part to their database, the Pirates' analytics department saw a buy-low opportunity in a pitcher who had an underutilized but effective sinking fastball. They saw a pitcher who had perhaps become too leery of pitching to contact in the cramped ballparks, against the power-packed lineups, of the AL East, meaning Burnett had focused on generating swings and misses from opponents, trying to blow four-seam fastballs by them, rather than attempting to induce weak contact and ground balls with slower, sinking fastballs.

"Being able to try to add that to a pitcher's arsenal was a concerted effort," Dan Fox said of the ground ball and two-seamer. "Targeting guys who you think might have that ability is one part [of the plan]. The ground-ball rate [increasing], the difference we saw with players we already had . . . that's all Ray [Searage] and Jim Benedict being able to teach it."

The Pirates' analytics department thought Burnett could have more success by leaning on his two-seam fastball, but getting him to employ it fell to the coaching staff. On Burnett's right arm is tattooed in Latin STRENGTH THROUGH LOYALTY, a tribute to his wife and family. Burnett had also become incredibly loyal to his simple, two-pitch mix—a four-seam fastball and a curveball. Unlike other aging pitchers he had never developed a third pitch. But he had now posted three straight seasons of 10-plus percent home-run rates.

Searage had his work cut out for him. His plan was to sell Burnett with a simple message: Searage was not looking to overhaul pitchers, he was trying to improve one or two elements. He was into tweaks, not reconstruction.

Did Burnett buy in? Check out his pitch usage with the Yankees in 2011 versus his pitch usage with the Pirates in 2012:

BURNETT'S 2011 PITCH MIX WITH THE YANKEES (PITCHF/X DATA)
Four-seam: 42%
Sinker: 13.6%
Change: 11.1%
Curve: 33.2%
BURNETT'S 2012 PITCH MIX WITH THE PIRATES (PITCHF/X DATA)
Four-seam: 24.6%
Sinker: 35.7%
Change: 5.6%
Curve: 34.4%

(Courtesy of BrooksBaseball.net)

Like Morton, Burnett's pitch mix radically changed with the Pirates. And like Morton, Burnett's results also evolved. Burnett's ground-ball rate soared. He went from posting a below-average ground-ball rate in all three of his seasons in New York to the game's second-highest ground-ball rate—56.9 percent—among qualifiers in 2012. He began to resemble the dominant pitcher he was earlier in his career.

That Searage and Hurdle could get buy-in from Morton was one thing. Morton was an amiable, thoughtful pitcher in need of help. That Searage and Hurdle could get buy-in from Burnett was remarkable. Burnett was a stubborn, headstrong veteran who had had success. He could be difficult to manage. His own teammate and friend Jeff Locke told the *Tribune-Review* there was "A.J." and there was "J.A." The *J.A.* was for "jackass." But somehow Searage and Hurdle were able to connect with all sorts, from the headstrong and macho Burnett to the analytical Morton. If they could get buy-in from Burnett and Morton, from both poles of the cooperation spectrum, could they get buy-in from everyone else?

Communication was key with the pitching philosophy. And the philosophy wasn't just about throwing a lot more two-seam fastballs, it was also about location. Pirates pitchers were told they were not just going to change what they threw, they were going to change where they threw. Unlike the shifts and pitch-framing philosophies, where the data was discovered or produced at the top of the front office and delivered down to the coaching staff and players, the third prong of the run-prevention strategy, the approach on the mound, was driven from the bottom up.

Hurdle wanted and needed his assistant coaches to be on board and feel ownership of this entire philosophy: from the defensive alignment to the pitching plan. That's the only way the effect would be maximized. He wanted his assistants to feel empowered. He wanted there to be collaboration. Hurdle asked the coaches and pitchers to buy in to the three-pitches-or-less doctrine. Searage and Benedict were on board with some of the concepts, they had their own ideas to add, and they had questions. Hurdle wanted his assistants—from Leyva to Searage—to ask questions. Hurdle didn't want to just hand down orders. He wanted his assistants to improve the big-picture plan. That would foster a sense of ownership and improve commitment and execution. Hurdle preached to his players, coaches, and front office staff that "We're trying to all get it right together." During the off-season and that spring, Hurdle wanted his staff to think of ways to enhance the plan, to test and share theories, and to make these plans better and more refined. More than anything else, he wanted them to ask questions of not just him but of the analytics staff, which was sending down an avalanche of data from the front office. He wanted his coaching staff to have the analytics staff test theories the coaches had, not just subscribe to those handed down to them. He wanted the coaches and analytics team to respect each other. That was the only way they would maximize and integrate the data. To get his position players to follow along, to get his pitchers to buy in, Hurdle had to present a united front. He had to have his assistant coaches on board. He had to have them accept not just the data-based message but the messengers as well. Creating a culture of respect and communication was still a formidable barrier.

Hurdle's assistants were all veteran coaches. Searage's hairline had receded after four decades of watching hundreds upon hundreds of pitchers. Nick Leyva's dark hair had grayed. Hurdle's bench coach, Jeff Banister, was a baseball lifer, a longtime minor league catcher and Texan, tall and broad-shouldered, his skin creased after thousands of hours under the sun on baseball fields. Banister had been part of the organization longer than anyone else. He was a twenty-fifth-round draft pick by the Pirates in the 1986 draft. He had only one major league at bat in his career, resulting in a basehit in 1991 against Dan Petry. Banister began coaching in the minor leagues in 1993. Entering 2013, he had been in the Pirates system for twenty-eight years, and mostly all he had experienced was losing.

For these coaches to lose any disdain they held for the analytics staff's invasion of the sacred space of their clubhouse and for the data to flow smoothly from the front office to the field, their voices had to be heard and their questions answered by the club's analysts. This was why the Pirates had Fox and Fitzgerald travel to spring training in 2013 and made them fixtures in the clubhouse. The two men had to be available to answer questions by players and the staff. They were there to become familiar faces throughout the season. Just as Hurdle had become more comfortable with and had gained trust in Fox and Fitzgerald in 2012, now he wanted the same for his entire staff and players in 2013.

Some of the assistant coaches were skeptical of having every pitcher trade in his trusted four-seam fastball for a two-seam fastball against every major league hitter. They felt to convince their pitchers to adopt this approach they would need evidence. And they didn't want generic, one-size-fits-all evidence; they wanted data tailored to each individual hitter-pitcher matchup. So the staff asked for the analysts to identify the pitch types, locations, and velocities that every major league hitter was most likely to beat into the ground.

Fox and his team had another project, too. Searage and Benedict had always believed in pitching inside, but most pitchers resisted buying in to this for several reasons. For starters, if a pitcher missed the inside of the plate, leaving the ball over the center of the plate, then the batter was likely to hit the ball deep for a home run in this modern era of shrinking ballpark dimensions and stronger hitters. That was perhaps the most humiliating scene in baseball, to stand in the center of the field alone and wait for a new baseball from the home-plate umpire while your opponent gleefully floats around the bases. Moreover, most pitchers did not enjoy missing inside toward the batter. If you hit a batter, retaliation against one of your own teammates was likely. Still, Searage and Benedict felt pitching inside was important and could accentuate the ground ball and a shift plan. They just needed some statistical evidence to show to their pitchers. The coaches wanted to see every major league hitter's performance against pitches on the outer half of the plate after being pitched inside earlier in an at bat. What was the psychological and performance effect of pitching inside?

When the coaches went to Fox and Fitzgerald with these questions, the coaches were struck by how receptive the two were to them. The analysts did not brush off the questions or roll their eyes; they were interested in the coaches' theories. Fox and Fitzgerald did not believe they and their algorithms had all the answers. They wanted to hear the questions.

"I have to find a way to not just encourage but to inspire and challenge these guys in different areas so I can help match them up in certain areas where their skill-sets will shine," Hurdle said of his staff. "Some of them found working with these analytics people was really fun and they probably didn't have that feeling going in."

The assistant coaches' questions led to research that might not otherwise have been considered by Fox and Fitzgerald. If every analyst in the sport is operating off the same big data—such as PITCHf/x and TrackMan information—then asking the right questions is paramount.

"A lot of times a coach or somebody will have something in the back of their head, but they won't write an e-mail. They are not going to compose something and give it to you," Fox said. "But they'll come over and say, 'From a player-development perspective, track this metric. I'd like to look at it in terms of player [performance].' I just try to be as available and visible as possible because you never know what you are going to get. They all have these vast databases of player comparisons and situations and strategy that I don't have."

Fox and Fitzgerald looked into the coaching staff's questions about pitching inside, and prior to the 2013 season they found that pitching inside would indeed have a psychological effect on batters that would create even more ground balls and further enhance the plan. The numbers showed opponents were more likely to pull outside pitches on the ground after being pitched inside earlier at bat. After being pitched inside, players were less willing to aggressively lunge at outside pitches. Now the coaching staff had the data they needed to get their pitchers to pitch inside, but would the pitchers execute the plan?

On June 13, 2013, the Pirates held their collective breath as Morton returned to the major leagues. He wasn't great in his first start since returning from surgery. He allowed 4 runs—2 earned—over 5 innings. The bull pen was worse and the Pirates were routed 10–0. But Morton did offer some evidence that the improvements he had made pre-surgery had stuck: he produced 2 fly outs and 6 groundouts. His velocity was steady, in the low 90s. And although not observable in the box score, Morton's movement had returned.

The ground-ball trend continued on June 18 at the home-run-friendly park in Cincinnati. In the first inning, Morton induced Zack Cozart to pound a 92 mph sinker into the ground to third baseman Pedro Alvarez, who began a key double play. In the fourth, Morton's sinker reached 94 mph as Brandon Phillips slammed it into the ground back to Morton, who flipped to first base for the out. With the Pirates leading 3–0 in the fifth, Morton found himself in his first jam of the game: runners on second and third with two outs, and the left-handed Jack Hannahan coming to bat. Morton threw a wicked 93 mph sinker that darted away from Hannahan, who grounded sharply to shortstop Jordy Mercer, who threw across the diamond to end the inning.

Morton's first two starts began a season-long trend of his opponents chewing up the turf with ground balls. He became perhaps the best ground-ball pitcher in the major leagues, and as the season went along, he became even stronger. Had he not missed the first two months of the season and had pitched enough innings to qualify, Morton would have led baseball in ground-ball rate at 62.9 percent. In a 5-start stretch in August, Morton posted an unheard of 43-to-5 ground-ball-to-fly-ball ratio.

And it wasn't just Morton who went on to have a career-best ground-ball season; it was nearly *every* Pirates starter. Almost every Pirates pitcher decreased his four-seam usage and increased his two-seam frequency, and nearly every Pirates starting pitcher produced a career-high ground-ball rate. According to PITCHf/x data analyzed by BrooksBaseball.net, Liriano did not throw a single four-seam fastball in 2013. Only sinkers.

On June 14 Jeff Locke took the mound at PNC Park against the Los Angeles Dodgers. Locke was in the midst of a surprising breakout year after entering the season with only 10 major league starts and a 6.00 ERA. After allowing a leadoff single to Yasiel Puig, Locke induced Nick Punto to pound a sinking fastball to Clint Barmes, who began a double play. In the third, a running two-seam fastball got in on the hands of Puig, the Dodgers' rookie sensation, who grounded out weakly to second base to end the inning. After crossing first base, Puig tossed his hands, rolled his eyes upward to the sky, and shook his head in frustration.

With the Pirates leading 2–0 in the fourth, Hanley Ramirez came to bat with one on and one out for the Dodgers. Ramirez beat another Locke two-seamer into the ground, leading to another inning-ending and threat-ending double play.

During a 3-start span that included 16 straight scoreless innings, Locke produced 23 ground-ball outs. The approach made him an All-Star.

"Our pitching program has by far been the strongest of the [plan's] outcomes," said Huntington. "It's a front-office [preference], but it's also a philosophical focus. We like guys that throw strikes and get ground balls. . . . If the ball is not leaving the [ballpark], you have a chance to make outs."

In June, the Pirates staff produced an amazing 53 percent ground-ball rate, and the club had gone 17-9 in the month, its third straight winning month to open the season, allowing just 0.7 home runs per 9 innings. The ground-ball trend continued all season. In 2013, the Pirates staff combined for the highest ground-ball rate—52.7 percent—since groundball-fly ball data began being recorded. The data is available back to 1988 at BaseballReference.com. In 2010 the Pirates ranked fifteenth in baseball in ground-ball rate at 44 percent. That ranking climbed to seventh in Hurdle's first year in 2011 and sixth in 2012, and in 2013, with the Pirates' concerted focus, the rate was 4 percent greater than that of the next-closest team, the St. Louis Cardinals.

Consider the remarkable changes by individual pitchers in the following charts:

GROUND-BALL RATES (PCT. OF BALLS IN PLAY AS GROUND BALLS)				
	2010	2011	2012	2013
Charlie Morton	46.8	58.5	56.5	62.9
A. J. Burnett	44.9*	49.2*	56.9	56.5
Francisco Liriano	53.6*	48.6*	43.8*	50.5
Jeff Locke	n/a	34.5	49.0	53.2
Wandy Rodriguez	47.9*	45.2*	48.0	42.3
Justin Wilson	n/a	n/a	20.0	53.0
Tony Watson	n/a	32.4	40.3	43.8
Jeanmar Gomez	46.8*	52.8*	48.4*	55.4
Vin Mazarro**	42.9*	43.1*	45.9*	52.2
Mark Melancon**	45.8*	56.7	50.0*	60.3

*Not with the Pirates.
**Mark Melancon increased his ground-ball rate by replacing his four-seam fastball with a cutter after being acquired by the Pirates; Vin Mazarro increased his ground-ball rate while throwing inside more with a four-seam fastball.

PIRATE PITCHERS TWO-SEAM FASTBALL RATE BY YEAR (PCT. OF TOTAL PITCHES)				
	2010	2011	2012	2013
Charlie Morton	27.3	61.1	42.3	57.4
A. J. Burnett	19.6*	13.6*	35.6	36.5
Francisco Liriano	24.9*	26.3*	27.9*	41.0
Jeff Locke	n/a	10.2	6.5	28.8
Wandy Rodriguez	17.3	22.0*	27.7	37.1
Justin Wilson	n/a	n/a	1.9	24.1
Tony Watson	n/a	0.0	66.9	64.3
Jeanmar Gomez	54.2*	60.1*	44.9*	61.1

PITCHf/x data via FanGraphs.com and BrooksBaseball.net.
*Not with the Pirates.

Four-seam fastballs were the traditional go-to pitch for major league pitchers. In 2008, the first year PITCHf/x began tracking and labeling every pitch in baseball, the vast majority of fastballs thrown were four-seam, accounting for more than 50 percent of all pitches. By 2014 the rate had decreased to 34.6 percent—a dramatic decline, in part tied to the Pirates. In 2008, 3.8 percent of all pitches in baseball were two-seam fastballs, according to FanGraphs.com, but in 2014, that number spiked to 14.7 percent. The two-seam fastball gave the Pirates a way to reinvent pitchers and create something precious—pitching depth.

There was one catch. To create as many ground balls as possible, the Pirates threw inside more than any other team. Their pitchers hit an MLB-high 70 batters in 2013. The Pirates batters were, not coincidentally, hit by an MLB-high 88 pitches. By late June the approach was clearly bothering opponents.

In the ninth inning of a game at Cincinnati on June 17, Reds closer Aroldis Chapman buzzed Pirates second baseman Neil Walker with an up-and-in, 100 mph fastball that dropped Walker to the dirt.

"You try to give players the benefit of the doubt, but given the history between us and Cincinnati, it makes you wonder," Walker told reporters afterward. "Balls should not be anywhere near anybody's head. I was hit by [Mat] Latos last time at our place. I was fine with it because he hit me right in the butt. . . . It's tough to get me fired up about things, but when you see a hundred-miles-per-hour fastball come near your face, you have to wonder a little bit."

The next night Charlie Morton began his start by drilling Reds lead-off hitter Shin-Soo Choo in the calf with a fastball. It continued a year-long feud between the Reds and the Pirates. Still, Pirates batters kept mostly quiet about being retaliatory targets. They knew the plan on the mound was working. They saw it was helping them win.

The Pirates led baseball for much of 2013 in defensive efficiency, which is the number of balls hit in play that are converted into outs. They finished fifth for the season, a meaningful improvement over the previous seasons of the Huntington Era, when the Pirates ranked in the twenties.

"Given the ground-ball nature of our staff, the difference shifts could make in the number of balls in play we turn into outs, and the impact it could have, was dramatic," Huntington said.

More ground balls being hit into the shifts helped the Pirates convert an extra 2 per cent of batted balls into outs throughout the season's first half compared to their 2012 level. This percentage might seem insignificant, but over the course of a season, when 4,500 balls are put in play that's equal to 90 hits being turned into outs. In the first half, the Pirates ranked first in baseball in defensive efficiency, the rate of converting batted balls into outs. They had ranked last, thirtieth in the sport in defensive efficiency in 2010 and twenty-fifth in 2011. By keeping more balls on the ground, the Pirates allowed a major league-low 101 home runs in 2013, 52 fewer home runs than they surrendered a year earlier. Thanks to the shifts, despite not having a single Gold Glove-caliber infielder, the Pirates limited opponents to a .224 batting average on ground balls, the fifth best mark in baseball. This was one of the greatest defensive improvements in baseball history. Ten runs added, or saved, is roughly equal to 1 win. With a 93-run improvement—from

68 defensive runs saved in 2013 compared to -25 in 2012—that converted to roughly 9.3 wins added.

To put it in monetary terms, consider the cost of 1 win above replacement on the open market. Wins above replacement (WAR) is an advanced statistic designed to boil a player's total value down into one number. On the free agent market in 2012–13, purchasing 1 WAR was estimated to cost clubs $5 million. For instance, a 3 WAR player is an above-average performer, and on the free agent market such a player would cost a club roughly $15 million per season. So to add 9.3 wins in free agent players would cost a club roughly $50 million per season. The Pirates had added 9.3 wins by shifting their defense and getting their pitchers to throw more ground balls, all this without adding a dollar to payroll. The Pirates were spinning gold.

For the first time in decades, the short-on-talent, short-on-dollars Pirates were in the midst of a pennant race as the season reached its halfway point.

The Pirates entered July having won 9 straight games, climbing to first place in the division. Halfway through the season they were 51-30, 2 games ahead of the Cardinals and 5 games ahead of the Reds. The two-seam fastball had improved questionable pitchers' productivity and had allowed the club to weather the rash of pitching injuries that threatened their season, while the shifting had saved runs.

However, because most of the changes the Pirates were making were invisible, the city was not buying it. Yes, the shifts were visible and working, but how much impact could they really have? No statistics tracking their value appeared on the nightly telecasts of games or in the newspapers. Not until the 2014 postseason did the MLB Network and Fox Sports begin using real-time graphics to show defensive positioning. The ground-ball philosophy was being played out completely under the radar. This was not like adding a free agent slugger whose home runs were dramatic and their impact obvious.

Pittsburgh had a trust issue. The city had seen the Pirates start off strong only to fall apart in the second half of each of the last two seasons, and since the roster had not dramatically changed, why should this season be any different? Pittsburghers were hesitant to emotionally invest in a team that had fooled them twice, and they weren't going to be fooled again. Despite having the best record in baseball at the end of June, through 38 home dates the Pirates were averaging just 23,203 fans, a decline of 1,652 fans per game from the same point the last season, and ranking twenty-third in baseball. Even their division rival the Brewers, mired in an awful season, were averaging 31,500 at Miller Park.

The city was still skeptical. In order to reach 94 wins, to get to the postseason, and ensure that Hurdle and Huntington would return for 2014, the club needed to find even more hidden value to produce even more wins.

9

THE MISSING ALL-STARS

On July 15, 2013, in the Jackie Robinson Rotunda at Citi Field in New York, a remarkable delegation of Pirates represented the team during the All-Star Game's media day. The Pirates sent five players to the midsummer classic—center fielder Andrew McCutchen, closer Jason Grilli, setup man Mark Melancon, third baseman Pedro Alvarez, and starting pitcher Jeff Locke. The last time the Pirates had sent that many players to the All-Star Game was 1972. All five had enjoyed productive first-half campaigns and helped the Pirates to be within a game of St. Louis.

The five All-Stars were given their own nameplates and podiums as hundreds of media members swarmed them in the vast rotunda of Citi Field, its brick edifice and open arches a nod to the legendary façade of Ebbets Field in Brooklyn. The five were asked to make sense of what was going on in Pittsburgh. How could they explain being 1 game behind St. Louis at the All-Star break with the league's fourth-smallest payroll?

While Grilli, Melancon, Alvarez, and Locke were all first-time All-Stars, the situation was most surreal for Locke, who had posted a 5.50

ERA in a limited season in 2012 and had to fight for a rotation job in spring training.

"We were getting on the plane [to New York], I look around, and we had the whole first-class section taken up. Just us," Locke told reporters. "I mean, people had their families with them, but I'd say that's still a pretty good sign."

But who wasn't among them on the plane was also notable. Where was Russell Martin? Locke knew Martin was deserving of All-Star consideration. He knew how much Martin had meant to his season. Martin was critical to the Pirates' first-half success, but his value remained largely hidden and underappreciated. Locke's dependence upon Martin's glove had shown up in the weeks preceding this surreal moment.

On a sun-soaked Sunday afternoon on June 9 on the north side of Chicago at Wrigley Field, Locke started the game with Martin behind the plate, his butt nearly scraping the dirt as he settled into his low squat. For a time in the late 1990s and early 2000s, several taller, offensive-oriented catchers had come into the game, suggesting a new prototype build for the position. Shorter catchers such as the five-foot-ten Martin believed that was just a fad, that being low to the ground was an advantage when receiving pitches.

Martin was important to Locke because the young lefty lacked elite velocity. He had to live on the edge of the strike zone to be successful in the major leagues. He *had* lived there to this point in the season, but to do so he was dependent on Martin's mastery of pitch framing. In fact, all the Pirates pitchers had degrees of dependence on Martin.

In the first inning, Locke got to a two-strike count on the Cub's right-handed Cody Ransom. Martin called for a two-seam fastball to be thrown toward the inner part of the plate, as the Pirates pitchers so often did in 2013. Locke went into his delivery, which included a brief turn of his back to the batter to add torque, then hurled a two-seam fastball. The pitch hissed near Ransom and just missed the inside part of the plate. Rather than reach out to his left to catch the ball and bring it back over home plate in a back-and-forth, herky-jerky motion, Martin demonstrated the art of pitch framing. He began with his glove inside near the batter and moved his hand to the pitch in one quick, subtle motion toward the strike zone. He caught the ball with his glove moving slightly back over the inside portion of the plate, getting the strike-three call on a pitch that was several inches off the plate. Ransom disagreed with the call. He muttered something and momentarily resisted leaving the batter's box, his small protest. As he finally walked back to the home dugout, he gave a long glare back at home-plate umpire Paul Nauert.

At the beginning of the bottom of the second inning, with a two-strike count on the Cubs' right-handed hitting Scott Hairston, Martin again called for a Locke fastball to be thrown inside. Locke fired a fastball that was slightly in off the plate. Martin made another slight but lightning-quick movement of his glove, moving from nearer the batter to over the plate, catching the ball in one subtle motion, making it appear that the pitch had grazed the strike zone. Hairston had jumped back from the pitch, hoping his dramatic body language would sway the umpire. Nauert turned and emphatically punched his left hand forward and drew his right fist back in unison, another strike-three call. Hairston dropped his head in disbelief and looked directly down at the pitch's invisible trajectory, as if it had left a vapor trail. He saw dirt and clay below the invisible flight path of the pitch, not a sliver of home plate.

Locke struck out the first two batters of the second inning with fastballs, then Cubs lefty Ryan Sweeney came to the plate. With a lefty up, and a 1–2 count, Martin called for Locke's knuckle-curve, a pitch that broke sharply away and down from a left-handed batter. Locke twisted and threw. The pitch began over the middle of the plate, then dropped sharply toward the outside corner, sweeping away from Sweeney. Sweeney could do little with the pitch so he didn't swing. The pitch grazed the outside corner of the plate, barely registering as a strike according to PITCHf/x location tracking. A less adept pitch-framing catcher might have allowed his glove hand to drift away from home plate with the ball, giving the appearance that the pitch was a ball. But not only were Martin's hands quick, they were strong. He reached forward and grabbed the pitch just as it crossed the plate. It was like nailing a landing in gymnastics, with no east or west movement of his frozen glove. Martin had gone straight out to meet the pitch before it could dive farther away from the batter. Had Martin let the pitch travel, even though it had caught the strike zone, the final inches of its path might have made it look like a ball. Again, Nauert turned and pumped his first—another called strikeout.

Locke—with a lot of help from Martin—had struck out the side. In the first two innings, Martin had helped frame three third-strike calls, and Locke took a no-hitter into the sixth before Dioner Navarro lined a single into left field.

It was the beginning of a remarkable monthlong push for an All-Star selection for Locke as he allowed just 6 earned runs in 32 innings in June, posting a 1.67 ERA. Martin had helped Locke to his remarkable first half of the season, when the lefty went 7-1 with a 2.06 ERA, and Martin was quietly making every pitcher on the staff look better through a completely obscured ability. Martin was worth nearly 3 wins above replacement in the first half of the season, giving the Pirates incredible value on his two-year, $17 million contract. And the WAR calculation did not include pitch-framing value. He was arguably the team's first-half MVP, but he was nowhere to be found on the All-Star flight.

★ ★ ★

The hidden value of Russell Martin began, fittingly, in obscurity. He was the son of a Montreal street musician and construction worker who cobbled together enough money to send his son to baseball camps and clinics so he could pursue his dream. In between rush-hour subway performances he took his son to practice his gift. Though

Martin played Quebec's first sport, hockey, he loved baseball and first started playing in the tree-lined, brick-duplex neighborhood of Notre-Dame-de-Grâce. After graduating from his Montreal high school, hardly a bastion for baseball, Martin sought a warm climate where he could play baseball year-round and secure the extra reps he had missed growing up in Quebec. He signed with one of the better junior-college programs in the United States at Chipola College in Marianna, Florida, where he played primarily on the left side of the infield, though he did appear in a few games as catcher in his final season.

Martin was a star at Chipola and was drafted as an infielder by the Dodgers in 2002. A natural athlete, he possessed a rare desire to work. In rookie ball with the Dodgers that summer, he played third base well, but there was a problem: Martin was blocked at the major league level by one of the game's best young third basemen, Adrian Beltre. The Dodgers also wondered if the squatty five-foot-ten Martin would hit enough and with enough power to play a corner position. The Dodgers also needed catching depth. A Dodgers scout suggested Martin had the abilities—the arm, the smarts, and the athleticism—to convert to catcher.

So in spring training in 2003, Martin began his catching education. The Dodgers' minor league catching coordinator, Jon Debus, began with an unusual drill that had nothing to do with crouching behind the plate and playing. During intrasquad games on the back fields of the club's Vero Beach, Florida, spring training home, Debus placed a batting-practice screen behind the catcher, behind which he placed two chairs, and there Martin was first exposed to the subtle technique of manipulating ball-strike calls.

A catcher must possess certain natural gifts to frame pitches. He must have naturally soft, strong, and sudden hands that eliminate excessive movement, actions that would catch an umpire's eye. As an exceptional athlete and former infielder, Martin possessed soft, calm hands, but most of the skill is acquired through thousands upon thousands of reps. A catcher must understand the angles of pitch flight and be able to execute a quick and fluid motion to create one of baseball's most important illusions. Martin explained to the *Tribune-Review* one of the first, critical concepts he learned from Debus: "I'm trying to go completely against what the ball is trying to do. If it's a slider going down and away, I'm going to try and catch it before it goes further down and away. If it's a two-seamer coming back, I try to catch it deeper in the strike zone so the natural two-seam action makes it look like a strike."

The education Martin gained on the back fields of the Dodgers spring training complex formed an important foundation, but to excel, Martin would have to build upon that foundation himself. He benefited by being innately curious. He gleaned important details from observation and learned through experience. He learned that lefties with heavy breaking balls force your glove away from the zone and cost you strikes. He learned that to catch these balls he would have to get down on one knee to allow his glove more room to operate horizontally in the strike zone.

In the Pirate City locker room in the spring of 2014, Martin knelt on one knee on the carpet to demonstrate to a reporter how much more freedom he had with his glove hand with one knee dropped to the ground. Getting the low strike is particularly important for Martin with the Pirates, as their pitchers often relied on sinking, two-seam fastballs. Moreover, PITCHf/x data proved that umpires were more willing to give a borderline low strike than a borderline high strike.

"Guys who are really good at getting low strikes are able to give a low target; and if they are catching the ball on the way up, it will look like a strike," Martin explained. "As opposed to if you give a high target and catch it on the way down, it looks like a ball."

Locke witnessed Martin's dedication to the craft early on, struck by his attention to detail. During some of Locke's first practices that February on the back-field bull pens in Bradenton, he was surprised when Martin cursed at himself for not catching a pitch in a certain manner, with the ball falling from his mitt. There was no audience besides Locke and pitching coach Ray Searage; they were surrounded by nothing else but chain-link fencing and windscreens. "No one is watching, but it didn't matter. He's competitive with himself," said Locke.

Martin attempts to maximize every hour of practice and has logged thousands upon thousands of repetitions to create muscle memory, the neural circuitry where skills are refined, if not born. He believes being an adept pitch framer is largely a learned skill, and that you have to want to do it and be passionate about it.

"When I'm catching a bull pen, I'm not just catching a bull pen. I'm working on my receiving constantly," he said. "I don't have to think about it anymore. I'm doing it. I think everyone should do it."

Martin also attempts to develop a relationship with umpires, making small talk between innings and pitches, something that couldn't harm his ability to influence their calls. Martin also has a voracious appetite for video as he likes to study his catching peers. The National League Central Division has not only one of the greatest collection of catchers in the game but the top collection of pitch framers. Along with Cardinals catcher Yadier Molina, one of Martin's favorite peers to study is Milwaukee Brewers catcher Jonathan Lucroy, who Martin feels is one of the best in the game at getting the low strike. Lucroy and Martin share an admiration for each other's work, like master painters in an obscure art form that few appreciate.

"When I'm hitting [against Lucroy] and know it was a little low, I look back at him and I'm like, 'You mother . . . ,'" Martin said.

Lucroy, like Martin, notes some of the ability is physical. While modestly built for a professional athlete at five feet eleven and 195 pounds, Lucroy has Popeye-like forearms that allow him to stop cold a ball moving at 98 mph. "There is a lot of forearm [strength]. A lot of this," says Lucroy as he quietly moves his left hand forward and mimics going out to stop and stick a ball. "For the most part what I do is, wherever the pitch is, I try to beat it to the spot. If you can do that, an umpire will give the pitch to you because he can see it."

But while Martin's magic impacted nearly every pitcher on the Pirates staff, the public, as they voted for All-Stars, couldn't see how he had improved the club by nearly 40 runs—equivalent to 4 wins—over the previous Pirates catchers simply through how he received pitches. This improvement had nothing to do with his bat or his strong and accurate throwing arm and couldn't be cited on the back of a bubble-gum trading card. It had everything to do with the hidden value of pitch framing, and it was the only way the Pirates could afford the improvement.

Between the defensive shifts, the ground-ball pitching plan, and Martin's glove, those hidden values would add up to the equivalent of 13 wins for the Pirates in 2013. At the All-Star break the Pirates had allowed 311 runs, the fewest in baseball. While Martin helped every pitcher on the staff, he perhaps helped none more than fellow free agent acquisition Francisco Liriano—who was also conspicuously absent from the All-Star Game.

★ ★ ★

Liriano had returned in May from rehabbing his broken arm in Florida and had immediately bolstered the Pirates' depleted rotation. He was the first reinforcement to arrive. In his first start as a Pirate, against the Mets on May 11, he allowed just 1 run over 5⅓ innings. He struck out 9, walked just 2, and hit 95 mph on the Citi Field radar gun. He looked strong. His fastball velocity was back and his slider was biting. One strong start followed another in the first half of the season, and remarkably Liriano began to resemble the highly touted pitcher he was prior to his elbow injury. His improvement was credited to his work with the coaching staff, which is not to be discredited. Liriano raised his arm slot in 2013, which helped him miss less often east-west with pitches, and tabled his four-seam fastball for a sinker, but catching the majority of his outings was Martin.

Several weeks before the All-Star Game, Liriano and Martin demonstrated their important in-game relationship on a misty, cool June night at home against the Cincinnati Reds. With one out in the first, Liriano got ahead of the Reds third baseman, right-hander Todd Frazier, 0-2. Frazier was forced to protect and expand his strike zone, which made him vulnerable to the slider. Martin called for a back-foot slider, meaning the pitch would begin tracking toward the middle of the plate, then in the last six to eight feet it would dive toward a right-handed batter's foot. Liriano perfectly executed the pitch, with Frazier swinging and missing over the top of a pitch that nearly smashed into his right foot.

Reds star Joey Votto followed Frazier. Votto was one of the most selective hitters in the league, a left-hander who rarely chased pitches out of the strike zone. Liriano again got ahead 0-2, in part because of Martin's deft glove influencing the fringes of the strike zone. With two strikes, Liriano again went to his slider, one of the best breaking balls in baseball. Votto swung and missed at the sweeping pitch that finished well out of the strike zone, ending the inning. Votto shook his head in disgust but could do nothing about it. When Liriano got ahead in the count, most hitters become susceptible to his excellent slider, which breaks late and is difficult to differentiate from a fastball.

With the help of Martin behind the plate, Liriano struck out batter after batter in this game. In the third inning Derrick Robinson chased Liriano's changeup out of the zone for the lefty's seventh consecutive strikeout, tying a Pirates record, and all but two of the strikeouts came on Liriano's hard-breaking slider. Liriano struck out 11 Reds that day, which would be his second-highest total of the season. Martin's pitch framing was crucial in allowing pitchers to get ahead in counts and set up batters for pitches that broke out of the zone like Liriano's strikeout slider.

In 2011, Liriano threw 52.9 percent of his fastballs for strikes, well below the major league average. During his trying 2012 season, he threw his changeup for a strike only 42 percent of the time. Hitters were better able to lay off his slider if they were ahead in the count. They could instead be patient and hunt for fastballs and elevated off-speed pitches. But with Martin catching him in 2013, Liriano's strike totals jumped dramatically. He threw his fastball for strikes at 58.1 percent, the second-highest rate of his career, and his changeup was called as a strike 20 percent more than in previous seasons.

Liriano did not make the All-Star cut since he had missed the first month of the season, but he had been the Pirates' best pitcher in the first half of the season with a 2.00 ERA. He had struck out 9.7 batters and walked just 1.7 batters per 9 innings, a remarkable improvement in command and performance. Moreover, Liriano's ground-ball rate also spiked thanks to the Pirates' staff's getting him to trade in his four-seam fastball for a two-seam, sinking fastball.

The Pirates were on record saying they could not afford free agent pitchers who could do all the things Liriano had done. Those pitchers were Cy Young Award candidates. Instead, the Pirates had made Liriano into a Cy Young Award candidate. Yes, Liriano had come to the team with the strikeout slider and changeup, but his adoption of a new philosophy had improved his ground-ball rate, and his throwing from a new arm slot to Martin's deft glove had improved his control.

Said Pirates television color commentator Bob Walk during Liriano's 7-inning shutout performance against a tough Oakland A's team in July, "He's been remarkably consistent since he started the year." No one had ever before said that about Liriano, and that's in part because Liriano—or most other members of the Pirates' pitching staff—had never had a catcher like Russell Martin making them look so good.

The Pirates paid Martin and Liriano a combined $10.25 million in 2013, after Liriano met his incentives. The pair produced a performance value of $39 million, giving the Pirates a surplus value of nearly

$30 million. Surplus value is a player's actual wages subtracted from his market value produced. A small-market club such as the Pirates had to find this type of value to win on an unfair economic playing field. The Pirates had to procure a significant return on investment. While the Pirates had unearthed hidden value in Martin, they had created value not just with Liriano, but with every other pitcher on the staff. The impact of Martin could be seen in the most traditional of statistics, ERA:

PIRATES SECOND-HALF ROTATION		
Player	2012 ERA (pre-Martin)	2013 ERA (with Martin)
Liriano	5.34	3.02
Locke	5.50	3.52
Burnett	3.51	3.30
Cole	n/a	3.22
Morton	4.65	3.26

While Martin's hidden talents were still underappreciated by the public, Liriano's first-half numbers were eye-popping, as were Locke's and the majority of the pitching staff's. A city that had doubted the Pirates was finally beginning to believe something had changed.

In early July the Pirates produced five straight sellouts, which is believed to be a record in the club's 132-year history. They entered the All-Star break with a 56-37 record, in the thick of the division race, and in a wild-card position. In suburban Pittsburgh, more and more houses proudly raised a Jolly Roger, the skull and crossbones a de facto club logo. More and more often, Pirates radio and television voice Greg Brown exclaimed, "Raise the Jolly Roger," at the end of broadcasts, his victory call. Pittsburgh-area department stores featured a strange sight: Pirates merchandise, T-shirts, and jerseys were being prominently displayed near the checkout lines, *not* Steelers or Penguins gear. In early July, Pirates merchandise sales jumped 50 percent, according to Forbes.com, ranking number two in the game. Hurdle was even noticing an uptick in the number of people wearing Pirates T-shirts and jerseys at his local grocery store and Starbucks. And people weren't just buying Andrew McCutchen jerseys. T-shirts boasting the names of the Pirates' five All-Stars, and even some Russell Martin shirts, were being spotted around the reluctant, tortured baseball town that had been skeptical for the first three months of the season. Finally, the city wanted to believe—even if it couldn't quite understand why or how this band of misfits was winning.

10

GEOGRAPHY TEST

A baseball field has a unique characteristic that differentiates it from every other field, court, or rink in other major professional sports: it does not have uniform dimensions. Every major league park has a unique footprint. Some have larger amounts of foul territory. Some parks feature deep left- or right-field gaps, some shallower. Unlike soccer pitches, football fields, basketball courts, or hockey rinks, major league fields do not have a uniform amount of territory, although the average field is 2.5 acres.

Using Google Earth and ballpark-dimension data from teams, illustrator Lou Spirito overlaid the outlines of every major league baseball stadium's on-field dimensions, meaning the perimeters of their outfield fences and the walls separating the grandstands from foul territory. He found that PNC Park had the deepest left field in baseball, deeper even than the vast swath of outfield of Coors Field. The deepest left field in the game consists of the outfield lawn from "the notch" to near the left-field foul pole. The notch is where the deep left-center field wall juts away from home plate and forms a triangular patch near the bull pen—410 feet away from home plate. It makes the park a night-mare for right-handed pull hitters seeking home runs to left field, or for left-handed hitters trying to go the other way. The dimensions also made defending left field difficult for a slow-footed player.

In 2013, the Pirates masked their athletic deficiencies in their infield through defensive shifts and their ground-ball-centric pitching. The infield is the one place on a baseball field with uniform dimensions and takes up much less ground than the outfield. There was no way to mask defensive liabilities among the Pirates outfielders at PNC Park. And major league hitters tend to spray fly balls more than ground balls. According to BIS, the average major league hitter pulled 73 percent of his ground balls but just 40 percent of his fly balls. It was yet another challenge confronting the Pirates.

Clint Hurdle knew the importance of outfield defense from his time in Denver. Because fly balls traveled farther in the thin, mile-high air of Denver—about 5 percent farther than at sea level—Coors Field had been designed with a deep outfield to try to normalize home-run totals. This park's dimensions led to an unintended consequence: because outfielders had to cover more ground and play deeper at Coors Field, it opened up more space for balls to fall in as singles and doubles. So not only were more balls flying over the head of Hurdle's outfielders, but more balls were likely to fall to the ground ahead of them or in the gaps between.

Hurdle was never a fleet runner. It was the one physical tool he lacked. At Coors Field, Hurdle grew to appreciate athletic outfielders who could cover ground. Teams typically employ their fastest, rangiest outfielder in center field, which most commonly has the greatest amount of ground to cover. But left field at PNC Park was actually larger than center. Hurdle knew that he essentially needed another center fielder to play left field. You could mask an infielder's limitations by aligning him more smartly via shifts, but even with data-based outfield alignment you couldn't hide lack of speed in the outfield or a player who ran poor routes to intercept fly balls and line drives. The Pirates needed an elite athlete to cover left field, and Hurdle needed someone to find him that player. That someone was Rene Gayo, who more than anyone else helped the Pirates meet their geographical challenges and take advantage of some of the game's other undervalued skills: speed and athleticism.

To find those underrated athletic players, assets difficult to find in the June draft as America's top amateur athletes often chose other sports, Huntington allowed Gayo to more than double the international staff under him, with the Pirates employing twenty-four full- and part-time scouts in Latin America in 2013. In Latin America, players were not subject to the draft, and a good scout could find cheap, undervalued talent there. Moreover, while on a visit to the Dominican Republic, Pirates owner Bob Nutting had been appalled at the conditions at the club's Dominican academy, where the Pirates' Dominican Summer League team plays along with other prospects invited to train there. Nutting paid $5 million to build a sparkling new facility, which opened in 2008, that *Time* magazine called the "Ritz of the Dominican." The facility, a jewel among Dominican academies, provided a competitive edge for the Pirates in recruiting. Still, it was Gayo's philosophy and his eyes that were paramount in solving the Pirates' outfield defensive dilemma.

The United States brought baseball to Cuba. And the brothers Ignacio and Ubaldo Aloma introduced baseball to the Dominican Republic when they fled Cuba and founded a sugar plantation there, forming the first two baseball clubs there in 1891, according to author Adrian Burgos, Jr. Today, no other place on earth generates as much baseball talent per capita as the Dominican Republic, which is located on the eastern half of the island of Hispaniola. Despite a small population of 10 million, equivalent to that of Ohio, nearly 11 percent of major league baseball players are Dominican natives. Baseball is the country's passion, and unlike in the United States, where the best athletes have a variety of options to choose from, baseball is the only sport in the island country, and excelling at it is for some a way to a better life.

Reno Gayo is a Cuban immigrant. Corpulent and mustached, charismatic and gregarious, he commands the attention of any audience before him. He is the Pirates' director of Latin American scouting operations, and few have excavated more value from the area than Gayo. In an era when top Dominican players sign seven-figure contracts like first-round picks in baseball's draft, Gayo signed the Pirates' number one overall prospect, Gregory Polanco, for $150,000, and their top middle-infield prospect, Alen Hanson, for a similarly modest bonus of $90,000.

Gayo's rise to prominence is an unlikely story. A second-generation American, he likes to say he was made in Cuba and born in the United States. In the early 1960s Gayo said his parents were members of the Student Revolutionary Directorate, a counterrevolutionary group in Cuba plotting against Castro. Gayo's godfather was the vice president of the organization, which worked with the CIA in an attempt to overthrow the Communist government. He still remembers overhearing dinner conversations as a child where the grown-ups talked about having taken apart machine guns and having set explosives. It seemed strange to him that his parents, aunts, and uncles had all been guerrillas.

"They were basically, I hate saying this, they were terrorists against Castro," Gayo said. "They were sneaking and ambushing like something out of a movie. Hard to believe these same people did that."

They fled Cuba after the failed Bay of Pigs invasion and settled in Miami, where Gayo's mother learned she was pregnant. Gayo was born in 1962. What helped Gayo's father assimilate was a love of baseball, an interest he passed down to his son. Gayo's father had played in the Cuban League, the second-oldest professional baseball league after the National League. The only time it has ever ceased to play was during the Spanish-American War. Gayo's father once saw Babe Ruth play, and he caught Tommy de la Cruz, who technically broke the color line in 1944 with the Reds. One of the few pictures in Gayo's office is of his father with de la Cruz.

Gayo only saw his father cry twice. The first time was when he listened to a speech by Pirates Hall of Fame outfielder and Puerto Rican native Roberto Clemente, who addressed a major league crowd in Spanish, and then in English. Clemente, who played from 1955 to 1972, was an advocate of improving race relations, and as a testament to his character, each year baseball acknowledges a player for his good deeds off the field by presenting the Roberto Clemente Award.

The second time Gayo saw his father cry was at Gayo's graduation from St. Mary's in San Antonio, Texas, where he got a degree in economics.

Gayo had the same dream as his father: he wanted to play professional baseball. He was a catcher at St. Mary's. He went undrafted but was signed by Reds scouting director Cam Bonifay, who later became Pirates general manager. Gayo's professional playing career lasted all of 30 at bats before his knees betrayed him. Gayo wanted to stay in the game, and Bonifay saw a young man with a feel for the game. In 1989, Cam Bonifay hired Gayo to scout Texas and Louisiana part-time for the Pirates. In 1994 he received his first big break when Jesse Flores, who was the scouting supervisor for the Indians, recommended that the Indians hire him as a full-time scout. Gayo became responsible for scouting south Texas, Louisiana, and New Mexico and drove tens of thousands of miles doing it.

Gayo says lots of people talk about working hard, but few actually do. Sometimes he'll look around at the scouts sitting near him, his competition. He'll see some look at their wristwatches disinterestedly. He calls them "watch lookers." He believes they have no chance against him. They don't have the patience or the desire to look under every rock for the next big thing.

Gayo said one competitive advantage he has tapped into in Latin America is simply outworking his rivals. Gayo said many scouts and scouting directors in the Dominican Republic do not stray far from the capital, Santo Domingo, and its plusher hotels. Gayo is willing to travel to the poorest towns and stay in cheap hotels at six hundred pesos per night so long as they have clean sheets. In short, Gayo is willing to collect more data on players. Said Washington Nationals international-scouting director Johnny DiPuglia to *Baseball America*, "A lot of guys won't do [what Gayo does]. They won't stay at hotels with no cable, no TV, dirty running water. I've done it. I try to avoid it now. I've done it plenty of times. I got tired of getting bacteria in my stomach."

In the winter, when there is no major league baseball and Gayo is home from international scouting trips, he'll watch old VCR videotape on his flat-screen television. He studies Tony Gwynn's swing. He watches film of Roy Halladay in high school, seeing what a great athlete with a hiccup in his delivery looked like before he became a Cy Young Award winner. It might seem like a waste of time, but Gayo is adding to his mental library of player comparisons or *comps*, as they are called in the scouting community. To many, comps are dangerous. They are subjective. For Gayo, scouting begins with learning history, learning what stars looked like before they were stars. These are his data points.

"I'll sit around and watch all that stuff, and the stuff in between like when the pitcher is walking around [after a pitch]," Gayo said. "I'll sit there and watch that. I've been doing that for years. You might think I'm crazy."

While Gayo has built an internal library of comps he has also created a philosophy. Over two decades of playing, watching, and scouting the game, he has learned through trial and error the type of player he prefers. The players he likes all have a common trait: they can run. These players were unlike Gayo, who was never fast, and now has balky knees. But he loved watching athletes run. He remembered seeing Bo Jackson run at Auburn and thinking it was the most beautiful thing he had ever seen. Gayo prized speed, in part influenced by

Whitey Herzog's speedy Cardinals and the Royals teams of the 1980s, teams Gayo loved watching.

Gayo has always been searching for fast athletes who can swing a bat. During the steroid era, in the 1990s and early 2000s, power had been at a premium while speed and athleticism were devalued. Teams simply tried to outslug each other with supersize batters. In today's game, Gayo likes to say, "the pharmacy is closed." With the advent of performance-enhancing-drug testing in 2004, speed and athleticism became more important. But even entering the 2013 season, defensive value was still not perfectly understood and therefore likely undervalued. The judgment of a player's range and ability to run efficient routes was still largely based upon subjective and anecdotal evidence. These undervalued players were the ones Gayo wanted.

"Running is a very important thing in baseball," Gayo said. "It's a common denominator in offense and defense. It's not just speed, it's the threat of it that makes a difference."

Despite being fluent in Spanish and English, Gayo had never scouted in Latin America until he was promoted to work as a Latin American scout for the Indians in 1999 by former general manager John Hart. Gayo was a perfect fit. In two years in that role, Gayo signed Willy Taveras, Jhonny Peralta, Roberto Hernandez, Rafael Perez, and Edward Mujica to modest deals, all of whom eventually became productive major league players. In 2001, the Indians came under the leadership of a new general manager in Mark Shapiro, who restructured their scouting department. Gayo was pulled out of Latin America. When the news hit, seven teams contacted him the following day. The first team that asked for permission to speak with Gayo was the Pirates.

The Pirates are known today as a data-heavy, forward-thinking organization that deploys analytics heavily in decision-making. While Huntington did not hire Gayo, he kept him in a senior role because Huntington believes traditional scouting remains paramount in amateur-player acquisition, particularly in Latin America. The Pirates have flooded the Caribbean with scouts in attempt to collect more intel on prospects than other organizations. In the Dominican Republic, play is far less organized than in the United States, so no meaningful statistics are produced like those at the Division I college level. No algorithms or databases can help you find talent on ramshackle diamonds where grazing cattle sometimes share the outfield. In the Dominican Republic, a scout must find lanky, malnourished sixteen-year-olds and have the ability to predict what they could become. Perhaps part of this is innate, but more than anything else, it is the product of intensive study over years.

"It's raw scouting in its purest form," Moises Rodriguez, the Cardinals' director of international operations, told *Baseball America*. "There are no stats. If you have scouts that know how to evaluate, and if you create a system to evaluate guys that are shown to you by your scouts, you're going to succeed a lot more."

This willingness to go where others would not and to see players as others had not had led Gayo to Starling Marte.

★ ★ ★

Santo Domingo, the Dominican capital, has two airports. The main airport, Las Américas International, to the east of the city, is where the vast majority of commercial traffic arrives and departs. To the north of the city is La Isabela, an airport with but one airstrip, which caters to small planes and charter flights. Adjacent to the airport exit, alongside an access road, is a ramshackle baseball field with a red-clay infield. Gayo travels to fields like this one on the outskirts of Santo Domingo, arriving with a lawn chair and two new, fresh baseballs he calls "pearls." He gives each team a ball, and he'll sit and watch under a searing sun.

Many scouts and evaluators in the Dominican Republic prefer to stay around their academy and have *buscóns* bring their talent and teams to the complex for workouts and games. *Buscóns* are quasi agents, sometimes coaches and sometimes even father figures, who represent young Dominican players. Gayo has always had a problem with people bringing talent to him. He's a scout. He reasons that he is supposed to go in search of talent, not have it brought to him. Moreover, when the talent is brought to the complex, the *buscón* controls the environment and showcases the talent. Gayo wants control. More than anything else he wants to see games—not batting practice and speed-pitch sessions.

Gayo plays a strategic sales game that often goes something like this: A *buscón* will approach Gayo and attempt to sell him on his shortstop, not knowing Gayo has his eyes on the right fielder. Gayo tells the *buscón* that the Yankees like the shortstop and will surely outspend the Pirates for him. He's too expensive, but what about the right fielder? You want $20,000? How about $25,000? That's how Gayo signed Willy Taveras. Gayo found Marte, like Taveras, on a field on the outskirts of the capital. In the spring of 2006, few saw Marte as a future big leaguer.

The opportunity to find an undervalued Marte was largely tied to his being showcased as a shortstop. When Gayo first saw him, he saw him the way all the other scouts did: a player lacking the instincts and hands for the infield. He didn't like Marte enough to sign him upon his first look. But Gayo was intrigued. He wondered how Marte would fare in the outfield.

"I remember back to [Ernest] Hemingway, he used to talk about bullfighters and the gracefulness of bullfighters. That's something I've always liked. Clemente had that. He played with fire but there was grace to his game. Starling had that. There was a grace to his game," Gayo said.

Gayo asked Marte to go to the outfield. Though a malnourished, 160-pound eighteen-year-old who was dealing with parasites like many Dominican teenage prospects, Marte began unleashing laserlike throws to the infield. Gayo's eyes widened to saucers. He then asked Marte to run. After watching Marte run several sixty-yard dashes on an unkempt playing surface, wedged between cattle-grazing grounds and tin- and sheet-metal-roofed homes, Gayo's jaw dropped. Marte clocked a 6.48-second sixty-yard dash. If you can run a 6.6, you can run very fast. If you can run a 6.5, you're flying.

"Not only 6.48," Gayo said, "but you could put a crystal glass on his head and it won't fall down. This guy is running and you're like, 'It's beautiful.' This is like the most beautiful thing you've ever seen."

But could he hit?

In a batting practice, Marte sprayed line drives all around the field. He demonstrated balance in his swing. Gayo still had questions; it was hard to tell if a young player would have an understanding of the strike zone or hit for power, but he saw that Marte could get his bat to the ball. In his swing, Gayo saw Marte had balance in his shoulders, waist, and knees, and power in his wrists. With a regular healthy diet and time in the weight room he could gain strength and really be something, Gayo thought.

Something else that Gayo liked in Marte was that he could compete. In game situations, when Marte struck out or made a poor play or decision, it did not carry over to his next opportunity, and he did not lose confidence. Gayo was sold. He offered Marte $85,000; he officially signed with the Pirates on January 4, 2007. Every other team had missed on Marte because of what he couldn't do: he couldn't play an adequate shortstop. Gayo focused on Marte's strength: he could cover ground like a deer.

Marte worked his way quickly through the Pirates system. With face-of-the-franchise Andrew McCutchen solidly entrenched in center field, Marte, a natural center fielder, was shifted to left field when he was first called up to the majors, near the close of the 2012 season. While a move off center field is usually viewed as a negative for a prospect, playing left field in PNC Park was more difficult and therefore more valuable. Marte proved that he was up for the job in his first full season in the majors in 2013.

On August 18 in the top of the twelfth inning in a tie game with the Pirates against the Diamondbacks, Arizona second baseman Aaron

Hill lifted a fly ball into shallow left field that to onlookers appeared would land and easily score the runner on second base to give Arizona a 1-run lead. Instead, Starling Marte came out of nowhere, at least from out of the edge of a television camera's periphery, to make a sliding blur of a catch to end the inning.

Had Marte been raised in the United States, he might have been a wide receiver or defensive back somewhere in the NFL. He's a sleek, six-foot, 190-pound athlete with muscle definition, the type of body rarely found in a major league clubhouse. On this August evening, Marte exploded out of his stance and took a perfect route to an interception point. Marte had been covering ground like that all season for the Pirates. His defensive range was a key reason why the Pirates remained a game ahead of the Cardinals in the middle of August.

According to the statistic defensive runs saved, Starling Marte ranked first among left fielders in 2013, saving 20 more runs than the average left fielder. This statistic used video scouting and analytics to attempt to measure the range of an outfielder. Teammate Andrew McCutchen ranked sixth among center fielders with 7 runs saved. According to ultimate zone rating, a statistic that uses a similar methodology to defensive runs saved, the Pirates had two of the top twenty outfielders in the game in 2013. Only Oakland, Pittsburgh, Arizona, and Boston had two outfielders in the top twenty. Boston won the World Series, and Oakland led the American League in wins. It spoke to the importance of defensive play, the importance of having an athletic outfield.

National League Central Division Standings as of August 18, 2013			
Team	W-L	Pct.	Games Behind 1st Place Team
Pittsburgh	72-51	.585	-
St. Louis	71-52	.577	1
Cincinnati	70-54	.565	2.5
Milwaukee	54-70	.435	18.5
Chicago	53-70	.431	19.0

But August 18 was the last game Marte played in for the Pirates for nearly a month. Eight days earlier in Colorado, a fastball from Rockies relief pitcher Josh Outman struck Marte on his left hand. Marte fell to his knees and grabbed the hand. The Pirates training staff came out to the batting area to examine Marte, who grimaced in pain. He continued to play through the injury for a week, but while it had not affected his fielding, he struggled to grip the bat and swing with full force and became hesitant to slide headfirst on the bases.

Marte complained of pain in his hand again following the August 18 game, and on August 24 the Pirates placed him on the disabled list. In his absence the Pirates played around .500 baseball. They lost 14 of 29 games and went from 1 game ahead of the St. Louis Cardinals in the National League Central to 2 games behind them, and just ½ a game ahead of the Cincinnati Reds, on September 18. The Pirates' lead in the wild-card race had shrunk to 5 games over the Washington Nationals and 7 games over the Arizona Diamondbacks. While their grasp on at least one of the two wild-card spots seemed firm, it was no longer automatic. The fans on their public forums of talk radio, Twitter, and Internet message boards collectively groaned, "Here we go again." "Ownership is cheap." "Epic Collapse III!"

Fueled largely by his defensive value, Marte finished the 2013 season ranked as the twenty-eighth most valuable position player in baseball with 4.6 wins above replacement, despite missing 30 games to a hand injury. Still, if he couldn't grip a bat and swing it effectively, he couldn't be in the starting lineup—a considerable loss. But it was tough to say exactly how effective Marte was since there was no perfect way to evaluate defensive performance. But that was all about to change.

Accurately measuring defense is one of the last great frontiers of on-the-field analytics, along with injury prevention and softer sciences such as a player's desire to compete and excel at his craft or clubhouse chemistry.

Throughout the twentieth century the public and teams largely made subjective judgments about defenders. Few analytical tools existed to measure defensive play. One of the few was the highly flawed statistic of fielding percentage, the number of successful assists and putouts divided by the total chances to either assist on or produce an out. But fielding percentage does not take into account the range of a player. For example, an error for one player might be a ball another player cannot reach. Moreover, an error is a subjective judgment of an official scorer.

John Dewan wanted to change baseball's thinking not just about overall team defense—by using defensive alignment and shifting—but also about individual player defensive value, by creating metrics such as defensive runs saved. Like Dewan's system, the Pirates' in-house defensive-valuation systems debit or credit defenders on their ability to turn batted balls in certain zones into outs. But Fox believes, like Dewan, that no system created to date is by itself enough to give a completely accurate portrait of an individual defensive player. Fox notes that the Pirates try to account for the ballpark and the type of pitcher the defender is paired with when evaluating a fielder's performance, but still, even the best of the current metrics are fraught with biases and unknowns. Since player movement is not being measured yet, there cannot be an accurate assessment of ability. An accurate portrait would require the new player-tracking system, Statcast.

★ ★ ★

On March 1, 2014, at the MIT Sloan Analytics Conference, Joe Inzerillo of Major League Baseball Advanced Media (MLBAM) took the stage at Hynes Convention Center in Boston for a much-anticipated presentation, akin to baseball's version of the late Steve Jobs unveiling an Apple product. Behind him on the stage was a large drop-down screen for the projection camera. At that time much of MLBAM's focus was on improving the digital reach and experience for its customers, which made MLBAM one of the most important and profitable baseball subsidiaries. Each major league team has an equal stake in MLBAM, and Bloomberg.com estimated each stake to be worth $110 million in 2013. The organization, baseball's digital arm, has turned away offers of more than a billion dollars from equity firms seeking to buy a stake in the company, according to media reports. But with the success of its partnership with Sportvision's PITCHf/x system, MLBAM became curious about creating its own data, and at the 2014 Sloan conference, Inzerillo announced its most exciting venture to date.

Before an eager audience of analytically inclined people in the baseball community, Inzerillo made the astonishing claim that he and his team had solved baseball's greatest mystery. He announced that every movement, every step, every throw on the field, would soon be measured and quantified.

"The Holy Grail has always been finding this defensive side, the runners, on an empirical basis that we could see," Inzerillo told the audience. "Now we are actually going to be able to see this phenomenon directly produced and then analyze the data and see what it means. . . . Baseball is a game of inches; now we are going to be able to tell you how many inches."

Then from his handheld tablet, Inzerillo began a remarkable video presentation of a single play from a 2013 Braves-Mets game at Citi Field. In the bottom of the ninth, the Braves had a tenuous grasp on a 2–1 lead against the Mets. The Braves' excellent relief pitcher Craig Kimbrel had struck out two but also hit a batter and walked another. The tying and go-ahead runners were on base when Justin Turner drove the ball into the left-center gap. Off the bat, the drive looked as if it would at least tie and possibly win the game. But Braves center fielder Jason Heyward, who typically plays right field, made a diving catch to end the game and secure a win for the Braves. It was a remarkable play, but the graphics that accompanied Heyward and Turner on the screen were even more incredible.

The graphics showed Heyward's real-time data. He had reached a top speed of 18.5 miles per hour, accelerated at a rate of 15.1 feet per second, begun 80.9 feet from the interception point of where the ball would fall for a hit, and covered that ground in 83.2 feet, nearly a perfect line to intercept the ball, a route efficiency of 97 percent. Heyward also displayed first-step quickness, his first reaction occurring just 0.2 seconds after the ball was hit. And it wasn't only Heyward that was tracked—*everything* was tracked. The ball left Turner's bat at 88.3 mph and had a 24.1 degree launch angle. It traveled 314 feet and had a hang time of four seconds. This was PITCHf/x on steroids.

For the first time in baseball history MLBAM demonstrated that just about every aspect of a remarkable play such as this could be measured. This was the next giant step for big data in baseball. It promised to push the total data points produced in the sport each season from the millions to the billions.

"We are just scratching the surface," Inzerillo said.

How does it work? Statcast combined the information from two different systems to pull its data together. Using the radar-based TrackMan to track the ball and its movement, Statcast also tracks the players on the field using a twin set of ChyronHego binocular cameras, which have 3-D capabilities due to their stereoscopic arrangement. The cameras record every player's movements on the field and are synced with the radar readings from TrackMan Doppler radar. The players' and the ball's movements are translated and turned into meaningful data by the system's software. The Statcast system was already set up and gathering real-time data at the Mets-Braves game at Citi Field in 2013 and was planned to launch in three more stadiums in 2014, with the goal being to have the system in place in every park by

2015. What PITCHf/x did for recording pitch movement, location, and speed, MLBAM's Statcast would do for every movement on the field.

But challenges are still ahead. While the data can be tracked and shared in real time, the accompanying real-time graphics have not been adapted. So much data—several terabytes—is produced per game that it limits who can process and have access to it. Unlike with PITCHf/x, teams do not want the Statcast data to become public, so that they can create their own proprietary metrics. Assuming the system does go into place, analysts will then have to create meaningful metrics from billions of new data points flowing into the game.

How is this going to change the game? What was once left to the subjective eye on the field will now be quantified. Just as John Dewan got the baseball industry to change the way it thought about collective defensive performance, Statcast has the potential to change the way we value and think about the performance of individual defenders, and also to help us better understand defense as a whole.

St. Louis Cardinals GM John Mozeliak feels Statcast will have a significant impact. "It eliminates the intuitive or subjective opinion on who's really good at defense," Mozeliak said. "This will allow you to really have a clear definition on someone that can cover ground and how they do it. Now it is still very subjective analysis. As much as we try to push the envelope, this type of tracking system will really change how people think about defense."

MLBAM's system could place an even greater premium on defensive value as qualities such as range, accuracy, route efficiency, and arm strength will for the first time be precisely quantified. The Pirates were already investing in the bet that individual defensive value was more important than many other teams thought in 2013.

But in the middle of August, with Marte's injury, that competitive advantage vanished. Now the Pirates would be challenged to give the city something it hadn't had in twenty-one years—a home play-off game—without him. Without Marte, the Pirates needed someone else to step up.

11

ARMS RACE

In early September of 2013, at Yinzers, a well-known sporting-goods store wedged between warehouses and the outdoor market near downtown Pittsburgh, a large placard was placed outside the storefront marking down the final six victories needed for the Pirates to reach win No. 82—thereby guaranteeing them their first winning season in twenty-one years. With each win, another number—77, 78, 79, and so on—was crossed off. Thousands walked past the sign every week as the strip's boulevard hosts the city's popular Saturday-morning market. The sign became the city's unofficial countdown watch. However, on September 9, there was a problem: Yinzers hadn't been able to mark off a win for five days because the Pirates hadn't won. The countdown was stuck on win No. 81. Though reaching 82 wins at this point in the season seemed mathematically inevitable, until it happened, Pittsburghers had a degree of doubt.

The last time the Pirates had secured a winning season was on September 12, 1992, four days after Gerrit Cole's second birthday. One day after turning twenty-three years old, with a city anxiously hoping and waiting for history to be made, Cole took the mound in

Arlington, Texas, to try to end the twenty-year losing streak against Texas Rangers ace Yu Darvish, one of the best pitchers in the American League. Texas paid nearly $100 million to Darvish and his Japanese league team for his services. The Pirates could never afford such a pitcher in free agency, whether the market was domestic or international. The only place they could find similar talent was at the top of the draft, where they found Cole. The Pirates needed Cole to be better than he had been over 15 mostly good but not dominant starts since entering the rotation in early June after Wandy Rodriguez left the game in Atlanta with elbow pain. Pirates top veteran pitchers Francisco Liriano and A. J. Burnett had been less effective in recent weeks. Starling Marte was still out. The entire Pirate team seemed to be sputtering at the wrong time, stalling before their final ascent to a summit—Win No. 82.

Clint Hurdle has said his thought-of-the-day e-mails are not typically designed for a particular player or member of the audience, which includes hundreds of recipients. Rather, he believes the message is often something that he, personally, needs to absorb that day. He often feels as if he is writing to himself. The once reality-deaf Hurdle had now become introspective and in search of truth. Still, his message on September 9 seemed tailored specifically for Cole, a UCLA product. This e-mail was first shared in an ESPN.com story on Hurdle, as more national reporters began circling around the Pirates and their compelling story, cramping Hurdle's office during pregame interviews:

> *Tim Wrightman, a former All-American UCLA football player, tells a story about how, as a rookie lineman in the National Football League, he was up against the legendary pass rusher Lawrence Taylor. Taylor was not only physically powerful and uncommonly quick, but a master at verbal intimidation. Looking Tim in the eye, [Taylor] said, "Sonny, get ready. I'm going left and there's nothing you can do about it."*

Wrightman coolly responded, "Sir, is that your left or mine?"

The question froze Taylor long enough to allow Wrightman to throw a perfect block on him.

It's amazing what we can accomplish if we refuse to be afraid. Fear—whether it's of pain, failure or rejection—is a toxic emotion that creates monsters in our mind that consume self-confidence and intimidate us from doing our best or sometimes even trying at all.

Make a difference today.

Love Clint

Hurdle wanted his players to perform without fear and for Cole to pitch without fear. Hurdle often spoke about "fearing nothing" but "respecting everything" regarding the game. He talked about the ideal mind-set of a player as being that of a "backyard ballplayer," thinking back to when there was no pressure in playing as a child. From that came a freedom from fear, a freedom to perform instinctively, Hurdle suspected.

The Pirates needed Cole to make a difference this day and going forward. The team's pitching depth had been tested due to a variety of injuries. With Marte hurt, the Pirates needed fewer balls hit into play. They needed more strikeouts from their pitchers and in particular from Cole, the number one overall pick in the 2011 draft.

Cole looked the part of a dominant pitcher. He was six feet four, 250 pounds, and broad shouldered, like a linebacker in the center of the field. He had grown a thick beard and mastered a piercing, no-nonsense glare on the mound. Cole's skill was never in question, but the dominance of his raw ability had not yet translated into results. Nearly 70 percent of his offerings were fastballs, an unusual reliance on one pitch, and he had gotten by mostly with rare velocity. His fastball averaged 96.3 mph, the top speed among major league starting pitchers in 2013. In a game earlier that season against the Los Angeles

Angels, Cole threw eight 100 mph pitches, topping out at 101.8 mph. Cole might have been a little too hyped up that night, performing as a major leaguer for the first time before friends and family in Southern California.

But despite his impressive velocity, Cole owned a below-average strikeout rate of 6.2 strikeouts per 9 innings over the first two months of the season at Triple-A Indianapolis. Cole had been a one-pitch pitcher, and to become something more he had to evolve, and he did on that balmy night in Texas.

Predicting what can become of someone's talent is one thing; developing it is another. The early-season question regarding Cole in 2013, and dating back to his college career, was "Where are the strikeouts? Where is the dominance?" Cole bristled at the question earlier in the year when reporters asked it. Some evaluators suggested the problem was that Cole threw everything so hard. He threw a 90 mph changeup and a 90 mph slider, so there was some truth to this. However, on September 9, a different Cole emerged and the strikeouts arrived.

In Texas, Cole unveiled a new weapon. Hurdle and the Pirates perhaps no longer wanted Cole to have any fear in throwing his new pitch, his curveball. The time to showcase a new trick was now.

On the sixteenth and most important start of his young career, Cole took the mound knowing that the club's veteran starting pitchers had faltered in recent starts. In the first inning, Cole struck out Elvis Andrus with a 98 mph fastball painting the outside corner of the plate. Fastball location had been a focus of his work in spring training and at Triple-A, and he had improved. But in the third inning, the baseball world saw his new weapon. Cole got Leonys Martin to swing and miss at a sharp-breaking curveball, and Ian Kinsler followed by badly missing another 83 mph curve. In the fifth, Mitch Moreland swung and missed an 84 mph curveball that had a sharp, sweeping breaking action. Geovany Soto also followed suit by swinging over the top of another breaking pitch. It wasn't just the movement of the curveball that helped Cole. The pitch, roughly 15 mph slower than his fast-ball, was disrupting the timing of the Rangers hitters.

"How do you create swing and miss? You get guys anxious, think-ing, 'I have to cover this,'" Cole said. "There is an art to striking guys out. [Milwaukee Brewers starter] Marco Estrada throws eighty-nine mph and struck out nine of our guys. He's clearly [messing] with some dudes. How is he getting them anxious?"

Cole produced anxiety in every hitter with a 100 mph fastball. The difference in speed on his curveball played on that anxiety. Cole con-tinued to match Darvish frame for shutout frame. In the sixth, Adrian Beltre grounded to short for the inning's final out on a 99 mph pitch. The fiery Cole pounded his mitt with his right fist and screamed something primal into the humid air as he walked off the mound toward the visiting dugout.

In the seventh, a 97 mph two-seam fastball from Cole trailed back over the plate for a strike against Moreland for his career-best 9th strikeout. He had allowed just 3 hits, 2 walks, and no runs. He team-mates congratulated him between innings.

A Pedro Alvarez double in the seventh allowed Clint Barmes to score the game's only run in a 1–0 Pittsburgh victory. The Pirates had reached the elusive 82nd win. They had ended the longest streak of consecutive losing seasons in North American pro sports history. On the cover the *Pittsburgh Tribune-Review*'s sports section the next morning were two simple, powerful, and golden numbers—82—designed in the Pirates uniform font and set against a black back-ground.

Pirates fans celebrated, sharing pictures of their celebrations on so-cial media. Some fans literally had champagne on ice at home. The Pirates played it cool—no on-field, impromptu mosh pit or plastic-encased lockers in the visiting clubhouse to protect wardrobes from showers of alcoholic beverages. No parade was planned along the Bou-levard of the Allies back in Pittsburgh, and Cole was not lifted upon his teammates' shoulders. Most of the players had experienced little of the losing streak. Only Neil Walker, who had grown up in suburban Pittsburgh and was drafted by the Pirates out of high school, had experienced all twenty consecutive years of losing. The win aroused different emotions in the clubhouse than in the fan base. Yes, reaching win No. 82 mattered to an embattled Pirates front office and coaching staff, but what mattered more to the Pirates clubhouse that night was seeing Cole take the next step and securing a critical win in a pennant race. But a troubling question hovered about: How long would Cole continue to pitch in 2013?

Just a year earlier, in early September, in the midst of a pennant race, the Washington Nationals decided to stop allowing young ace Stephen Strasburg, a former number one overall pick like Cole, to pitch as he reached the team's self-imposed innings limit. Strasburg's shadow loomed over Cole. Injuries to young pitchers in the game were epidemic. Of the ten hardest-throwing starting pitchers in 2014, only Gerrit Cole and Angels starter Garrett Richards had not required Tommy John surgery to date in their careers. Only two universal tools are designed to protect pitchers and prevent injury, and they are simplistic—counting the number of pitches a starter throws per start and the number of innings he throws in a season—and the effectiveness of these were extremely doubtful. The Nationals had set an arbitrary innings limit to protect their young ace from overwork in his second year back from surgery, and this triggered speculation about Cole. Would he, too, be shut down in the midst of a pennant race?

Much like the Pirates' march to win No. 82, Cole's innings were also being counted and monitored by the public. As the calendar turned to September, Cole was on a pace for 190 pitched innings between the majors and Triple-A, more than a 25 percent jump from his 2012 total of 150. Major league teams are often hesitant to increase a young pitcher's workload by such a percentage. Unlike the Nationals, who announced their plans publicly for Strasburg a year earlier, the Pirates remained quiet about Cole. When asked if Cole had a specific innings limit, Pirates general manager Neal Huntington told a reporter, "If we ever get there, we'll let you know."

People had the false impression that the 2013 Pirates were a young team. That narrative was created to explain their unlikely and difficult-to-comprehend success. People thought of the team as a group that had found its way and matured. But in truth the Pirates were a middle-aged baseball club. The average age of the twenty-five-man roster was 28.4, the twelfth-oldest in baseball. The Pirates division rival, the first-place Cardinals, who were headed to a sixth straight winning season, were a much younger club, the fourth youngest in MLB. While building up the farm system was a key tenet of Huntington's master plan, the farm system that he inherited was ranked 26th by *Baseball America* in 2008, and few in the first five draft classes under Huntington had impacted the major league club. Unlike in football or basketball, it takes years to develop prospects in baseball, even first-round selections.

After years of nickel-and-diming the draft, Huntington had finally convinced the ownership to concentrate spending there, on the one talent-acquisition tool that a small-market team shouldn't skimp on, the one place they could expect to find future star talent at a relatively reasonable cost.

The shift in strategy began in 2008 when the Pirates selected Pedro Alvarez second overall. He was ranked as the draft's top talent by *Baseball America,* and he eventually signed for a club record of $6 million. Huntington and club president Frank Coonelly began implementing a plan for the Pirates to play catch-up, to try to jam two draft classes into one. They pushed to spend on the draft. Not only would the Pirates pay the asking price for premium talent selected in the first round, they heavily engaged in overslotting, meaning that they exceeded Major League Baseball's recommended signing bonuses for draft positions lower in the draft for talented players who had slid due to their hefty signing demands. Some of Dan Fox's first assignments from Huntington were to study the amateur draft. From 2008 to 2012, Huntington's first five seasons with the Pirates, they spent

$51.4 million on draft bonuses, more than any other team in baseball and a record in the sport for a five-year period.

Moreover, Huntington and the Pirates knew they could not compete in the free agent marketplace for top-of-the-rotation pitching, so instead this became a focus of their draft efforts. From 2009 to 2011, in the top ten rounds of the draft, twenty-two of the Pirates' top thirty selections in each of those three drafts were pitchers (and seventeen were selected out of high school). They signed eighteen of those arms to bonuses totaling $25.6 million—more than they paid their major league starting pitching staff in 2013. They doled out seven-figure contracts to high school pitchers such as Colton Cain ($1.2 million), Stetson Allie ($2.3 million), Zachary Von Rosenberg ($1.2 million), and Clay Holmes ($1.2 million), who each fell out of the first round due to signing demands and were drafted at positions—such as in the seventh round—where players typically sign for thousands, not millions, of dollars.

The Pirates weren't just spending on any pitchers. They were seeking a specific type of pitcher: one with a tall, lean body that produced promising throwing velocity and had the potential to fill out and become stronger. The front office challenged their scouts with finding the next Justin Verlander and Stephen Strasburg, and with the first overall pick in the 2011 draft the Pirates selected a pitcher comparable in size and talent: Gerrit Cole. In June of 2013, Cole was the first potential impact starting pitcher to arrive to the major leagues from the Huntington draft classes. He was the bluest of diamonds in baseball: a young, relatively polished power arm who was under club control for six-plus seasons.

The Pirates had employed Dan Fox's math to find hidden value in shifts and free agents such as Francisco Liriano and Russell Martin, but to sustain success and be competitive every year they had to have a productive farm system. With injuries mounting in 2013 and their veteran starting pitchers struggling in the second half of the season, the Pirates needed some of the talent from the drafts to begin helping the club. They needed players such as Cole to arrive and make an impression. And just as important, they needed pitchers such as Cole to remain healthy.

Cole had always been carefully handled in a dangerous environment. He was raised in Santa Ana, California, just south of Los Angeles, where pitchers are the most at risk for elbow injury in the world. According to Jon Roegele's Tommy John database, which includes all known 839 Tommy John surgeries performed on pitchers through September 2014, more minor and major league pitchers who have had the surgery are from the Los Angeles metro area than from any other metro area in the country, or from Canada, Mexico, and Japan combined. This apparently has happened for a variety of factors. For starters, Southern California's mild year-round temperatures permit year-round throwing. Moreover, affluence enables parents to send their promising sons to private instructors. As draft bonuses and major league salaries increase, it further spurs the sports-specialization culture in Southern California, and the wear on the elbow in baseball.

While Cole came from a well-to-do family and received private instruction, his family made sure months off from throwing were included in his pitching program. Two-month breaks twice a year were built into his year-round pitching schedule.

Unlike most fathers with sons playing baseball at a high level, Cole's father, Mark, was a man of science with a degree in physiopathology, the study of the mechanisms of disease, from the University of Southern California. He was interested in how data could prevent injury and was particularly fascinated by *Sports Illustrated* writer Tom Verducci's data-driven piece in the early 2000s that linked substantial year-to-year innings increases with injury for young professional pitchers. Mark began counting Gerrit's pitches as early as Little League.

In high school, Mark created a system where Cole rated his soreness and stiffness levels on a scale of 1 to 10 after every start. Cole was permitted to throw just once a week while pitching for his Orange Lutheran High School team and at UCLA. So while scores of other young, high-velocity arms were breaking down across the game,

Cole entered professional baseball with less mileage on his arm. He was also carefully managed by the Pirates. His Triple-A strikeout totals were lower than expected and his strikeout-generating curveball did not come into play until September by design. There was a reason why observers in Indianapolis said they rarely, if ever, saw Cole throw the curveball. While the Pirates are secretive about their injury-prevention strategies, it's believed they do not treat all pitches as equal. It's thought that the Pirates believe some pitches place more stress on young arms than others.

Cole notes that a pitcher such as Miami Marlins star Jose Fernandez, who had Tommy John surgery in 2014, would not have been allowed to throw his curveball and slider so often if he had been drafted by the Pirates. "As good as some of our guys' breaking balls are, that's just not the emphasis," Cole said.

Cole suggested that even in college at UCLA he was not leaning on his breaking pitches as much as Stephen Strasburg did at San Diego State University, perhaps where the damage to his elbow began.

"If you look at pitchers and look at longevity, not only throughout a season but throughout a career, the guys who stick around are the guys that have the best fastball command," Cole said. "That's driven probably from statistics, but I don't need statistics to tell me that matters."

As analysts and fans wondered why Cole wasn't striking out batters at a high rate at Triple-A, and where the dominance was in his first months in the big leagues, he explained strikeouts were not his focus; developing fastball command was the first building block.

Will Carroll lives in Indianapolis and often travels to Victory Field there to watch top young arms when they come through either playing for or against the Pirates' Triple-A affiliate there. Carroll has dedicated his career to studying injuries in sports, authoring a book titled *Saving the Pitcher,* and was the one who hired Dan Fox to write columns for BaseballProspectus.com. Carroll is frustrated by the industry's general lack of interest in data-based injury-preventive practices, and technological solutions, but believes that Fox is employing a "smarter pitch count" that should help benefit his players.

Carroll notes that when he and Fox worked together at *Baseball Prospectus,* Fox was particularly interested in the notion of "pitch cost," the idea that not every pitch places equal stress on the elbow and shoulder. Moreover, a prevailing thought is that higher-stress situations in games result in even more stress and fatigue on elbows and shoulders. With smarter pitch counts, pitches would be weighted differently depending upon the type of pitch and the stress level of the game situation in which the pitch is thrown. For instance, pitching with the bases empty is thought to be less stressful than pitching with the bases loaded.

While watching Cole in Indianapolis, Carroll rarely saw him throw curveballs, rather, fastballs, changeups, and occasional sliders. Carroll believes Fox has developed "a smarter version of a pitch count" and that the Pirates measure the workloads and stress levels of their pitchers using sophisticated mathematical models, favoring math over the eye test to decide when to rest pitchers or take them out of games.

Injury prevention is one of the final frontiers of big data. If a team could employ better injury-preventive practices, perhaps data-driven practices, and shave down even 10 percent on its injury rate of pitchers, it would gain an enormous competitive advantage.

Tampa Bay is believed to be one of the first teams to employ PITCHf/x data to monitor its pitchers' health and predict and preempt injury. PITCHf/x tracks release points of pitchers, and a deviation from a normal release point may indicate injury. According to research from Jonah Keri's book *The Extra 2%,* Tampa Bay had only one pitcher in the entire organization undergo Tommy John surgery from late 2005 to mid-2009.

The Pirates were believed to be gathering similar data in the summer of 2013 on Cole. They monitored what he threw and how much he threw. In his first 19 starts in the major leagues in 2013, Cole threw more than 100 pitches in a game only twice and threw fewer than 90 pitches in 6 of his starts. Several times in the second half of the 2013 season Cole either had his start pushed back several days or skipped, although the Pirates were not open about their specific inning, pitch, or workload limit for Cole.

"We do have some proprietary stuff we do in terms of workload. That information is made available to the coaches, and they have asked for various parts of it at various times. Not only starters but also relievers," Fox said. "I don't know how everything was arrived at [with the Cole situation], but I do know the stuff we provided was part of the process."

So what was involved? Pitch types? High-stress innings? Total pitches?

"All of the above and some other [measurements]," Fox said. "A lot of the [preventive health models] work better with the more detailed information you have, so the PITCHf/x era is sort of the demarcation line."

Clint Hurdle used some of that data with Cole and his other pitchers. Hurdle was careful with workloads. The Pirates ranked last in the major leagues in pitches per start in 2013, with their starting pitchers averaging just 90 pitches per appearance. Hurdle also tracked the bull-pen workload, consecutive days pitched, and how many times relievers were up and throwing in the bull pen.

While the Pirates lost several starters due to injury, their bull pen remained mostly healthy. The data approach reached beyond smarter pitch counts and analyzing PITCHf/x data such as velocity trends and release points. According to Carroll, in 2013 the Pirates were one of only twelve major league teams to put at least several of their prized arms through biomechanical evaluations, where pitchers were brought into a lab and had markers attached to their body. They went through their throwing motion and had the stress on their elbows and shoulders measured and compared to a database of healthy and unhealthy pitchers. But the biomechanical lab testing is imperfect as it is difficult for pitchers to throw normally while wearing a compression suit with dozens of electronic markers attached. Carroll, who writes for the *Bleacher Report,* reported in 2014 that the Pirates and the Baltimore Orioles were testing a compression sleeve from the company Motus. The sleeve fits easily over a pitcher's throwing arm and elbow so he can throw naturally. The sleeve's monitoring device is touted as being able to measure stresses on the elbow in real time and will perhaps be a breakthrough tool in injury prevention.

By 2014, the Pirates also had their minor league pitchers start to record their daily nutrition, hydration, rest, and workout routines. In spring training they began having their players wear Zephyr monitoring vests, on a voluntary basis. The tight-fitting compression shirt, which had a black, circular, detachable electronic device—about the size of a quarter—attached near the center of the chest, collected data from a sensor that records a player's heartbeat and energy consumption.

Cole did not show any signs of fatigue as he kept pitching into September. He only got better. His performance data didn't decline and his velocity was stable as his ability to prevent runs increased. His breakout performance was in win No. 82 against the Rangers, as he unleashed a sharp curveball that allowed him to strike out 9 batters.

Five days later against the Cubs, Cole was again masterful, allowing just one run while striking out seven in seven innings. Perhaps his most dominant outing came against the Padres on September 19, when he struck out a career-high 12 over six innings, allowing just four hits and a run. After that win the Pirates had moved to within a game of St. Louis. Cole won four straight September starts. Instead of being shut down at an arbitrary innings mark, he ended up being the club's best pitcher in September, striking out 10.97 batters per 9 innings with a 1.69 ERA and a 4-0 record. The surge was tied to the increased use of his curveball. After throwing it sparingly early in his rookie campaign, he had nearly tripled his use of it to 20 percent of his pitches in September.

The Pirates never revealed what Cole's red line was. Maybe he crossed it, or maybe he didn't. Perhaps the human element—Hurdle's observations—allowed Cole to cross that line. Or maybe the data-based workload monitors kept his arm fresh. Whatever the case, Cole kept pitching. He helped the Pirates continue to play great baseball into late September, propelling them to the cusp of a postseason berth.

★ ★ ★

September 23 was a cool night on the north side of Chicago. Temperatures dipped into the fifties. Autumn had arrived with a cool breeze coming off Lake Michigan. This season was rarely associated with important baseball in Pittsburgh. With a win over the Cubs the Pirates would clinch their first play-off appearance since 1992. A week earlier, Hurdle had sent out a daily e-mail message designed to mitigate any anxiety or mounting pressure:

> *"I never worry about the future. It comes soon enough."*
> —*Albert Einstein*
>
> *Make a difference today.*
> *Love Clint*

NL Central Standings as of September 22, 2013			
Team	W-L	Pct.	GB
St. Louis	91–65	.583	–
Cincinnati	89–67	.571	2.0
Pittsburgh	89–67	.571	2.0
Milwaukee	69–86	.445	21.5
Chicago	65–91	.417	26.0

Pirates starting pitcher Charlie Morton was matched up against the hard-throwing Jeff Samardzija, who had given the Pirates trouble in several meetings this season with a combination of his mid-90s fastball and hard-breaking curve. The matchup played out as expected, as a late-season pitchers' duel.

Morton was excellent. Hitting his mid-to-low-90s sinker was akin to hitting a bowling ball, his opponents said. Batters thought the sinker seemed "heavier" than most other fastballs. The pitch induced ground ball after ground ball, and Morton threw seven shutout innings, allowing just three hits. He induced 11 groundouts against no fly balls.

Samardzija was nearly as good. He allowed one run over six innings as the Pirates took a 1–0 lead into the eighth inning. As the game neared an end, plastic sheeting akin to shower lining went up to protect lockers in the cramped visitors' clubhouse at Wrigley Field, and twelve cases of champagne were wheeled in.

Hurdle removed Morton after he threw just 89 pitches. Setup man Mark Melancon would pitch the eighth with closer Jason Grilli ready for the ninth.

Melancon had been the game's best setup man for the first five months of the season, but he had struggled in September. He had thrown a career-high number of cut fastballs—61.4 percent—and the pitch seemed to lack the same blistering effectiveness as it had earlier in the season. Brian Bogusevic singled off Melancon, a line drive to center field, to begin the bottom of the eighth. He advanced on a groundout and scored on a Donnie Murphy single to left field. Melancon got out of the inning without further damage, but the Cubs had tied the score at 1. For the third straight game the Pirates had allowed a lead to slip away after the seventh inning. Prior to these three games, the Pirates had won 76 of 77 games when leading after seven innings.

Kevin Gregg came into the game to pitch the top of the ninth for Chicago. With two outs and the bases empty, Starling Marte walked into the right-hander's batter's box. He was back in the lineup but was still struggling from his hand injury in August. On a 2-1 pitch, Gregg threw a hanging slider that stayed up in the hitting zone. At that moment, Marte appeared to be completely healthy. He crushed the pitch. He knew it was gone as he took several steps toward first base, then punched both of his hands into the air. The ball landed in the sixth row in the left-field bleachers. Cheers rose from the several thousand dots of gold sitting in the cold, dark grandstand. Pirates fans had grown in number at road venues during the season's second half. The Pirates took a 2–1 lead into the bottom of the ninth as Pirates closer Jason Grilli completed his warm-up throws in the makeshift bull pen that rests along the right-field line and then jogged toward the center of the diamond with a chance to pitch the Pirates into the postseason.

Grilli recorded two outs in the inning but also allowed a Nate Schierholtz single. Ryan Sweeney then came to the plate and rifled a Grilli fastball to the right-center-field gap. The Pirates' outfield was playing deep to prevent an extra-base hit, and right fielder Marlon Byrd attempted to intercept the ball in deep right-center field, but failed to field it cleanly. As the ball deflected off Byrd's glove and trickled away from him, Schierholtz sprinted around second base as Cubs third-base coach David Bell waved his arm violently like a propeller, urging Schierholtz to head toward home plate.

Pirates first baseman Justin Morneau saw Bell's signal and tried to anticipate what would happen next. He drifted toward the middle of the infield. Morneau had not hit as the Pirates had hoped when they acquired him from the Twins at the end of August via a trade, but he remained one of the game's better defensive first baseman. Morneau had been with the club less than a month, but at that moment he found himself the key man in a historic play.

"It's probably not too often going to be a play at home on that kind of ball," Morneau told reporters afterward. "I stay at first and try to keep [Sweeney there] and drift toward the middle once I see something different happen. Then I saw [the ball] kick away. That's my cue there. I go back to the instincts. Something told me to go [to the center of the infield]."

In center field, Andrew McCutchen had moved over into a proper backup position and collected the ball that had deflected off Byrd's glove. McCutchen was a great player but lacked one skill: a first-rate throwing arm. He had worked to strengthen it in the off-season through hundreds of long-toss sessions with his Florida neighbor and former Pirates player Steve Pearce. McCutchen fielded the ball and made an accurate one-bounce throw to Morneau near the pitcher's mound. Morneau collected the toss and quickly pivoted and delivered a perfect throw to Pirates catcher Russell Martin, who was blocking the plate.

Martin had played the second half of the season with a bad left knee, and he was the last line of resistance between clinching a play-off berth or going to extra innings. Martin took the throw from Morneau and hung on to the ball as Schierholtz collided with him. On his knees, minus his catcher's mask, which he had tossed away for a better view of the action, Martin lifted the ball triumphantly above his head. Home-plate umpire Mike DiMuro punched the air to signal the final out. The moment was captured by Associated Press photographer Charles Rex Arbogast and became an iconic image of the season. The game was over. The Pirates were in the play-offs.

When the Texas Rangers had clinched a postseason berth several years earlier, star outfielder Josh Hamilton, who was battling alcoholism, asked the team to celebrate with alcohol-free beverages for fear a champagne-and-beer celebration could trigger a relapse. As the likelihood of the Pirates clinching a play-off berth had approached, several veteran players had approached Hurdle and asked him if he preferred that the team celebrate with nonalcoholic beverages. His battle with alcoholism was not a secret, and he had not had a sip of alcohol in fourteen years. The visitors' clubhouse at Wrigley Field was the smallest in the game, and twelve cases of champagne would not only drench the worn carpet but fill the cramped confines with a mist of alcohol.

"I told them it didn't bother me," Hurdle told the *Pittsburgh Post-Gazette* earlier in the day. "I wasn't going to lick my lips. I'm way past that. I'm a grown man. . . . I know what I can't do. I could be a drunk tomorrow if I had one beer. Like I always say, one is too many and a million aren't enough. I wanted to embrace the moment. I wanted to be a part of all of it. I wanted to get wet. I wanted to be soaked. I wanted it dripping down my face. I wanted my eyes to sting."

For twenty minutes after the final out, Hurdle and the Pirates participated in a baseball ritual that hadn't happened in a Pittsburgh-occupied clubhouse since the Pirates captured the National League's East Division in 1992. They doused themselves with champagne and cheap beer. They wore eye protection of every variety, from ski goggles to dollar-store swimming goggles to the bulky eye protection you'll commonly find in an introduction-to-chemistry classroom. The motley crew of veteran cast-offs, bonus-baby draft picks, old-school coaches, and mathematical wizards had got there by becoming a sum greater than that of their individual parts. They had to accept new voices, new ideas, and collaboration. That was their story and their accomplishment in 2013. And by the end of September, they weren't ready for the ride to end.

12

MAGIC ACT

Black-and-white math blended with the various colors of subjective observations and insights several hours before each series. In 2013, prior to the first home game of every series, Dan Fox and Mike Fitzgerald sat in on the strategy meeting Clint Hurdle held in his office at PNC Park, along with the usual crowd of assistant coaches and video coordinators. In every such meeting that season, Fox and Fitzgerald were present. Beginning in 2013, in addition to preseries meetings before home games, Hurdle included Fox or Fitzgerald on a conference call during pre-series meetings on the road, and Fitzgerald even began traveling with the team on a number of road trips. While nearly every club had hired at least one nerdy mathematical genius number cruncher, by 2013 few if any such quantitative analysts had been integrated into meetings and even the team's traveling party as Fox and Fitzgerald were with the Pirates.

The Pirates had let their quantitative analysts out from where some might have imagined them to reside, a basement surrounded by computer servers. They were allowed to enter the ego-filled, exclusive atmosphere of a major league clubhouse. And what was most remarkable was Fox and Fitzgerald were accepted there. In 2013, a communication barrier, and even a lack of respect, still often existed between old-school and new-school camps throughout the sport. Quantitative analysts and on-field staff and players were often very different people, with very different backgrounds, temperaments, and prejudices. One common complaint heard from analytics staffers in the game is that their data-based findings do not always reach the field. But this complaint was not heard in Pittsburgh.

Since the middle of the 2012 season, the Pirates' analytics team had begun to play more and more of a role. Fox's and Fitzgerald's job responsibilities grew beyond making off-season evaluations on potential player acquisitions. They were useful in more than just implementing big-picture strategies, such as shifting, identifying the value of pitch framing, or finding inefficiencies in the draft. Their roles extended beyond macro-level analysis. In 2013, the Pirates leaned on their analysts more than ever for help at the micro level, the daily game-planning.

"It started with Clint really reaching out and saying, 'Hey, I want you guys to be more involved and be here more in terms of the meetings,'" Fox said.

Hours before the start of every series is a general meeting with Hurdle and his assistants, as is the case with most major league teams. Then specialized meetings follow: the hitting coach goes over scouting reports and video with his hitters; the pitching coach does the same with his starters and relievers; and the infield and outfield coaching staffs meet with the position players. But before those specialized meetings, preparation against an opponent starts with a comprehensive scouting and strategy-setting meeting in Hurdle's office, where members of the major league coaching staff, advance video scout Wyatt Toregas, and someone like special assistant to the general manager Jim Benedict, who is on the road scouting the next opponent, meet. In 2012, Fox or Fitzgerald were integrated into opponent-scouting meetings at the start of all home series, which often comprise multiple series. Come 2013, they were each involved in every preseries meeting, home and road.

"[Before 2012] it was more e-mail-type exchanges. [In 2013] we were talking every three days, opposed to once during the homestand," Fox said. "That leads to just hanging around, more face time, more off-the-cuff conversations. In every little conversation is something we can learn from and help with. [Trust] I think is tied to time and exposure."

In part because of Hurdle's openness and increasing trust bred through familiarity, Fox and Fitzgerald counseled Hurdle on day-to-day lineup construction and bull-pen usage in addition to defensive alignment. Hurdle also encouraged his assistant staff and players to ask questions of Fox and Fitzgerald. Some players, such as reliever Mark Melancon, frequently interacted with Fitzgerald in the clubhouse. "There were some skeptics early on and even now," Fitzgerald said of the clubhouse's view of PITCHf/x data. "So it's good to be [available]." Fitzgerald didn't preach sabermetrics ideology to players, he did not try to convert nonbelievers, nor did he try to explain WAR—unless asked. Rather, Fitzgerald made himself available. Over time in a clubhouse wary of outsiders, as most major league clubhouses are, he became a familiar face. In these meetings, particularly the preseries meetings with Hurdle, the art of subjective, observational scouting—such as getting a feel for a player's recent mechanical changes or weaknesses, or even mental temperament—met science, the streams of data flowing from the Pirates' proprietary database.

Even beyond identifying the nearly invisible potential of Russell Martin as a must-have free agent, Fitzgerald considers his most important work to be gathering and analyzing day-to-day material for opponent-scouting meetings, which are a combination of reports and voices. The advance video scouting is done by Toregas, a former backup and minor league catcher for the Pirates, who by August and September was breaking down the last 45 games of each opponent in advance of each series. Reports also came from live scouts in the field, following upcoming opponents, who were responsible for providing up-to-date anecdotal snapshots of players and teams, findings that do not show up in a box score. And beginning in 2012, and playing an even bigger role in 2013, was the analytical data supplied by Fox and Fitzgerald. Fitzgerald says much of the work done is to try to confirm findings or observations by advance scouts through objective analysis. Ideally, they want evidence everyone can agree on and work from.

"It's math-y, but there's still the whole arts-and-science debate," Fitzgerald said of implementing big data. "I'd argue there is an art to that sort of stuff. I think that's the biggest thing."

But where do the subjective and the objective meet? Fitzgerald cites an example. Say a batter excels against fastballs on the outer half of the plate from left-handed pitchers. But then what about the two lefties in the Pirates bull pen? Tony Watson and Justin Wilson both have rare, for left-handed pitchers, upper-90s fastball velocity. Maybe that batter has done damage against four-seam fastballs on the outer half, but how many 97 and 98 mph fastballs has he actually seen and hit? Here is where Fitzgerald and Fox dig deeper, seeking more subjective and objective information.

"So it's an art in the sense of what we get from the raw information doesn't always tell the whole story. How were the pitches set up? Were there runners in scoring position that were tipping pitches [to the batter]? At the end of the day you can make the argument that [the art] is just refining the data, but in a way there are still situations that come up where there is gray area and you have to massage through it," Fitzgerald said. "I like to think that is where we do damage, where we can get value out of it."

Fitzgerald says that five years from now every team will have incorporated data into their day-to-day operations. So the question then becomes how well will individual clubs do on the tough, fifty-fifty calls? What is the decision-making process? Will the field staff consistently stick with decisions made in advance meetings? That's where the new advantages will reside. Through a growing respect and appreciation for the different skills sets of old-school and new-school camps, made possible by time and familiarity, the Pirates created a massive communication advantage. It not only allowed data-based findings to reach the field in 2013, but the communication allowed the data to be refined by coaches and players asking the right questions, questions sparked by observation.

Part of the sport's struggle in communicating big data ideas to on-field staff is undoubtedly tied to presentation flaws, and in the 2012–13 off-season, Fox and Fitzgerald focused on how they could overcome this and better present their data to best get it adopted on the field. This went beyond selling the team on shifting. How could all data findings most easily be accepted by players and coaches in advance meetings?

"The biggest thing I've found, and I think Dan and the other guys would agree, is these guys understand visuals like that," said Fitzgerald as he snaps his fingers, "versus if we give them some [statistical] data laid out on paper."

Recall, one change for presentation the Pirates made in 2013 was to purchase a video and information tool from TruMedia that allowed for the easy creation of data-visualization heat maps from the Pirates' statistical databases linked to video. These are critical tools in the pregame scouting meetings.

"Say, so-and-so has a thirty percent miss rate against changeups below the zone. We can pull up all the video on that," Fitzgerald said. "Or, 'Here's the cluster he's done damage against a certain pitch, and then here's the video that ties to that.' You can say, 'I see a hole here; let me go look at this hole on video.' I think it kind of speeds up the process of finding weakness."

Ray Searage brings an important piece of luggage with him on every road trip, a large plastic crate, roughly nine cubic feet in size. When he opens the crate, all that is visible at first are towels, as if he does not trust hotels to launder their bathroom essentials. But after the Pirates pitching coach removes several layers of fabric, his most important ally in game planning emerges: a laptop.

"Two have already been smashed," said Searage of his previous laptops when explaining his seemingly overly cautious packing.

There in the middle of any road clubhouse, surrounded by players' lockers and near the center-of-the-room sofas and televisions of a common clubhouse layout, Searage can often be seen before games with his laptop opened, examining various heat charts of opposing hitters and Pirates pitchers. Searage looks at the screen and then writes down his thoughts on a legal pad, formulating a recommended game plan. Fox and Fitzgerald supply him with their analytical findings, having combed through the video advance report and having tried to identify areas with likely question marks. For instance, a switch-hitter might have been strong from the left side lately but historically is a much better right-handed hitter. What should the recommended plan of attack be? That is where art meets science and objective meets the subjective.

Searage prefers to receive the advance statistical and video reports on opponents two to three days before a particular pitcher's start. Then he begins poring over the data, consulting with Russell Martin and the pitchers to outline a plan. During the last series of the regular season in Cincinnati, never was there a more important strategy session during the last two decades in Pirates history.

The Pirates arrived in Cincinnati on the final weekend of September already knowing they would play the Reds in a one-game playoff to determine which team advanced to the National League Division Series (NLDS). The Pirates and the Reds had clinched the NL's two wild-card berths, and the Cardinals had secured the division title, but something critical remained to play for: home-field advantage. The Pirates had a 50-31 record at PNC Park, a .617 winning percentage, compared to a .525 mark on the road. Home field was even more valuable to the Reds, who owned a .636 winning percentage at the Great American Ball Park and were just a .500 team on the road. The winner of the weekend's series would gain roughly a 10 percent edge in advancing to the NLDS.

What most influences home-field advantage is not what you might think. It is not primarily tied to park dimensions, travel fatigue, or familiarity. It's umpire bias. University of Chicago behavioral economist Tobias Moskowitz and *Sports Illustrated* writer L. Jon Wertheim concluded in their book *Scorecasting* that home-field advantage is predominately tied to the home-field team's enjoying the benefit of more borderline strike-ball calls, with umpires either consciously or subconsciously influenced by the environment. Moskowitz and Wertheim based this on examination of millions of pitches tracked by PITCHf/x and QuesTec—computerized systems that track pitch location.

"In baseball it turns out that the most significant difference between home and away teams is that the home teams strike out less and walk more—a lot more—per plate appearance than road teams," Moskowitz wrote.

Moskowitz also found that the larger and louder the crowd, the more umpire bias—whether consciously or subconsciously—could be created. A one-game play-off, such as the wild-card game, could make for a raucous environment.

But home-field advantage was also important because Cincinnati's Great American Ball Park was one of the most hitter-friendly venues in the National League. The Reds were built for run production with sluggers such as Joey Votto, Shin-Soo Choo, and Jay Bruce. While the Pirates were built for run prevention at pitcher-friendly PNC Park.

While the Pirates arrived in Cincinnati knowing whom they would play in the wild card play-in game, they also entered knowing who would pitch for them: left-hander Francisco Liriano.

The analytics, the video scouting, and the advance reports all agreed: the top three Reds hitters—Votto, Choo, and Bruce—were all left-handed, and all struggled with the low-and-away slider, Liriano's best pitch. Searage could see these weaknesses clearly on the heat maps generated on his laptop. A package of printed statistical reports and heat maps were placed in each player's locker prior to a series. In those reports they could learn of the .321 on-base plus slugging percentage (OPS) left-handed batters produced against Liriano in 2013. The mark was the all-time single-season best by a left-handed pitcher who had faced at least 100 left-handed hitters, according to Baseball-Reference.com's "play index" tool. Liriano was even better than Randy Johnson, who might have been the most terrifying left-handed pitcher for a lefty hitter to face in the game's history, and who in 1999 limited lefties to a .331 OPS. The six-foot-ten Johnson threw in the mid-90s with a sidearm motion and also had a wipeout slider. Liriano's improved ability to get ahead with a low-to-mid-90s two-seam fastball—in part tied to Martin's pitch framing—allowed for his slider and changeup to become even more effective. Hitters were facing less favorable counts, more susceptible to either missing or pounding Liriano's off-speed pitches into the ground.

Securing home-field advantage for the winner-take-all game was not just critical for the Pirates as a whole, it was critical for Liriano. In 2013 his ERA was 1.47 in pitcher-friendly PNC Park versus 4.32 on the road. After a series-opening win on Friday, September 27, against the Reds, the Pirates smashed six home runs against them on Saturday to secure home-field advantage. Come Tuesday, Liriano would be on his home mound, and Pittsburgh would be hosting a postseason baseball game for the first time in two decades. Finally, meaningful baseball would be played in October in Pittsburgh.

★ ★ ★

Russell Martin's father never wanted a nine-to-five job. He refused to live a traditional lifestyle. Jazz was his passion. He worked in construction and was good with his hands. He built decks and took on other odd jobs. He did that work so he could frequent the Montreal subway as a street performer during morning and afternoon rush-hour crowds. His pleasure came from having a commuter pause, stop, and listen. He gave Russell the middle name Coltrane in homage to the great jazz performer John Coltrane. Russell senior told *The New York Times* the middle name was not simply meant as a tribute to

Coltrane's music but also to his free and independent spirit, which he hoped his son would emulate.

With the Pirates, Martin presided over the stereo in the clubhouse, hooking up his iPhone and scrolling through the saved playlists. Attached to the exterior of Martin's wood-grained locker is a list of music designations for each day of the week. There's a day for rap and hip-hop, a day for alternative rock, and a day for Latin music. To create a more subdued Sunday-morning atmosphere following Saturday-night games, there's reggae as players sporadically file into the clubhouse, often toting Starbucks coffee-to-go cups. Martin controls the playlist much the way he sets the tone in the clubhouse, players say. He comes to work every day setting a standard. He works as hard as any other player in recent memory with the Pirates, running stadium steps at 2:30 p.m. in September five hours before a night game, part of what he calls a pregame "activation" period. The songs Martin chooses to play all have a repetitive beat, which is a defining criterion for rock and roll and much of the modern pop/rock and hip-hop genres. Jazz lacks a repetitive beat. Jazz, the love of Martin's father, is improvisational.

"Jazz is still a huge part of his life, but I never really understood that music. I like a beat, a pattern," Martin said. "In jazz they are just like one guy is going one way, another guy is going off that, the other guy is going off that. It's like you are all playing together but there is no pattern. It's strange."

However, Martin tries to avoid a repetitive beat as a catcher, endeavoring to be without patterns in one of his most important tasks. Despite all the data at the hands of coaches in the dugout, professional catchers still have an important in-game task: they call the pitches. In the NFL and the NBA, coaches call the plays. Even in college baseball catchers turn to the dugout for pitch signals from coaches. But in professional baseball, catchers are responsible for calling pitches.

Martin takes the responsibility seriously. Being an analytical player, he plays a significant role in designing game plans, examining the strengths of opposing hitters versus that day's starting pitcher, and reviews scouting reports created by the analytics team. In particular Martin likes to study first-pitch swings, percentage of swings, percentage of out-of-zone swings, and two-strike approaches. He wants to get a sense of the hitter's tendencies, but also of his psychological disposition: Is he aggressive or passive? Martin studies heat charts trying to locate the areas of a strike zone a hitter is effective in. For instance, in a start at San Diego, the Pirates television broadcast displayed a heat zone, a data visualization, of how Padres left-handed hitter Seth Smith performed against pitches in certain parts of the strike zone. Smith hit well against pitches in the middle to outer half of the plate. So Martin had Pirates starting pitcher Gerrit Cole pitch in, under, and over the hot areas to record a three-pitch strikeout.

Martin understands the importance of big data; for him it provides an edge at the margins. But the game is still largely instinctual for him, and he relies heavily on observing and adjusting off what he sees. If his middle name and his father's love of jazz have impacted him in one area, it is on the baseball field in pitch sequencing. Martin strives to avoid patterns.

"My style of catching and calling a game is a little like jazz," he said. "There's no beat to it, there's no sequences. There's just feel. I almost feel that's how I can call a game. I'll call eight changeups in a row or eight sliders in a row if I feel like that's the right thing to do."

In observing Martin and seeing the way he interacts with teammates, Fox was struck by something, another hidden value. While it was perhaps impossible to value intangible elements such as leadership and baseball makeup, Fox was blown away by Martin's work behind the scenes and thought that these skills must have value. Fox was impressed by Martin's ability to articulate his methods from pitch framing to pitch sequencing to hitting approach. It wasn't just Martin's pitch framing that Pirates pitchers raved about; they also praised him for his ability to game-plan. Jeff Locke lauds Martin's ability to keep hitters off-balance. Although quantifying such skill through data is not known to have been accomplished, Locke believes it does have value. For example, earlier in the season against one of the National League's best hitters, Joey Votto, Martin demonstrated his master pitch-sequencing psychology.

"We went with back-to-back fastballs in the first at bat to Votto on [June 1]. We went right after him. It's oh and two and he didn't take a swing, and I'm sure that was kind of weird for him," Martin said. "He knows how he is going to be pitched. When you throw something that doesn't make sense, he's like, 'Whoa, he just threw me a change-up?' He has to reprogram the possible sequences that are going to happen in his mind. It's knowing who you are playing against. . . . If he's beat in a certain way, does he come up in his next at bat looking for that type of pitch? There is no piece of paper that tells you that."

To Martin, pitch-sequencing is an art form that could benefit from some data analysis. While he's able to employ some of the data at his disposal to create a rough plan, once the game starts, he has to adjust and evolve based upon his reads from the batters. Sometimes it's observing how comfortable a batter is in taking a pitch. Was he jumpy or was he "soft" on the landing, tracking the ball with ease and letting it drop out of the zone without so much as a triggering of his hands? While a pitcher's slider might be his best pitch according to data from PITCHf/x, if Martin doesn't like its movement in a bull-pen session or feels it lacks its typical life during the game, he'll stay away from it.

"It's always good to review [data]," Martin said. "But instinctively you have to do what you feel is right. You have all that information to fall back on, but you don't want it to cloud your judgment during the game."

Most important, Martin knows his pitch-sequencing ability won't matter if he can't get pitchers to trust him and his process. He knows his pitch calls are merely "suggestions" and the pitchers have the ultimate veto power with a simple negative, horizontal shake of their head as they look in for signs from the mound.

Entering spring training in 2013, Martin knew little about the pitchers Locke and Liriano. Locke was young with little of a major league track record, and Martin had never played with Liriano. Prior to spring training, Martin asked Pirates video coordinator Kevin Roach for video on the two pitchers so he could study them. In spring training Martin felt he connected with Locke as they rotated from hot to cold tubs during a treatment session. They spoke for forty minutes and it was not all about baseball. Martin was trying to learn Locke's temperament and level of aggressiveness. Martin also shagged fly balls with Liriano and others, picking their brains, searching for nuggets of their pitching philosophies. More than anything else he wanted his pitchers to feel confident on the mound. He doesn't want them overthinking. He wants them to trust the call.

"That's the thing about baseball, it's not a perfect science," Martin said. "There's not going to be one moment where that was the perfect pitch. . . . Typically, if a pitcher has conviction and he attacks, we are going to get a good result."

Pirates reliever Jared Hughes told a story to a reporter of how he learned to trust Martin that spring. In an early exhibition game, Martin called for a slider, and Hughes, a natural sinker-ball pitcher, in need of a ground ball to get out of a jam, shook off Martin's call. Martin then called time-out and walked to the center of the McKechnie Field diamond to chat with Hughes. He wanted to know why Hughes had rejected Martin's pitch selection. Hughes explained he needed a ground ball, he needed his sinker. Martin told Hughes he believed his slider could be a ground-ball pitch, too. Hughes thought about this. It was a spring training game after all, the stats didn't matter much, and he was sure to make the team. He agreed to throw the slider, and the pitch did generate a ground-ball out. Through small moments like that, Martin built trust.

Martin's art-combined-with-science, jazzlike approach would never be more important than on the day Liriano was to start the wild-card play-in game on October 1 at PNC Park versus the Reds. The pitch

Liriano had the most conviction in and the pitch the Reds hitters were most vulnerable to was the slider, and Martin knew this.

That Tuesday, fans began streaming early to Pittsburgh's North Shore, the land adjacent to the city's central business district north of the Allegheny River. The North Shore's signature neighborhood, Mexican War Streets, its narrow roads lined with trees and 150-year-old, brick row homes, was designed by Alexander Hays on land owned by Mexican War veteran General William Robinson. The streets were named after generals and famous battle sites from the Mexican War. PNC Park's main entrance rests at the intersection of General Robinson Street and Mazeroski Way. After years of neglect, the neighborhood was being revitalized, and so was its baseball club.

Students from Duquesne and the University of Pittsburgh cut class and commuted down the city's elevated east end toward the North Shore. Car traffic was shut off earlier than normal on the Roberto Clemente Bridge, which spans the glistening Allegheny River with its gold towers and cables, connecting downtown to the North Shore. In an outbreak of some undiagnosed ailment, scores of children and businessmen called in sick to school or work in western Pennsylvania. The previous night, the team, particularly backup catcher Michael McKenry, had taken to social media to rally support. On Twitter, McKenry called for a "blackout," asking fans coming to the game to wear black T-shirts, jerseys, sweatshirts—anything black—to better promote unity, and perhaps intimidation. On the streets, tickets were going for hundreds of dollars above face value. A single baseball game is typically not a huge event. It's not a football game or a scarce product in what is a long season with 162 games. But on this day, this was an event.

Around two o'clock that afternoon, Neal Huntington approached the window of his front office to see what was causing a commotion on Federal Street, which borders the east end of PNC Park, beyond the left-field wall.

"I was in my office. . . . I'm locked in as we are beginning prep for

2014," Huntington said. "All of the sudden I hear a 'Let's go, Bucs' chant out my window because my office overlooks Federal Street, and I remember thinking, 'That's awfully early, this is going to be crazy.' I looked out of my office window unaware that the blackout is taking place and seeing eighty to ninety percent of people in black, and Federal Street is jammed. Everything else is kind of a blur. . . . I realized we were really in for something special that night."

Two hours before first pitch, Federal Street was swamped with fans, along with the sounds of music and revelry. Thirty minutes before the first pitch, Hurdle entered the dugout as was his custom. He likes to sit there alone, take in the soft light of the setting sun, and feel the energy of the crowd. He had never felt a pregame energy quite like this, and he had played and coached in the World Series.

"I haven't been to a World Cup soccer game, but I can only imagine that is what it is like," Hurdle said. "For our guys to throw the blackout thing there. And the fan base to show up. You talk about hunger, passion, twenty years without . . . they let it all out."

It was crowded and loud in PNC Park, and alone in the center of that atmosphere were Liriano and Reds starting pitcher Johnny Cueto.

Ten months earlier the majority of the league had given up on the enigmatic Liriano. In 2013, he had gone from baseball's bargain bin to the National League Comeback Player of the Year. He was to start the club's most important game in twenty-one years, given the most important assignment since Doug Drabek took the mound in Atlanta–Fulton County Stadium for Game 7 of the 1992 National League Championship Series. Interestingly, the now gray-haired Drabek would throw out the ceremonial pitch prior to the game.

Hurdle was criticized at times throughout the season for some of his day-to-day management, such as continuing to bat Starling Marte in the leadoff spot despite his below-average walk rate and his struggles with right-handed pitching. But Hurdle and his staff had the foresight to align the rotation so Liriano would pitch in the one-game play-off game. He had allowed only two extra-base hits to left-handed hitters the entire season. Yes, two extra-base hits the entire season.

The crowd was in lively spirits before the game, and Andrew McCutchen rose to the top step of the third-base dugout to appreciate it prior to the first pitch. McCutchen's mother had sung the national anthem, further elevating the crowd's electricity. Several hundred fans unable to get tickets stood on the Clemente Bridge over the Allegheny River, trying to get a peek at the action from behind center field, eager to be a part of the atmosphere, to say they were there. Flags waved and "Let's go, Bucs" chants were sung.

Following pregame introductions, during which the Reds were viciously booed, PNC Park pulsated. Anticipation welled up as if the more than forty thousand people were waiting for the main act at a concert to take the stage. The field was empty for a moment in a brief calm before the Pirates emerged from their dugout in black jerseys and white pants. The first of many roars erupted from a crowd that had twenty years of pent-up baseball frustration to vent, that had endured twenty years of baseball misery before hosting a play-off game. Liriano jogged to the mound and picked up the first ball of the evening, as chants of "Let's go, Bucs" began around him.

As he went through his warm-up pitches, he knew the game plan well, it was simple. Liriano was to get ahead with his fastball and bury the lefty Reds sluggers with his slider. Liriano's first two pitches of the evening were 93 mph, two-seam fastballs, one for a ball, one for a strike, against the normally patient Reds leadoff hitter, Shin-Soo Choo. Martin then called for the game's first slider. Liriano unleashed a wicked one that broke sharply away from the left-handed Choo. Choo swung violently over the top of the ball. From his crouched position Martin looked up at Choo briefly, surprised to see the normally calculating Choo swing so aggressively and miss so badly. Martin called for another slider. Liriano again snapped off a slider and buried it deep below the strike zone. Choo again swung and missed. The black-clad crowd roared. Choo headed back to the dugout as the ball was thrown around the horn, from Martin to third baseman Pedro Alvarez to second baseman Neil Walker to shortstop Clint Barmes and back to Liriano.

Martin started Reds number two hitter Ryan Ludwick with a slider, which sailed out of the zone for a ball, then called for the game's first changeup, which Ludwick swung over the top of for a strike. Liriano next threw a slider, which tempted Ludwick into another swinging strike. Ludwick pounded yet another slider into the turf bounding toward shortstop Barmes, who threw across the infield for a putout.

The Reds had two of the game's most patient, selective hitters in Choo and their number thee hitter, Joey Votto. That season Choo had seen 4.23 pitches per plate appearances, the eighth most in baseball. Votto was thirteenth, at 4.18. Votto stepped into the left-hander's batter's box and twisted his cleats into the dirt to develop a more stable base. He then did something he rarely ever did: he swung at the first pitch. His swing was atypically aggressive and out of control. His front foot came uprooted from the ground and he nearly stumbled out of the box as he grounded weakly to Pirates first baseman Justin Morneau, who flipped to Liriano for the final out of the inning.

As Martin made his way into the dugout between innings and consulted with Liriano and pitching coach Ray Searage, he noted the Reds were being uncharacteristically aggressive. The energy in the ballpark was palpable, everyone felt it. Heck, Votto was thought to be an emotionless, baseball-smashing robot, and even he looked to be caught up in the moment. Martin thought the energy combined with the stakes of the situation—win or go home—had changed the approach of the normally patient Reds stars. Martin felt Choo and Votto were trying to do too much. The Reds were looking for fastballs early in counts they could drive, and Martin knew this made them susceptible to off-speed pitches. The game plan was for Liriano to get ahead in the count with his fastball and then bury the Reds lefties with his slider. Martin decided Liriano wasn't going to go to the slider just as a strikeout pitch; it would be his *everything* pitch. He would throw it early and often until the Reds adjusted.

After the Pirates went scoreless in the bottom of the first, Liriano got right-handed Reds second baseman Brandon Phillips to ground out on two pitches. The best Reds power hitter, another lefty, then came to bat. Jay Bruce had the most power in the lineup, and like Choo, Bruce was one of the more selective hitters in the game. He saw 3.96 pitches per plate appearance that season, which ranked forty-fourth in baseball. Against Bruce, Martin went away from a typical pitch-sequencing pattern and did something unorthodox. Bruce did not swing at the first pitch, a slider from Liriano, which went for a ball. Bruce swung at and missed the next two pitches, both sliders, which broke down and away from Bruce's swing. After three straight sliders, Martin quickly glanced up at Bruce to make sure he wasn't trying to steal a sign. Martin again gave Liriano the sign for a slider, putting down two fingers, burying the sign close to his body. Liriano nodded in agreement, then twisted and fired off another sweeping slider, which Bruce missed badly with a swing for another strikeout. The next batter, Todd Frazier, grounded out on a changeup to end the inning.

"In those types of the games the energy is [high], guys are going to swing the bat. You think they are going to take pitches and work the count? Are you kidding me? It's a freaking play-off game," Martin said. "Everyone is feeling like me. They are really amped. They want to swing the bat. You know what? They are going to get a crap ton of sliders, and we are going to see what happens."

While Martin's pitch sequencing and Liriano's execution was crit-ical, the most unforgettable memory of the game would be tied to something Cueto did with a ball and what Martin would do with his bat. "Let's go, Bucs" chants had begun in the first inning, and in the second they had grown in volume. Dozens were waving the Jolly Roger; forty thousand were clad in black. Through the unifying color and the noise the fans had taken on an intimidating oneness. The environment, no doubt aided by Yuengling and Iron City beer, was reminiscent of that of an English Premier League soccer match.

In the bottom of the second inning, Cueto made the first mistake of the game. He left a pitch out over the plate that late-season acquisition Marlon Byrd belted for a home run. The crowd noise picked up in ferocity as the ball was swallowed by the crowd and Byrd began his trot around the bases. A new chant originated at some ground zero somewhere in PNC Park and grew in volume to a tidal wave. In a taunting, haunting crescendo forty thousand chanted, "*Kwaaaayyyyy-toe . . . Kwaaaayyyyy-toe*," toward the center of the diamond. Under this avalanche of noise, with the misfortune of having a two-syllable, perfect-for-chanting surname, Cueto was thrown a new game ball by the home-plate umpire. Cueto literally dropped the ball. Seeing this, the crowd went into a frenzy, believing the dropped ball signaled that they had got inside the head of the Reds starting pitcher. On the very next pitch, Cueto allowed a fastball to leak out over the plate. Waiting for it was Martin, who smashed the ball into the left-field bleachers for another homer. The crowd was euphoric. Twenty years of pent-up misery was released on this night, manifesting itself in a sound that felt like being at the bottom of a waterfall.

"I think as the legend grows," said Martin to reporters afterward, "it will be like the sound waves of the people making all that noise grabbed the baseball out of his hand and made it drop and messed with his rhythm."

The Pirates held a 2–0 lead after two innings. Liriano buzzed through the bottom of the Reds lineup in the third inning. During the Pirates at bat in the third inning, McCutchen reached on a single and later scored on a sacrifice fly by Pedro Alvarez.

In the top of the fourth inning the Pirates led 3–0 as Liriano faced the vaunted top third of the Reds lineup for the second time. Martin was even more aggressive with his game-calling, but it did not begin well. After starting the inning with a slider to Choo, Liriano let a fastball get away and hit the Reds leadoff man, placing him on first. Martin called for another slider against the right-handed Ludwick. The pitch caught too much of the plate, and Ludwick singled sharply into left field. With two Reds on base and none out in the inning, the crowd quieted for the first time since the game began. Coming to the plate was Votto, one of the most feared and disciplined hitters in the game. If Liriano made another mistake, the game could be tied with one swing.

On the first pitch to Votto, Martin called for a slider, which was fouled away. On the second offering, Liriano buried a slider in the dirt, which Votto chased for another strike. Martin dove to his knees and blocked the ball with his chest protector to prevent the runners from advancing. To Martin's bewilderment, Votto was continuing to be ultra-aggressive, so Martin made the unorthodox decision to go with yet another slider. Unlike in the first inning, Votto choked up on the bat slightly and made a more controlled swing. But he again swung over the top of the breaking pitch for a strikeout. Several thousand people in the stands jumped to their feet, thrusting fists into the air and waving towels.

Against the following batter, Brandon Phillips, Martin called for a changeup with no balls and two strikes, which Phillips popped to Walker for the second out. The left-handed Bruce followed and saw his fifth and sixth pitches of the night, all of which were sliders. Bruce swung and missed at the second slider to even the count at 1-1. Martin finally called for a fastball, which Bruce connected with, beating the shift with a single to the left to cut the Pirates lead to 3–1. To Martin's amazement the Reds were still hunting fastballs, continuing to be overly aggressive in their approach, even though Liriano had thrown 12 sliders to lefties in the first 4 innings, and 8 were swung at and missed.

With runners on first and second and two outs, Martin called for four straight off-speed pitches to Todd Frazier, including an 88 mph slider that broke below his flailing bat for a strikeout. Liriano had limited the damage to one run.

The Pirates scored two more runs in the bottom of the fourth with Walker scoring Marte with a double and then later coming around to score on a fielder's-choice groundout, giving the Pirates a 5–1 lead after four innings. The noise was changing now as the fans' nervousness dissipated and confidence grew that the Pirates would advance. Those that were there swear that PNC Park's upper deck vibrated like a rickety set of bleachers in a high school gymnasium.

Liriano went through the top of the Reds lineup for a final time in the sixth inning. Choo tapped out weakly to first base. Votto once again swung over the top of a slider for a strikeout, then slowly walked back to the visitors' dugout with his head low. Against Liriano and with the crowd on the side of the Pirates, the Reds seemed to realize that they had no chance. Reds manager Dusty Baker looked blankly out to the field as the television camera panned the crowd and then the Reds dugout, creating a striking juxtaposition. In the seventh, with two outs and a runner on, Liriano induced Reds catcher Ryan Hanigan to ground out to third. It was the last batter of the night for Liriano, who allowed four hits and one run over seven innings, walking one and striking out five.

The Pirates' analytics department had identified Liriano as a strong bounce-back candidate, but rebuilding Liriano was a team effort. It took Ray Searage's being something of a pitcher whisperer. Rather than trying to make a multitude of changes, he focused on several critical tweaks, raising Liriano's arm slot to cut down on east-west misses of the strike zone. Liriano was aided in getting strike one called more often by Martin's pitch framing, setting up Liriano's wipeout slider, and Martin's game planning and pitch sequencing was also valuable. Crucially, Martin was able to connect with pitchers and earn their trust. It all came together on this night. Liriano's slider and Martin's game-calling and pitch framing was another example of new-age and traditional baseball blending to form a powerful result for the Pirates in 2013.

In a the bottom of the seventh inning a victory seemed certain as Martin struck again, sending a 96 mph fastball from Logan Ondrusek over the left-field wall to give the Pirates a 6–1 lead. The "blackout" crowd rose again as one; black towels were twirled, fists were raised, and high fives were exchanged as Martin clapped his hands together as he touched first and rounded the bases. Victory seemed inevitable as Jason Grilli came out from the left-center-field bull pen and jogged to the center of the diamond in the top of the ninth inning. The roar was becoming hoarse now after forty thousand fans had sustained an incredible volume for more than three hours. With two outs, the crowd rose to its feet in anticipation of a final, joyful release.

When the Reds' Zack Cozart slammed a Grilli fastball into the infield, Grilli bounded from the mound with both arms raised in anticipation of the final out. Walker scooped up the ground ball and threw to first baseman Justin Morneau to complete the 6–2 victory. A mosh pit formed in the center of the field, while in the stands strangers hugged and high-fived each other, and fans at the bars along Federal Street poured into the street. One overzealous fan jumped from the Roberto Clemente Bridge into the Allegheny River and lived to tell the tale.

The victory was in large part credited to Liriano's brilliance. He was at the top of his game, showing at times what scouts would label a plus-plus slider with two-plane break. In English, it meant that the slider was breaking late and hard with significant movement down and away from left-handed hitters, and it was difficult to distinguish the pitch from his fastball. But Martin also deserved credit for not only framing pitches, but for correctly diagnosing the Reds' strategy and calling an ultra-aggressive game plan. Against the lefty trio of Reds stars—Choo, Bruce, and Votto—Liriano threw his slider on 20 of 27 pitches. Against Liriano, the three went 1 for 8 with 4 strikeouts. Overall, Liriano's arm nearly came off as he threw the slider a whopping 44 times versus 23 fastballs and 23 changeups. Of the 44 sliders, 34 went for strikes—13 of which went for swing-and-miss strikes. It was a rare rate of whiff-producing pitches. Liriano recorded only 4 swing-and-misses with his fastball and changeup combined.

"By the time the hitter has made up his mind to swing, it hasn't broke yet, and within the last six to eight feet, that's when the tightness and the depth comes in," Martin said of Liriano's slider. "Right out of his hand it looks like a fastball. You can tell yourself a slider is coming, but your mind is telling you it's a fastball."

Another celebration ensued in the clubhouse. More champagne and more Coors and Miller Lite were carted into the Pirates clubhouse. Plastic sheeting again protected lockers. Before popping the corks on champagne, the Pirates waited for Martin and Byrd to enter the clubhouse. A circle was formed, and pushed into the center by several players was Clint Hurdle. Hurdle raised both of his arms into the air, shaking both fists in jubilation as he was soaked in champagne.

Minutes later he spoke to reporters through squinting, irritated alcohol-soaked eyes in a rowdy clubhouse: "Did you feel that out there? That's incredible. It was awesome. The fans made a difference from the time we took the field. I don't know if it can scare the other team, but you can feel it."

In the raucous clubhouse the man perhaps most responsible for the victory was nowhere to be found. Liriano was not part of the celebration. Local reporters waited and waited for him to appear, but he never did. One by one reporters gave up their quest for an interview and departed for the press box to try to beat deadline, attempting to eloquently put into words the madness they had just witnessed. When the locker room was nearly empty of reporters, Liriano finally appeared. He walked slowly to his locker in street clothes and explained why he had been absent, why he had not been able to talk, as he picked up an orange-tinted pharmacy bottle from his locker. Liriano had pitched with a sinus infection. This was a Jordan-toppling-the-Utah-Jazz-Blazers-while-battling-the-flu moment.

Liriano used but few words to explain the performance: "I was very calm. I wasn't trying to do too much. I tried to do the same thing I was doing the whole year."

What he had done the whole year was to trust Martin and the

coaches. Liriano had also outperformed his contract by such an amount that if he wasn't the greatest free agent value of the off-season, the man catching him that night was. Math had played such a big role in the Pirates' turnaround—from the data-driven shifting and pitching philosophies to identifying the hidden value and skills of Liriano and Martin. Math and big data had helped the Pirates to their first winning season and postseason win in twenty-one years. But to get over the wild-card play-in game hurdle, to advance to their first postseason series since 1992, the Pirates also required the art of Martin's ingame intuition and the magic of one of the greatest baseball crowds anyone had ever heard. Afterward, Reds third baseman Todd Frazier said it was the best crowd he had ever seen, and A. J. Burnett, who had played in the play-offs and in New York, said he had never experienced any other crowd like it. Neither had the veteran beat writers or the Pirates' longtime official scorer. A disillusioned baseball city had once again fallen in love with its team. That had nothing to do with big data or complex algorithms. That was raw emotion.

EPILOGUE

A PERFECT CIRCLE

February 18, 2014, marked the first day of full-squad workouts for the Pirates in Bradenton, Florida. Clint Hurdle called the team to the cafeteria as he did every season to present a new message. At last year's meeting he had introduced the team to Dan Fox and Mike Fitzgerald and unveiled the radical defensive plan to a guarded and curious club.

This meeting was different. It was different from all of the other first-day-of-spring-training meetings since 1993. That's because for the first time in two decades the Pirates had entered the spring coming off a winning season and a play-off berth. They weren't able to reach the ultimate goal of every team, winning the World Series, but they took the formidable St. Louis Cardinals to the fifth and final game of the National League Division Series before losing. Hurdle figured the club would battle new adversaries in 2014: they could no longer sneak up on opponents and could ill afford any complacency.

To focus on new goals and challenges and move on from last season, Hurdle asked video coordinator Kevin Roach and a local cable producer to compile a six-minute highlight clip from 2013, which was set to Aerosmith's "Dream On." The staff set up a digital projector and began to play the video. The cafeteria roared as they all relived moments from the previous season. As the video reached its climax, the play that began the streak of twenty consecutive years of losing—when the Braves' Sid Bream beat Barry Bonds's throw home in the 1992 NLCS game—was alternated on the screen with the play that ended a twenty-year playoff drought when Justin Morneau's relay toss to Russell Martin beat the Cubs' Nate Schierholtz at the plate at Wrigley Field on September 23, 2013. That play clinched the Pirates' first post-season appearance in twenty-one years. The closing still frame was the iconic image of 2013: Martin holding the ball triumphantly above his head on his knees at home plate at Wrigley Field.

"Honestly, seeing that moment again like that made the hairs on the back of my neck stand up," said Martin to then *Pittsburgh Tribune-Review* columnist Dejan Kovacevic who first recounted the video. "That belonged to all of us, to the whole city."

As the video ended, one word flashed on the screen, *NOW*, in all caps. The message was clear: 2013 was over. Last season's magic was over. It was time to go back to work and write a new story, to find new ways to improve, to find new hidden advantages. And it wasn't going to be easy.

While the video revisited magic from the 2013 season, much of that magic had been the product of using math and taking advantage of underutilized skills and strategies. But this was a new season, and the three prongs of the Pirates' aggressive defensive plan—shifts, ground balls, and pitch framing—would no longer provide the competitive advantage that they did in 2013, or at least not to the degree they had. These data-based concepts were not like player talent. They were not unique skills possessed by the Pirates. These successful practices were in a way like Coca-Cola having to reveal its recipe. As in any other industry, baseball teams always copied the successful strategies of rivals. More teams would be shifting, more pitching staffs would be focused on attempting to generate more ground balls hit into the shifts, and pitch framing would no longer be a hidden value possessed by catchers. And now, for the first time in more than two decades, the Pirates were wearing a target.

Hurdle, like his team, wanted his focus to be on the present. He could not afford to bask in the previous season's accomplishment. He was named the National League Manager of the Year in November by the Baseball Writers' Association of America, earning 25 of 30 first-place votes. While this prestigious award was voted upon by some of the more traditional writers, who often recognized a manager's worth based upon wins and losses, Hurdle was also named the NL's top manager by the Internet Baseball Awards, which were voted on by a new-age, analytically inclined constituency. Hurdle was what stat geeks had long waited for: a manager who embraced analysts' findings and was willing to move away from tradition.

Many view the major league manager's office as having diminished influence in the modern age, with more and more control over the roster being concentrated in the front office. But the manager remains a key gatekeeper in allowing data-based practices to flow onto the field. Working with people will always be part of the game. The manager is still largely responsible for creating a clubhouse culture and must persuade and lead a team down a new path, as Hurdle did successfully in 2013. He also played an integral role in helping to create a culture of respect that enabled the Pirates to better integrate their quantitative analysts into the clubhouse to maximize their effect. Leadership is the ability to influence and persuade, and Hurdle did just that in 2013.

Pirates general manager Neal Huntington was also acknowledged for his good work, finishing second to Red Sox GM Ben Cherington for Major League Baseball's Executive of the Year honors. Huntington's signature moves were the signing of Russell Martin and Francisco Liriano, the top two free agent bargains of the off-season. He also traded for an elite setup man in Mark Melancon and acquired Marlon Byrd and Justin Morneau for the postseason push. Huntington also had the vision to build the club's proprietary database and to hire Dan Fox, and those decisions began to pay off in 2013.

After many in the public called for regime change in the fall of 2012, both Huntington and Hurdle were instead awarded three-year contract extensions in the spring of 2014. Through taking big risks, they had earned security. Still, they wanted to prove their success was not a fluke, and they knew repeating it would be more difficult than ending the streak. Said Huntington after the season, "We've said from day one it's going to be one thing to build it but it's going to be even harder to sustain it."

★ ★ ★

In late March 2014, Dan Fox stood behind home plate on the crushed-brick warning track of the Red Sox's spring training home in Fort Myers, Florida, watching batting practice. The Pirates had made the two-hour trip down I-75 to play the Red Sox in a rare spring training night game. Fox was approached by a reporter, and the pregame talk turned to pitch framing and how the Pirates had identified Martin as a bargain in the previous off-season and had taken advantage of pitch framing sooner than most other teams. Rather than bask in the prudent decision, Fox lamented that that competitive advantage was now gone.

For Fox and Fitzgerald, it was time to get back to work. Catchers who can frame pitchers and can hit were now going to be signed to mega-contracts. One such catcher, Brian McCann, signed a five-year, $85 million deal with the Yankees just months earlier. Even catchers who couldn't hit but could frame pitches were also being sought. The punchless Ryan Hanigan—who had hit just .198 with the Reds in 2013—was aggressively targeted by the Rays in an off-season trade, and the team had also signed thirty-eight-year-old catcher Jose Molina despite his advancing age and negative value as a hitter.

Not only was the hidden value of pitch framing unearthed in 2013 by Pirates analysts and then copied in 2014. The Pirates anticipated that shifting would become more accepted throughout the game. While they were not the first team to shift, because their remarkable turnaround season was tied to a 500 percent increase in the use of shifting—an unheard-of pivot in strategy in a conservative industry that is slow to change—it got the sport's attention. Recall, according to BIS, shifts more than doubled in the game in 2014. Not only were more teams shifting more often, but opposing hitters also began fighting back with more bunt attempts and with some more often successfully targeting the opposite field.

The Pirates' approach with their pitchers was also replicated. In 2014, the percentage of pitchers who'd traded in their four-seam fastballs for two-seam fastballs continued to increase, and more clubs employed a pitching philosophy similar to that of the Pirates, loading up on ground-ball pitchers. In 2014, 14.6 percent of all pitches in baseball were two-seam fastballs, up from 13.6 percent a year earlier, and an increase from 3.8 percent in 2008, according to PITCHf/x data. As pitching staffs began throwing more sinking fastballs, one team began a creative counterpunch. In Oakland, A's general manager Billy Beane began hoarding fly-ball hitters. In 2013, Oakland hitters combined for a 60 percent fly-ball rate. No other team in baseball lifted more than 39 percent of their batted balls into the air. The importance of fly-ball hitters was written about in a BaseballProspectus.com article by Andrew Koo titled "More Moneyball." Koo wrote, "In *The Book: Playing the Percentages in Baseball,* authors Tango, Litchman, and Dolphin found that fly-ball hitters had an advantage over ground-ball hitters, simply because they are better hitters—you can't homer on grounders, after all. They also found that fly-ball hitters are especially good against ground-ball pitchers, because the former tend to swing under the ball while the latter want the hitter to swing over the ball."

The A's offense in 2013 and 2014 was among the game's best despite their playing in an extremely pitcher-friendly stadium.

The game is constantly evolving. A constant cat-and-mouse game is played between hitters and pitchers, between opposing managers, and even between opposing analysts. This punch and counterpunch does not have an end point; rather, it is circular. Fox saw clearly that he and the Pirates would have to adjust, they couldn't remain static, and for Fox, that is part of the fun.

★ ★ ★

A year ago to the day after the Pirates had clinched their first play-off berth in two decades at Wrigley Field, Pirates longtime equipment manager Scott Bonnett—or Bones as he's known to everyone around the club—made his way back to the visiting clubhouse at Turner Field in Atlanta in the seventh inning and began prepping for an event that he had hosted just once before: celebrating a play-off berth.

Per MLB stipulations, every member of the team's traveling party is allotted two bottles of champagne. The Pirates party included players, coaches, club officials, and members of the ownership. So Bonnett ordered twenty cases of champagne. He filled several deep plastic carts with ice, where he placed the bottles, and he helped hoist plastic sheeting to protect the lockers. He had also had ordered dozens of goggles and towed with him from Pittsburgh hundreds of commemorative T-shirts and sweatshirts.

Exactly a year after beating the Chicago Cubs to clinch their first play-off berth in two decades, the Pirates beat the Braves, 3–2, to clinch another play-off berth. The Pirates again soaked a visiting clubhouse carpet with champagne, and for the remainder of their series in Atlanta dehumidifiers and fans hummed in vain to dry and rid the space of the sour smell. One year after winning 94 games, the Pirates won 88 games and again finished second in the National League Central Division to again be a part of the select one-third of major league teams invited to the postseason. The Pirates managed to become one of the sport's best teams yet again despite having one of the lowest payrolls—twenty-seventh out of thirty teams, at $78 million.

In some ways their path back to the postseason was similar to that of the previous year. While much of the sport had begun to shift in 2014, the Pirates shifted their defense even more often and in even more sophisticated ways. They stayed ahead of the pack not just by raising their overall number of defensive shifts from 494 to 659, but also by shifting their infielders not just based upon a hitter's overall batted-ball distribution history, but also based upon his tendencies in each ball-strike scenario of an at bat. The Pirates knew hitters were more likely to pull the ball when the count was in their favor, and more likely to go to the opposite field when trailing in a count. Moreover, few teams positioned their outfielders away from conventional starting points as aggressively as the Pirates. Positioning outfielders based upon batted-ball data is more complex and nuanced than shifting infielders, since batted balls to the outfield have a variety of trajectories, speeds off the bat, and distances traveled. While the Pirates' shifts were not quite as successful in 2014 as they were in 2013, they still ranked sixth in baseball with 36 defensive runs saved.

While pitch framing was no longer a secret in 2014, the Pirates doubled up on the practice. Prior to spring training, they quietly traded for Yankees catcher Chris Stewart to back up Martin even though Stewart was a significant offensive liability. In 2013, Stewart was even better than Martin at framing pitches. In 110 games for the Yankees, he had created a value of 21.7 runs saved through pitch framing, second only to Yadier Molina in the major leagues. Stewart's pitch framing was worth roughly two wins above that of an average catcher. The acquisition of Stewart was significant since catchers receive the most off days of any position player. By acquiring him the Pirates could field an elite pitch framer not in just 120 games a year—the average workload of a catcher—but in all 162 games of the regular season.

The Pirates continued to seek and rehab pitchers who were coming off career-worst seasons but had raw talent and the ability to be better. Just as the Pirates were criticized for trading for A. J. Burnett and signing Francisco Liriano, they were also ridiculed for agreeing to a one-year, $5 million deal with Edinson Volquez. Volquez was a lot like Liriano. Despite great raw ability—a mid-90s fastball and a changeup with so much fade that it seemed to fall off an invisible cliff, Volquez struggled to harness his arm. He posted a 5.71 ERA in 2013 with the San Diego Padres and the Los Angeles Dodgers, the worst ERA among qualified major league starting pitchers, and that despite playing in pitcher-friendly environments. But the Pirates were able to work their magic yet again in 2014 as pitching gurus Ray Searage and Jim Benedict—and Martin's glove—helped Volquez throw more strikes and better trust his defense and two-seam fastball. Volquez cut his ERA by nearly three runs (3.04 ERA) and became the fourth straight first-year Pirates pitcher to lead the club in wins with 13 victories.

The secretive preventive medical practices that the Pirates were investing in continued to yield results as they tallied the fewest days lost to injury in baseball in 2014, according to Grantland.com. They also began using more data-based medical practices as a number of players started to wear the Zephyr bio-harnesses during games, compression shirts worn under jerseys that contained an electronic, medallion-like monitor in the center of their chests, which measured their heartbeats and calories consumed among other metrics. It allowed players not only to better monitor their diets but also to see how performance correlated with adrenaline during games.

The analytics staff continued to grow with the hiring of another full-time quantitative analyst in September of 2014, a former blogger named Stuart Wallace. Wallace was to be based in Bradenton, Florida, year-round and would work directly with the club's minor league and player-development staff based there. After seeing the benefit of having the major league staff engage daily with analysts, the Pirates wanted their minor league and player-development staff to have a similar resource.

The reach of analytics is expanding to the minor league level as a number of teams—including the Pirates—have equipped their minor league ballparks with PITCHf/x and TrackMan technology. Since clubs had seen the value in pitch tracking at the major league level, they now wanted it at the minor league level to measure everything from curveball movement to prospects' pitch-framing ability. Moreover, with the player-tracking system Statcast slated to be operating in every major league stadium by 2015, teams will only be adding more analysts to make sense of the new crush of data, which is expected to grow exponentially.

Perhaps most important to the Pirates' efforts in 2014 was their continued focus on marrying their new-school and old-school personnel. After having Fox be a part of planning meetings with Hurdle in the 2012 season, and then having both Fox and Fitzgerald involved in all home strategy sessions and on teleconferences for meetings on the road in 2013, the Pirates took it a step further in 2014 by having Fitzgerald travel with the club on the majority of its road trips. Fitzgerald had made about half the trips in 2013. The Pirates always wanted to have an analyst in the clubhouse to counsel, making them the first known major league team to have a quantitative analyst among its traveling party.

On that celebratory night in Atlanta, as the party wound down and the champagne was exhausted, Pirates second baseman Neil Walker found Mike Fitzgerald standing quietly in the corner of the clubhouse away from the epicenter of the celebration, where the players and coaches were massed. Walker took a Budweiser from an ice-filled bin and walked toward Fitzgerald, dousing the analyst with beer. Fitzgerald, the math genius who had never played professionally, and Walker, drafted out of high school and having spent years in the minors before emerging as an everyday major league player, laughed and celebrated together. The dichotomy between them and yet their acceptance of each other was a snapshot of how far the Pirates had come in creating a culture of respect, a culture that would allow important data to be embraced.

While much was similar about the 2013 and 2014 seasons, as the Pirates tried to reinforce and deepen the sophistication of successful strategies of the previous campaign, one dramatic change played a salient role in returning the Pirates to the postseason.

Just as the Pirates adopted a strategy to improve each of their pitchers' performance in 2013 by creating more ground balls hit into the shifts, in 2014 hitting coach Jeff Branson got his hitters to collectively buy into a new hitting approach. The focus was less on trying to smash fastballs into the seats and more about using the whole field, not trying to pull pitches on the outside of the plate, but trying to hit them to the opposite field, which would result in more line drives, and being more competitive and contact-focused with two strikes. The Pirates cheated on too many fastballs in 2013 and were susceptible to getting out in front and swinging and missing at off-speed pitches. It's one reason why they fell in the 2013 NLDS as they flailed at curveballs and changeups from Cardinals starting pitchers Adam Wainwright and Michael Wacha. But in 2014, after adopting the new approach, the Pirates jumped to third in on-base percentage in baseball from eighteenth in 2013—despite not playing in the American League, where the designated hitter bats in place of the pitcher. Despite no significant external additions outside of trading for part-time first baseman Ike Davis, the Pirates improved from twentieth in runs scored in 2013 to tenth in 2014. The Pirates improved from eleventh in the National League in two-strike, on-base plus slugging percentage in 2013 to first in 2014.

The communication of ideas within the organization was better than just about every other team. When Hurdle hired assistant hitting coach Jeff Branson to fill the void left by Jay Bell, who left after the 2013 season for Cincinnati, Hurdle was criticized for making a "cheap" hire. But Branson had the trust of the players, having worked with so many of them at the minor league levels where he was a long-time minor league hitting coach. His message of competing better with two strikes and using the whole field was not unique, what impressed rival NL scouts and executives was how he got an entire lineup of various personalities, skill sets, egos, and backgrounds to buy into a systematic approach. The improved offense helped make up for pitching performances from the bull pen and the starting pitchers that were not quite as good in 2014 as they had been 2013.

But the hitting approach worked not just because of Branson, but also because of Russell Martin, who had the respect of his teammates. He was a key veteran presence in the clubhouse, and when younger players saw Martin buying in to trading power for contact, they followed suit. In 2014, Martin choked up on his bat with two strikes to be quicker to the ball and to better avoid strikeouts. He focused less on power and more on putting the ball in play and now offered obvious value.

In 2014, Martin cemented his status as the top free agent signing in club history. He continued to add value not just with his pitch framing, throwing arm, and uncanny way of connecting with thirteen different personalities on the pitching staff, but also with his bat. Not even the Pirates' analysts saw this coming. Martin finished the season with a .402 on-base percentage, the fourth best on-base mark in the sport had he had enough plate appearances to qualify. He finished with a career-best 5.3 wins-above-replacement season, the twenty-first best in baseball. It's also worth noting that WAR is an accumulative stat, and the twenty players ranked above Martin had played at least 29 more games than him. In his two years as a Pirate, Martin produced 9.4 WAR, or a value of about $50 million on the free agent market, yet the Pirates had paid only $17 million for two years of Martin. The upturn in his offensive performance helped Pittsburghers appreciate him, but the city had also learned that he brought value in ways that could not be measured, from his mound visits and pitch sequencing, to the standard of work ethic he set in the clubhouse. They also loved his enthusiasm and competitive nature. He made the game fun.

The appreciation for Martin was heard as much as it was seen in the ninth inning of the Pirates' 2014 wild-card game versus the San Francisco Giants. While there was another "blackout" crowd at PNC Park, Giants ace Madison Bumgarner had quieted the Pirates bats—and the crowd—for much of the night. It was in Pittsburgh, where Bumgarner began is historic 2014 postseason performance. He was a few pitches from completing a masterful shutout effort, as the Giants held an 8–0 lead in the ninth inning, when Martin was introduced by the public address announcer. The atmosphere of the game was starkly different from a year earlier, but the silence was broken in the ninth inning as Martin walked toward the plate for perhaps his final at bat as a Pirate. Martin was to be a free agent after the season and had greatly increased his value. The crowd knew that this might be the last time they saw him wearing PIRATES embroidered across his chest. Just as with the "*Kway*-toe" chant a year earlier against the Reds, the chorus started at some unidentified ground zero with one voice exclaiming, "Re-sign Russ. . . . Re-sign Russ," and it spread like wildfire, the chant roared throughout the stadium. The fans that had once questioned the signing of Martin now understood his total value and that he was an integral part of the Pirates' two straight play-off appearances.

A glassy-eyed Martin said afterward when surrounded by reporters that it was one of the "coolest" moments of his career. Martin had never before been embraced the way he was in Pittsburgh. In New York and Los Angeles he was just another guy in the shadow of stars. In Pittsburgh, he was beloved as much as the 2013 NL MVP Andrew McCutchen. Perhaps that moment was the greatest validation for the Pirates' big data approach. That emotional outpouring was not enough to keep Martin in Pittsburgh. After the 2014 season, Martin entered free agency and signed a five-year, $82 million deal with the Toronto Blue Jays. The contract suggested that the industry saw the magic Martin worked with the Pirates, and that defense was no longer being under-valued in the game.

Fitzgerald played a big part in bringing Martin to Pittsburgh. He found the mathematical component that led the Pirates to Martin's hidden talents. But a magical intangible remained in how Martin made every pitcher better, and how he always seemed to rise to the moment. His standard of passion and of work ethic, and even the way he organized the clubhouse's music playlists, also had value. He added to clubhouse chemistry. There's not yet a way to measure those traits, though some believe the future of analytics will be to focus on soft science. Perhaps much can be gleaned in quantifying psychology and chemistry, where soft-science meanings might be hidden in an exponentially growing stack of data. But no matter how adept we become at measuring the game, there will always be a mystery to it and there will always be those, such as Fox and Fitzgerald, seeking to explain that magic.

After the Pirates' loss in the wild-card game, the clubhouse was subdued. A long season had abruptly ended. Players exchanged well-wishes, hugs, and handshakes as they cleared out their lockers and headed their separate ways to off-season homes scattered across the country. While the Pirates had again finished as one of the best teams in the sport on one of the smallest payrolls, only one team in the sport—the World Series champion Giants—did not have their season end on a sour, somber note.

As the clubhouse slowly emptied, Fitzgerald emerged from the video room. He was in a hurry but stopped to reflect with a reporter on the season. He did not seem depressed. If anything, he seemed eager to get started again. He felt the team's best days were ahead. The Pirates had a talented, young core and could perhaps be even better in 2015, 2016, and beyond, if of course Fitzgerald and Fox could continue to find underappreciated free agents and stratagems to supplement the roster. After a brief conversation Fitzgerald continued on his way and vanished around a corner in search of the next big thing, another hidden advantage. In baseball's big data age, there is no off-season, there is no end to the quest of identifying the next big thing.

ACKNOWLEDGMENTS

I had the good fortune—and timing—to be hired by the *Tribune-Review* to cover the Pirates in 2013. During my first year on the beat, like a lot of folks in Pittsburgh, I was having trouble understanding the surprising success of the Pirates during the first half of the season. After all, the Pirates had not gone out and purchased a bunch of free agent stars. Their farm system had not suddenly graduated a number of talented young players to the majors. As I spent time around the team, I was impressed by the club's culture, its willingness to accept new data-based ideas. While I had covered college athletics for most of my journalism career, I have always been fascinated by sabermetrics thought in baseball. In Pittsburgh, more than in most places around the game, I saw these data-based theories getting to the field. I've always loved writing about trends, new technologies, and challenging conventional wisdom. And trends, technology, and challenging tradition reached a confluence with the 2013 Pirates in the three-river city.

I suspected some of the surprising success of the Pirates was tied to the club's defensive shifting. In the early months of the season the team's increased commitment to radical defensive alignment was obvious from the press box or television screen. My digging into the shifting and understanding how it worked in concert with a pitching plan led me to writing an article titled "Shifting Gears" in September 2013 for the *Tribune-Review*. I received tremendous feedback on the story. I began to think the Pirates' story was too important, too big, to be confined to one newspaper article or even a series of articles.

Many people involved with this book deserve a hearty thank-you, starting with my managing editor at the *Tribune-Review*, Duke Maas. Not only did Duke hire me, he gave me the freedom to pursue this idea when I approached with him my idea for this book in November 2013.

This book also did not come to fruition without the Pirates' willingness to draw back the curtain.

Big Data Baseball is not about one key actor or one transcendent genius. This story is about an entire organization. It is about the power of collaboration. I am thankful to all those in the organization—front-office officials, coaches, players, and scouts—who were willing to be interviewed for this project. I spoke to dozens of people in the organization, some named in the book, and some not, but they all played a role in this story. I am specifically grateful to the Pirates general manager, Neal Huntington, manager Clint Hurdle, and quantitative analysts Dan Fox and Mike Fitzgerald, who were willing to discuss some of the strategies and practices that led to their success. They could have shut the door, but instead they allowed me to tell what I think is an important story of progress and teamwork.

Big Data Baseball isn't just about the Pirates. It's about the thirst for knowledge from folks such as John Dewan and hundreds of hobbyists. Their passion combined with improved technology and computing power led to baseball's big data age. I constantly badgered Dewan and his BIS president Ben Jedlovec for data for the better part of a year, and to their credit they kept cooperating. Ryan Zander and the folks at Sportvision, which gave the sport its first true big data tool,

PITCHf/x, were also incredibly helpful to me in this project. The game's bloggers and hobbyists were also an incredible resource. I believe we are in a golden age for baseball writing, in large part because of the data-based writing. Incredible research is going on at a variety of sites across the Web. I often referenced these amazingly talented and bright analysts, the types of folks once barred from the game that are now integral parts of many major league front offices. In particular, database journalist Sean Lahman answered my questions and offered support on this project.

Getting a book from a proposal to realization is about much more than having an idea. It's imperative the idea find the right and able hands.

I will be forever indebted to fellow author and *Grantland* baseball writer Jonah Keri. Jonah helped get the proposal for this book in the right hands. For a first-time author, one of the most difficult steps in getting a book published is to get your proposal or manuscript to a publisher. Jonah was willing to pass along my proposal to the Susan Rabiner Literary Agency, which represents him. At Rabiner my proposal found its way to Eric Nelson. Eric had no idea who I was, but he believed in the idea and sold the proposal.

Eric led me to Flatiron Books and Bob Miller. Ultimately, *Big Data Baseball* wouldn't have happened without Bob's believing in a rookie author and the idea. Bob also named the book! I worked closely with Flatiron Books editor Jasmine Faustino, who was extremely patient and helped mold the book into a better product. Jasmine's fingerprints are all over this book.

I have many other people to thank and won't be able to name them all, but I must start with Mom and Dad. Dad gave me a love of baseball and statistics, and Mom gave me an appreciation for the arts. This book is an intersection of those interests. They were also early—and free—copy editors and have always been there to listen and support. No one sacrificed more than my wonderful wife, Rebecca. When you commit to a book, it requires a lot of time alone and brief periods of insanity. Reporting and writing this book took place over a year, in addition to my day job, and I'll always be grateful for Rebecca's total support. She was the first to read and critique early versions. She was always available as a sounding board. I am very aware of my good fortune in finding such a partner.

REFERENCES

Much of this book was based upon original reporting, interviews, and first-hand observations. *Big Data Baseball* was also influenced by my reporting for the *Pittsburgh Tribune-Review,* and I have cited below a handful of articles that were critical in the development of this book. Also included are a number of other publications from which I drew quotes, critical facts, and inspiration.

Arangure, Jr., Jorge. "Former 'phenom' Hurdle finds true calling as manager." *ESPN The Magazine,* October 23, 2007.

Bell, Robert; Koren, Yehuda; Volinksy Chris. "Statistics can find you a movie." *ATT.com* http://www.research.att.com/articles/featured_stories/2010_01/2010 _02_netflix_article.html?fbid=vA7w673gpqL.

Burjos Jr., Adrian. *Cuban Star.* New York: Hill and Wang, 2011.

Bowman, Bob, and Joe Inzerillo. "MLBAM: Putting the 'D' in Data." Sloan SportsConference.com, March 1, 2014. http://www.sloansportsconference.com /?p=13950.

Calcaterra, Craig. "Dan Turkenkopf got a job with a major league team. This tells us something." *HardballTalk,* NBCSports.com, June 16, 2013. http://hard balltalk.nbcsports.com/2013/01/16/dan-turkenkopf-got-a-job-with-a-major -league-team-this-tells-us-something/.

Cook, Ron. "Cook: Pirates manager's goal is to make a difference every day." *Pittsburgh Post-Gazette,* September 25, 2013.

Daugherty, Paul. "How Pirates' Morton fine-tuned his motion and saved his career." *Sports Illustrated,* June 5, 2011. http://www.si.com/more-sports/2011/06 /15/charlie-mortonpirates.

Dewan, John. "To shift or not to shift." *Bill James Online,* March 30, 2012. http://www.billjamesonline.com/to_shift_or_not_to_shift/.

Fast, Mike. "Spinning Yarn: Removing the Mask—Encore Presentation." *Baseball Prospectus,* September 24, 2011. http://www.baseballprospectus.com/article.php?articleid=15093.

Fox, Dan. "Schrödinger's Bat: Simple Fielding Runs Version 1.0." *Baseball Prospectus,* January 24, 2008. http://www.baseballprospectus.com/article.php?articleid=7072.

Friend, Tom. "Love Clint." ESPN.com, September 30, 2013. http://espn.go.com/mlb/playoffs/2013/story/_/id/9726637/pirates-manager-clint-hurdle-inspiring-others-daily.

Isaacson, Walter. *The Innovators.* New York: Simon & Schuster, 2014.

Keith, Larry. "The Eternal Hopefuls of Spring." *Sports Illustrated,* March 20, 1978.

Keri, Jonah. *The Extra 2%.* New York: Random House, 2011.

Knight, Molly. "The Hurt Talker." *ESPN The Magazine,* August 13, 2012.

Kovacevic, Dejan. "Full text of Kyle Stark email." *Pittsburgh Tribune-Review,* September 20, 2012. http://blog.triblive.com/dejan-kovacevic/2012/09/20/full-text-of-kyle-stark-email/.

———. "Kovacevic: Pirates aim to be . . . Hells Angels?" *Pittsburgh Tribune-Review,* September 12, 2012.

———. "Kovacevic: Pirates' 2013 tale ends 'NOW.'"

———. "Russell Martin vs. Matt Morris, cage match." *Pittsburgh Tribune-Review,* November 29, 2012. blog.triblive.com/dejan-kovacevic/. "Mistakes . . . I've made a few" *Pittsburgh Tribune-Review,* June 24, 2013.

Lahman, Sean. "Baseball in the Age of Big Data." *SeanLahman*, August 4, 2013. http://www.seanlahman.com/2013/08/baseball-in-the-age-of-big-data/.

Laurila, David. "Prospectus A & A: John Dewan." *Baseball Prospectus,* March 13, 2009. http://www.baseballprospectus.com/article.php?articleid=8616.

Mangels, John, and Susan Vinella. "Nothing Personal." *Cleveland Plain-Dealer,* September 22, 2013.

McCracken, Voros. "How Much Control Do Hurlers Have?" *Baseball Prospectus,* January 23, 2001. http://www.baseballprospectus.com/article.php?article id=878.

Oliver, Jeff. "Ex-Pirates Owner Lustig: Nutting 'Too Rational.'" *Pittsburgh Tribune-Review,* April 2, 2013.

Renck, Troy. "Hurdle on hot seat in '07 season." *Denver Post,* January 19, 2007.

Sawchik, Travis. "Despite illness, Liriano's mastery continues in victory over Reds." *Pittsburgh Tribune-Review,* October 2, 2013.

——. "Meet the man who built the Pirates' analytics department." *Pittsburgh Tribune-Review,* September 21, 2013.

——. "Pirates' catcher Martin offers hidden value." *Pittsburgh Tribune-Review,* June 10, 2013.

——. "Pirates' Gayo finds hidden gems." *Baseball America,* November 18, 2013.

——. "Pirates pitching coach Searage builds trust, foundation with pitchers." *Pittsburgh Tribune-Review,* March 13, 2014.

——. "Shifting Gears." *Pittsburgh Tribune-Review,* September 15, 2013.

Spirito, Lou. "Baseball's many physical dimensions." *Los Angeles Times,* March 31, 2013. http://www.snd.org/wp-content/uploads/2013/08/LAT_03312013-page-001 .jpg.

Surowiecki, James. *The Wisdom of Crowds.* New York: Anchor, 2005.

Turkenkopf, Dan. "Framing the Debate." *Beyond the Box Score,* April 5, 2008. http://www.beyondtheboxscore.com/2008/4/5/389840/framing-the-debate.

REFERENCES

Waldstein, David. "One Hard Way to Play Ball." *New York Times,* June 16, 2012.

Other valuable resources where data or reporting was drawn from include Baseball-Reference.com, FanGraphs.com, MLB.com, BrooksBaseball.net, Grant land.com, the SABR BioProject, Forbes.com, CBSSports.com, TheSportingNews .com, PiratesProspects.com, Bloomberg.com, Deadspin.com, *The Wall Street Journal,* Jon Roegele's Tommy John database, *ROOT Sports,* BillJamesOnline .com, and of course Bill James's *Baseball Abstract*s. The *Baseball Abstract*s are where the big data revolution began, with James's call to gather better and, most important, a greater volume of data so we can better understand this beautiful and yet mysterious game.